JOURNEY INTO
THE UNKNOWN

JOURNEY INTO THE UNKNOWN

British Football's Early Adventures
in European Club Competitions

NEIL FREDRIK JENSEN

First published by Pitch Publishing, 2025

1

Pitch Publishing
9 Donnington Park,
85 Birdham Road,
Chichester, West Sussex,
PO20 7AJ
www.pitchpublishing.co.uk
info@pitchpublishing.co.uk

A CIP catalogue record is available for this book
from the British Library.

ISBN 978 1 83680 158 0

Typesetting and origination by Pitch Publishing

Printed and bound on FSC® certified paper in line with
our continuing commitment to ethical business practices,
sustainability and the environment.

Printed and bound in India by Replika Press Pvt. Ltd.

Contents

About the Author

Neil Jensen is a football and finance writer, based in Hitchin, Hertfordshire. His books include *Tales of the Town* (2017), *Mittel: Stories from European Football* (2018), *The Great Uncrowned* (2022) and *The Summer of Total Football: World Cup 1974* (2024). He has written for a broad range of publications, including *The Economist*, *The Blizzard*, the *New European* and *World Soccer*.

This book is dedicated to Richard and Robert Jensen and Anne-Marie Blair (nee Jensen). In memory of many hours kicking a Frido ball around a disused allotment and the recreation ground in South Ockendon village.

Acknowledgements

As ever, a big thank you to Pitch Publishing for helping bring this project to fruition.

The Warm-Up

MY EARLIEST memory of European club competitions was the 1968 European Cup Final at Wembley. I had a teacher, Mrs Parks, who was very keen on football. She would cycle to school every day and if, at breaktime, the tennis ball we were kicking around the playground went her way, she might kick it back. She was in her 50s, she liked Manchester United and, in particular, Bobby Charlton. Mrs Parks, on the afternoon of 29 May 1968, asked me if I was going to watch the big game that evening – United versus Benfica. She had an *Evening News* special edition in her hand, with colour photos on the front page of the two teams. She asked me if I wanted to borrow it and said she could pick it up on her way home from school. We all urged United to win as it was really a case of England against Portugal – I was the only Chelsea fan in the school at the time because almost everyone was a United fan. But given they were effectively representing Britain, we all rejoiced at school at their 4-1 victory, especially dear old Mrs Parks.

It was not long before my football lexicon started to include phrases like 'aggregate', 'away goals', 'first leg' and 'second leg'. I also became fascinated by club names such as 'Dynamo', 'Spartak', 'Lokomotive', 'Borussia', 'Eintracht', 'Internazionale', 'Real', 'Fortuna' and 'Sporting'. Another influence from the period was the *Goal* magazine correspondent Leslie Vernon, whose column on the world

11

game was the first page I turned to. I discovered teams like Ferencváros, Rapid Vienna, CSKA Sofia and Ajax and read about the great stadiums of Europe, places like the Nép, the Prater, the Bernabéu and the San Siro, all of which I have since visited.

A couple of summers later, I was sent on a football training course hosted by former West Ham United forward Alan Sealey. On a typically rain-soaked summer holiday afternoon, he told us about the time he scored two goals in the European Cup Winners' Cup Final of 1965 against TSV Munich 1860. He even unpacked a cine film to show us how it was done. Sealey took part in the games with us, very visibly enjoying himself when he scored a goal or two. It was all a little reminiscent of Brian Glover in the movie of Barry Hines's novel, *Kes*, except the former West Ham forward was 'Sealey … it's a goal'. Sadly, Sealey died when he was just 53, of a heart attack, but I never forgot his tips on how to trap the ball properly and how to effectively use the outside, the inside and the toe of the boot. At the time, we did not realise just how important he had been in the story of our local Football League club.

I was fascinated by the three European competitions at the time and discovering where each team came from really enhanced my knowledge of geography. Chelsea were in the curiously named Inter-Cities Fairs Cup in 1968/69 and I was very disappointed that they were drawn against Morton of Scotland in the first round. They easily disposed of the team from Greenock on the Clyde and then they came up against DWS Amsterdam. They drew 0-0 at Stamford Bridge and then, on the morning after the second leg, I dashed downstairs to grab the *Daily Mirror* as it fell through the letterbox. I worked feverishly to find the score (there was no report) and noted that the scoreline was 0-0. Through my bleary sleep eyes, there was a line in italics that said 'DWS won on toss of a coin'. What the hell was this? I thought. I could not believe that a Dutch guilder had been our downfall, and neither could Ron Harris, the skipper of Chelsea. Similarly, the away goals rule was deeply criticised by my teenage self when Åtvidaberg, in 1971/72, knocked my team out of the Cup Winners' Cup on my birthday!

Another glimpse of the future was captured at a Cub Scout Jamboree at Gilwell Park in 1969. It was an international event and the organisers had arranged a mini-World Cup involving teams from eight countries. We saw French, Swiss, Belgian and German players, along with English and Scottish teams. The passion and rivalry was exciting and stirred up memories of the 1966 World Cup three years earlier. I believe the Swiss won the competition.

I was fortunate to see a lot of European football in London, including the first UEFA Cup Final in 1972, between Tottenham Hotspur and Wolverhampton Wanderers. Although not a Spurs fan, I queued in the early hours of a bright Sunday morning, along with thousands of others, with my friend and his father as well as my brothers to try to get tickets for the game. I could not help feeling a little disappointed that the final was between two English clubs, but I will always remember the traffic jam in the Tottenham High Road and the fans banging on the side of our coach as we snaked through the crowds to the stadium. And I also recall the sight of the newly designed UEFA Cup, a period piece if ever there was one, shining in the floodlights as it was paraded around the pitch after the game amid the sheer mayhem.

I saw Ajax, Feyenoord and Cruyff, West Ham's run to the Cup Winners' Cup Final in 1976, and teams like Red Star Belgrade, Juventus, Bayern Munich and Barcelona, all of whom leapt out of the atlas at me. European football fascinated me and still does, although the plethora of competitions and their size has made it an everyday item of indulgence.

Not even being mugged by three opportunist Ajax fans in Stockholm at the 2017 Europa League Final has dulled my enthusiasm. There was something special about two-legged ties and the sense of mystery about teams of men from the east, south or north. The world has become a more globalised place, so we are no longer in awe of teams of 'crack' Eastern Europeans, ultra-efficient Germans and cunning Italians and Spaniards. One reason is that the top clubs are no longer standard-bearers for their domestic football, they are multicultural squads of hired hands drawn from across Europe, South America, Asia and Africa. A team wearing the colours of Real Madrid could so easily be a team from England and vice versa. We have certainly lost some of the curiosity and wonder, but we have also gained plenty as the game has evolved.

Fortunately, there is still much to enjoy, but whether it was because I was just 11 years old or because the 1960s and 1970s were still a time of exploration in pan-European competition, those early days when you discovered that they also played football in every country were indeed quite magical. This book is the story of the pioneering years, the glory of the late 1960s and early 1970s, right through to the moment the madness took over in 1985 in Brussels. However awful the events at the Heysel Stadium were that night, they provide a suitable bookend for the period 1955–1985.

1

Continent Cut Off

SOME PEOPLE have always found the prospect of pan-European football competition a little romantic. The thought of travelling to far-off places, testing football abilities and mixing with foreigners was exciting and gave people the opportunity to add to their education. Travel, they said, broadened the mind and made for more rounded individuals. This was sold to people in much the same way that eating fruit and vegetables or reading good books and appreciating culture like opera, ballet or drinking fine wine. Of course, not everyone could afford to travel, certainly not in the 1950s, but by the 1960s holidays abroad became accessible, and eyes, if not always minds, were opened.

From a football perspective, healthy competition against overseas nations and club teams was a way to learn from others and perhaps borrow a few ideas and techniques. The Second World War was ended by a united Europe in collaboration with the United States and the Soviet Union. Was there any greater motivation to further the cause of integration than sport, seemingly a benign and healthy form of nationalism that might strengthen harmony and cooperation?

The United Kingdom, in some respects, still longed for the days of Empire. Schools were slow to remove pull-down maps that were covered in pink to represent British territories that had gradually turned to a different colour on most globes. Britain hung on to its wartime mentality for a long time, with corrugated metal air-raid shelters remaining at the bottom of gardens for decades and a deep-rooted suspicion of foreigners. Mention of Germans, Italians and Japanese was often met with a 'spit-on-the-ground' response, in sentiment if not in action, and the reference points for most aspects of daily life were 'before the war', 'during the war' or 'since the war'.

Britain was supposed to be the world leader in football. 'We invented the game' was the popular view of the nation's favourite pastime. England was slow to realise that other nations just might be more skilful, tactically savvy and better organised. The British Empire did its bit in spreading the word and several coaches and administrators moved across Europe and beyond to teach local people about the ways of association football. Some popular overseas clubs were established with a British influence; scratch the surface of clubs in South America, Spain, Italy and elsewhere and it is possible pioneering figures such as John Gramlick, a founder of the First Vienna Cricket & Football Club, or Herbert Kilpin, the son of a butcher from Nottingham who was involved in the development of AC Milan, will emerge.

Central Europe certainly liked the idea of competition among countries and their clubs. This, of course, may have been easier in landlocked Europe where railway connections were being established between cites such as Budapest, Vienna, Prague, Paris and Berlin. But for the UK, the English Channel was an obstacle and an economic barrier for many sporting organisations. Between 1897 and 1911, the 'Challenge Kupa' matched teams from the Austro-Hungarian Empire. It was dominated by Austrian teams such as Wiener SC, and only once did a Hungarian club, Ferencváros, win the competition. Britain did try its hand at cross-border competitions, the rather presumptuous 'Football World Championship' that was inaugurated in 1876. This was a match between the FA Cup and Scottish Cup winners, but the world was undoubtedly a smaller place in the 19th century.

By the turn of the century, teams were travelling to Continental Europe on close-season tours. This was not just big clubs but also amateur organisations such as Ilford, West Auckland and Bishop Auckland. In 1909, West Auckland went on a fortnight's break to Italy, travelling to Turin, Milan and Genoa. They took part in the competition for the Sir Thomas Lipton Trophy, held in Turin. Lipton, of Lipton's Tea fame, was very generous to sports such as yachting, rowing and football. The Football Association (FA) was invited to send a team but declined. West Auckland beat Stuttgarter Sportfreunde and Winterthur of Switzerland to win a huge trophy that cost around 'one hundred guineas'. Two years later, they won the trophy again, beating Juventus 6-1 to keep the glittering prize permanently.

It was not just British football pioneers that left their mark on Europe, as the French were also renowned administrators and innovators. It was a Frenchman, Pierre de Coubertin, along with the Greek, Demetrious Vikelas, who founded the International Olympic Committee in 1894, and in 1904 the first FIFA president was Robert Guerin. Later, Jules Rimet became president and it was his idea to launch a World Cup.

England did not join FIFA until 1906 and saw little value in France's proposal for a European federation. Two years later, England travelled to Europe for their first tour and found the opposition far too weak – they netted 28 goals in four games against Austria, Bohemia and Hungary. However, their relationship with FIFA was, at times, fractious, and in 1928 they, along with the other British countries, withdrew. This meant that when the World Cup was introduced, they could not enter. Regardless, their response did not really paint a positive picture: 'I am instructed to express regret at our inability to accept the invitation.'

It was not until 1950 that they first participated, by which time Italy, Brazil, West Germany and Uruguay had all made significant progress in developing their football knowledge. The British sides played their Home International Championship games, not really aware that their position at the table was coming under severe threat.

All through the 1920s and 1930s, many teams went abroad in the early summer, visiting Scandinavia, the Low Countries, Germany, Switzerland, and venturing even as far as South Africa, Australia and Canada. Some of this football tourism, especially in the early days, was tantamount to missionary work, but a few more open-minded football people also saw it as a fact-finding expedition.

If any area of Europe was to have a profound influence on British sport, it was Austria and Hungary. Arsenal's Herbert Chapman, the most innovative figure in English football in the inter-war years, had more than one eye on developments in Central Europe, where coffee houses attracted football intellectuals who would discuss tactics and ideas amid cups of thick, dark Viennese coffee. Chapman developed relationships with some of the top coaches in Continental Europe, such as Hugo Meisl and Italy's World Cup-winning coach Vittorio Pozzo, and had tried to take some of their methods to England. Meisl was full of respect for Chapman, claiming he was the world's leading football man.

While Chapman's Arsenal dominated English football in the 1930s, they were never able to test themselves against foreign opposition in serious competition, so much of their reputation was gained through hearsay. Chapman admired the Central European Mitropa Cup and the enthusiasm that it generated in the late 1920s and 1930s, and predicted that a West Europe Cup would emerge sooner or later. Needless to say, not everyone trusted foreign football. In the early 1930s, when France introduced a professional league, some British players were enticed abroad by what the insular media called 'the French menace'.

Hugo Meisl was the driving force behind the competition that Chapman had been so impressed by. Its full name was La Coupe de l'Europe Centrale but it became more commonly known as the Mitropa Cup. Meisl, a child of the Habsburg Empire, was Jewish, multilingual and eager to travel. His experiences in the First World War helped formulate a belief that sport, and football in particular, could help develop bonds between nations. And in *mitteleuropa*, it was relatively easy to cross borders to play football matches.

Meisl's idea was to bring together eight teams for a modest competition in which all ties were two-legged. Two teams from each of Austria, Czechoslovakia, Hungary and Yugoslavia took part in the inaugural tournament in 1927: Sparta and Slavia from Prague, Ferencváros and MTK from Budapest, Admira and Rapid from Vienna and Hajduk Split and OFK Belgrade from Yugoslavia. The final was won by Sparta Prague, who beat Rapid Vienna 7-4 on aggregate. The crowds were raucous and occasionally nationalistic as evidenced by the second game of the final in Vienna, which was held up because of pitch invasions. Nevertheless, the blue touchpaper had been lit and the Mitropa Cup had provided audiences with a glimpse of the future.

It also provided encouragement for other organisations to introduce similar types of competition. In 1930, for example, Servette FC of Switzerland organised the Coupe des Nations (or Small Club World Cup). This was supposed to comprise 12 teams but two possible entrants, Sheffield Wednesday, from non-FIFA England, and Benfica, did not accept the invitation. The ten teams created a relatively strong field; there were champions from Italy, the Netherlands, Switzerland, Czechoslovakia, Germany, Belgium and Hungary, as well as cup winners from Austria, France and Spain. First Vienna of Austria, who had beaten the hosts Servette in the first round 7-0 – only for the Swiss side to get a second chance in the consolation round of losers – emphasised their superiority by beating them once more by an emphatic scoreline. Seven years later, France hosted a tournament to coincide with the Exposition Internationale des Arts et Techniques dans la Vie Moderne. Eight teams were involved: Austria Vienna, Leipzig, Slavia Prague, Phöbus (Hungary), Chelsea, Olympique de Marseille, Bologna and Sochaux. Bologna were the winners, beating Chelsea quite easily by 4-1 in the final.

Although British teams were still visiting the continent right up until the summer of 1939, it was directed by the advice of the Foreign Office. The political situation in Germany and Italy was now influencing the way people saw Germans and Italians. In 1934, the infamous 'Battle of Highbury' took place between England and Italy. Italy's manager, Pozzo, used the sort of language that Benito Mussolini would have been proud of, speaking of his team as 'soldiers' playing on 'battlefields'. Italy were world champions and England were desperate to show them they were their equals. The game ended with multiple injuries and an England win by 3-2. It was a brutal, uncompromising contest, but both teams were guilty of overplaying it.

The newspapers the following day were full of criticism about the Italian approach to the game. Some reporters even called for the FA to cease all games against the evil Continentals. The reaction to the game almost incited a diplomatic incident. Frank Carruthers of the *Daily Mail* commented: 'England beat Italy, but should these games be played? [...] They [Italy] were not greatly concerned with the ball.' The *Dundee Courier*'s post-match comments hinted that Italy's tactics signalled a sea-change in attitudes. The newspaper claimed that 'this was not a match but a battle [...] It is evident that the rules of the game as played on the continent bear little resemblance to the laws that govern football in this country [...] These continental teams, backed by the uncontrolled enthusiasm of their countrymen, have no regard for the safety of their opponents [...] The bitterness of feeling that is creeping into all forms of international sport is something which all true sportsmen deplore.' Referee Otto Rudolf Olsen also went public: 'I had to pull the Italians up and I gave them an awful warning. I said to them: "You must stop this rough, dirty play."' Nobody seemed to be listening.

A year later, England welcomed Germany to London. When it was announced that England would play Germany in a football match in London, on 4 December, public sentiment became inflamed. The Trade Union Congress called for the game to be postponed and that the entry into Britain of German football supporters should be prohibited. The *Daily Mail* added fuel to the fire by reporting that swastika-adorned motor coaches, packed with Germans, would proceed through central London. There was a touch of irony about the choice of venue for the game – Tottenham Hotspur's White Hart Lane. Tottenham had a strong Jewish contingent among its clientele. There were media reports, driven by local Tottenham and Edmonton newspapers and the *Jewish Chronicle*, that German supporters would march through known Jewish neighbourhoods. There was little substance to such rumours but, in an age where stereotyping was not a crime and political correctness was unheard of, the British press portrayed the Germans as bull-necked, bespectacled and noisy. Every one of them was a Nazi. The head of German football, Herr Linnemann, was called a 'Nazi football dictator' as he warned travelling supporters not to sing political songs. When they arrived, it seemed to be a surprise when it was revealed that 'all were smartly dressed and almost every other man carried a camera and pair of binoculars'.

The German supporters were escorted all the way to White Hart Lane. In Park Lane, a policeman was placed every ten yards along the route. German messages were blasted out from loudspeakers wherever the supporters went. The friendly spirit of the game – England won 3-0 – was something of a relief. The *Daily Mirror* commented: 'Doesn't sport reconcile, doesn't it bring nations together, can't we kill war with perpetual football?'

The Second World War put a stop to major football matches, although in Britain regional competitions tried to bolster the population's morale. The post-war boom in attendances confirmed the popularity of the sport and its role in the lives of working-class people. Obviously, with all the devastation of the war, competitions like the World Cup were put on ice, but clubs ventured abroad to play in France, Belgium and the Netherlands, from the top clubs to amateur outfits. British clubs were very popular in the countries that had suffered during the war, and their presence, which some saw as a sign of unity and empathy, was often greeted with affection and appreciation.

Just six months after the war in Europe ended, Russia's Dynamo Moscow visited Britain, a tour that was a combination of goodwill gesture, a show of strength and a fact-finding mission. The Soviets had a list of conditions before they agreed to travel to the UK, not least that they would eat all their meals at their embassy and only play club sides. The media in England was quick to write them off, claiming they would not be good enough to play the classy professionals from the Football League. There was a great deal of curiosity about these visitors from a nation that had been Britain's ally in the war and had suffered tremendously during the conflict. They were also Communists, which in itself aroused suspicion in British people.

Dynamo played four games and left Britain unbeaten. They drew 3-3 at Chelsea in front of a huge crowd approaching 100,000 and they beat a strangely constructed Arsenal XI that included guests such as Stanley Matthews and Stan Mortensen. 'This is not Arsenal,' claimed the Russian media. 'It is a representative team.' From British football authorities' perspective, the most worrying result was Dynamo's 10-1 win at Cardiff City's Ninian Park. Their final game of the tour was a 2-2 draw with Rangers in Glasgow. While the smarter members of the sporting community admitted the Soviet visitors had exposed the limitations and crudeness of the British game, other reports suggested not everyone was impressed: 'The view of the football experts is that while the Dynamos are a good team, they are not world beaters and that good play and solid tackling could knock them out of their stride.' Regardless of local bias, Dynamo's passing game, which they referred to as *passovotckka*, was very eye-catching.

Dynamo Moscow passed off into the night, but their brief stay in Britain did spark off some interest in overseas football. But there was still enough arrogance and xenophobia in the game to portray England as the cradle of football, and with that exalted status came the right to believe the national team would always be able to emerge victorious.

After the Second World War, they rejoined FIFA and in 1950 entered the World Cup for the first time. The war had robbed football of the peak years of some players and, in the aftermath, some clubs were often short of talent. The England 21-man squad had few youngsters, and eight members were over 30. Another five were close to 30 and only two were under 25. Stanley Matthews (35) and Tom Finney (28) were both included. England went to Brazil confident of success, but they won just one of their three group games, against Chile, and suffered the humiliation of losing 1-0 to the United States. The US team was built around the St. Louis Simpkins-Ford club and had some younger players than England.

Contrary to some opinions about the game, most of the team was US-born, with others, such as Joe Maca, Ed McIvenny and Joe Gaetjens, becoming US citizens. This should have been a wake-up call, but three years later Hungary beat England 6-3 at Wembley, and then the following year thrashed them by 7-1 in Budapest. The Continentals had not just learned how to play football, they were now making England look very pedestrian and somewhat clueless. One report after the Wembley debacle, by journalist Bob Ferrier, was blunt and to the point: 'Shed no tears for England. Seek no excuses. There were no excuses.' He went on to call for dramatic change to the game in England. 'Defensive, lusty passing, furious kicking tactics which dominate our league system, must be wholly abandoned and we must learn to master the ball and relearn the art and craft and elegance and flowing rhythm of this great game which we gave the world.'

Six months after Wembley, Hungary inflicted upon England their worst-ever defeat but still people were slow to learn. Some tried to talk up the possibility of English success in the Hungarian capital: 'We were told the Hungarians had lost their zip. They were slowing down. The machine was clogging a little,' wrote Walter Pilkington. It was, sadly, wishful thinking and Hungary merely emphasised how much work needed to be done by England at both club and national team levels. Critics felt clubs needed to spend more time and money on coaching rather than scouting for bargains and that footballers had far too much time on their hands outside of playing games. This was time that could be used to enhance training and developing strategies and better ball skills. Everything about the Hungarians appeared to be modern and professional, from their fitted shirts to their slimline boots, while England were still wearing heavy, restrictive kits and cumbersome footwear. Change was needed if the home of football was to adapt to the new order.

In the 1950s, another major competition emerged in Europe. The Latin Cup involved the top sides from France, Italy, Portugal and Spain. The first edition was in 1949 and included Barcelona, Sporting Clube de Portugal, Torino and Stade de Reims. Over the next eight years, Real Madrid, Benfica, AC Milan and Juventus were among the entrants. The competition was not a financial success, although attendances were very good. It was no coincidence that when UEFA's European Cup got under way, Real,

Benfica and Milan would all emerge as contenders for the trophy.

Something was moving in Britain, however, and the introduction of floodlights at many Football League grounds provided an opportunity to stage prestige matches under the lights against foreign opposition. The lights, of course, had to be funded, so the novelty of games at night, along with the chance to see overseas teams and players, was an ideal way to cover the considerable cost of modernisation. In the mid-to-late 1950s, clubs from Austria, Belgium, Czechoslovakia, Denmark, Hungary, Israel, Russia, Spain, Turkey and West Germany, to name but a few, arrived to play at newly illuminated stadiums. Not all pundits felt these games would be a success, predicting the average football supporter would not find games on dark winter nights much of an attraction. Generally, the curiosity value led to some very good attendances.

Nobody staged the prestige friendly better than Wolverhampton Wanderers, who were league champions in 1954. Wolves, who had spent £30,000 on their new lights, carried the flag for England in trying to restore some pride after Hungary had destroyed the national side twice in a matter of months. They beat South Africa, Celtic, Racing Club of Buenos Aires and Spartak Moscow, before Honvéd of Budapest arrived at Molineux. Five of the Hungarian team that had been so tragically beaten in the 1954 World Cup Final were in the Honvéd line-up. Wolves manager Stan Cullis, aware of the flowing style of the Hungarians, tried to gain an advantage by ordering the ground staff to saturate the Molineux pitch. Honvéd raced into a 2-0 lead inside 14 minutes but Wolves came back to win 3-2 in front of 55,000 people. Cullis believed Wolves were 'champions of the world' because they had beaten a team as talented as

Honvéd, but such a claim was interpreted as arrogant and rather short-sighted across Europe.

In the offices of the French sports newspaper, *L'Équipe*, the editor, Gabriel Hanot was rather annoyed. He and his colleague, Jacques Ferran, laughed a little at suggestions that Wolves were an unbeatable combination and that English football had been vindicated. 'We must wait for Wolves to visit Moscow or Budapest before we proclaim their invincibility,' said Hanot. His caution was understandable for England had failed to impress in the 1954 World Cup but reached the last eight before losing 4-2 against Uruguay. Hungary, by contrast, had scored 27 goals in their five World Cup games but were deprived of a fully fit Puskás in the final. Scotland had also featured in 1954 and were hammered 7-0 by Uruguay.

Hanot acted quickly and set out plans, in the form of an open letter, for a European club competition involving the champions of domestic football across the continent. Initially, both FIFA and UEFA were not over-enthused, but momentum soon gathered for the concept, which would involve midweek games under floodlights. Unsurprisingly, the Football League was not over-enthused either, officially because of the threat of fixture congestion, but maybe they also feared further blows to the fragile ego of the English game.

In July 1955, the draw for the first round of the competition involved 16 clubs. Interestingly, eight were the champions of their respective leagues in 1954/55, including Chelsea, who had surprisingly won the Football League for the first time. AC Milan, Real Madrid, Reims and Anderlecht were also among the participants. If the various associations had sent their champions, then Benfica and Honvéd would have undoubtedly made for a stronger field.

Chelsea, arguably the most ill-equipped of post-war league champions at that point, were discouraged from taking part by the Football League. The draw had already paired them with Swedish club Djurgården, so a replacement had to be found. Gwardia Warsaw, who had finished fourth in the Polish league in 1954/55, took Chelsea's place. UEFA was not happy about Chelsea's decision, particularly as the games with Djurgården had already been arranged. The attitude of the Football League can only be interpreted as an expression of the narrow- mindedness that existed at the time, but it also denied Chelsea the chance to be the first English side to compete in European competition. The media felt that it was simply a case of the League not wanting to be represented in the European Cup. Shortly afterwards, Aberdeen, the Scottish champions in 1955, and Chelsea announced they would be meeting in September to determine the 'British Championship', the newspapers overplaying the importance of the game that was little more than a friendly.

Meanwhile, Hibernian, who had finished fifth in the Scottish League in 1954/55, were confirmed as Scotland's representative. Some sceptics wondered whether Hibs were equipped to play in the competition, but both Partizan Belgrade and Servette had finished at the back end of their domestic top six. Hibernian were drawn to meet Rot-Weiss Essen of West Germany, but there were doubts about them continuing as the German Football Association considered them to be too weak to compete, although they were the champions. Hibernian and Rot-Weiss Essen did meet, presumably because the authorities relented. The Edinburgh team was the first British team to enter Europe.

Some felt Hibernian had arrived at this moment a little late. The late 1940s and early 1950s were a golden period for the club, with three Scottish League titles won in 1948, 1951 and 1952. They had an all-star forward line that included Gordon Smith, Eddie Turnbull, Lawrie Reilly, Bobby Johnstone and Willie Ormond. In both 1954 and 1955, they had finished fifth in the final league table. Their opponents in the first round of the European Cup, Rot-Weiss Essen, had won the German championship in the play-off final against Kaiserslautern, who had World Cup hero Fritz Walter in their line-up. They were coached by Fritz Szepan, the former Schalke star forward from the 1930s.

Hibernian flew out to Germany to a city that had suffered considerably during the Second World War. As a prominent city in the Ruhr industrial region, it had been identified as a target for strategic bombing. The match in Essen on 14 September 1955 went almost unnoticed in the British media. Hibernian flew out to Düsseldorf, taking a 13-man squad. It took some time for any news of the game to hit the newspapers, and then the information was scant. Hibernian won 4-0, putting on an impressive display. The goals came from three members of the 'famous five', two from Turnbull and one apiece from Reilly and Ormond. Hibernian had every reason to be optimistic, but German domestic football was some way behind Britain, Spain and Italy. Rot-Weiss improved in the second leg, which was drawn 1-1 at Easter Road. Hibernian's next opponents were Djurgården, who had comfortably disposed of Chelsea's replacements, Gwardia Warsaw.

There was no overseas trip for Hibernian this time as the Swedish winter made it difficult to play on home soil. Djurgården 'hosted' Hibs at Partick Thistle's Firhill on 23 November but were beaten 3-1. The second leg, just five days later, was a 1-0 win for Hibs, sending them through to the last four.

Things were now getting serious; Stade de Reims were the reigning French champions and had beaten the crack Hungarians, Vörös Lobogó, who were also known as MTK, in the quarter-final. Reims' star player was Raymond Kopa, a compact, clever forward who would eventually join Real Madrid. Over the two games, the overwhelming conclusion was the French team were far more savvy than Hibernian. They won 3-0 on aggregate, winning 2-0 in Paris before grabbing a 1-0 victory at Easter Road, with 45,000 in attendance. Hibernian's pioneering sojourn was over, but the crowds, the excitement and the games themselves had sparked off something that English football had missed out on in 1955/56. The first European Cup was won by Real Madrid, who came from 2-0 and 3-2 down to beat Reims 4-3 in the Parc des Princes, Paris.

Although the game was on television in the UK, most newspapers consigned the result to the stop press. The perception of foreign football was still negative. Neil Bentley of the *Evening Chronicle* noted: 'The European Cup final was exciting for football fans. At every incident, I was expecting trouble for British referee Arthur Ellis, but the continental blood didn't quite boil over in spite of Madrid's exciting win.'

2

The Rise and Fall of the Babes

EXCITEMENT FOR the new European competition was considerable across the continent. The first final, between Real Madrid and Stade de Reims, had excited the French public and the demand for tickets was such that the game was switched from the Paris Velodrome to the Parc des Princes. The average crowd for the 29 ties was over 30,000, with Real Madrid attracting two attendances over 100,000. Chelsea, who had been advised not to take part, must have been kicking themselves, for their own campaign in 1955/56 had been a severe let-down after their league championship success.

Chelsea's successors were Manchester United, who had assembled an extraordinarily talented team of young players, most of whom had been developed through the club's pioneering nationwide youth system. In the post-war world, some clubs had been short of playing resources as well as money, so home-grown talent was clearly a direction that would not only provide squad members, but also avoid the need to buy players for increasingly rising transfer fees.

Matt Busby was something of a football visionary and saw the direction football was heading. Like Santiago Bernabéu in Madrid, he was enthused by the prospect of matching his team against the best. 'I've always been

European Cup-conscious; the only way to become the best team in Europe is by winning the European Cup,' he said some years later.

Interestingly, Chelsea never commented about their withdrawal from the European Cup in 1955, but it is clear now they let a massive opportunity pass when they allowed themselves to be talked out of entering that inaugural competition. They attended the initial meeting in Paris, along with 16 other clubs, and chairman Joe Mears, who would eventually become chairman of the FA in 1963, was keen for his club to join such a forward-looking venture. Had they taken part, they may have developed into a very different club instead of one of the great underachievers for so many years.

Manchester United, a year later, were very enthused. Sir Stanley Rous wrote to the club and invited them to enter for 1956/57. Rous might have looked like the archetypal English gentleman, but he was an advocate of pan-European competition. Busby asked him whether the FA could stop United playing in Europe, and Rous confirmed there would be no hurdles. The Football League was a different matter, and it should be remembered that the FA and League were often at loggerheads. It was suggested, however, that the Football League could pressure United to withdraw from the European Cup if the ties caused a fixture congestion. Even as United were planning for a brand-new adventure, the League was planning to expand its constitution to five divisions of 20 teams with a new midweek competition. This would, presumably, evolve into Alan Hardaker's 'baby', the Football League Cup.

United's ground, Old Trafford, did not have floodlights, so any European ties would have to be played at Manchester City's Maine Road. Busby saw an additional benefit from attractive games involving some of Europe's best teams, and the profits made from the anticipated big crowds could effectively fund the club's floodlights.

Twenty-two clubs entered the 1956/57 competition – including Manchester United – in the preliminary round. United were drawn to meet Anderlecht, a club that had been Belgian champions seven times since 1946. Included in their team was Joseph Mermans, known as 'Jef', who played over 400 games for the club and was captain of Belgium. United were going well in the league and were expected to get through to the next round. The first leg, in Brussels, was won 2-0 but went largely unnoticed by the media.

However, the newspapers were very quick to proclaim United as the best side in Europe and that, as England's champions, it was more important for Busby's team to win the European Cup in 1956/57. A crowd of almost 44,000 packed into Maine Road for the second leg at the end of September 1956 and they were treated to a sublime exhibition. United won 10-0, an incredible scoreline in any era, with Dennis Viollet scoring four and Tommy Taylor a hat-trick. Duncan Edwards, Eddie Colman and Billy Whelan were all in excellent form – in fact the entire United team was praised for one of the great team performances in the club's history. Anderlecht were quick to acknowledge the team that ended any hopes they had of progress. 'I've never played against a team so adept at the best continental style of football,' said Jef Mermans. 'These United players have the craft of the Hungarians and the stamina of the Russians. It was an education to see the kind of football I never expected from an English side.'

The Belgian press joined in the praise of United. *Le Peuple*, a Socialist daily newspaper, commented: 'Eleven Belgian players served as training partners for Manchester,' while *Sportswereld*, added: 'It looks as though Manchester are taking over where the Hungarians left off.' Others, such as *Les Sports*, emphasised how United did not resemble the popular image of an English football team: 'In Manchester we saw the future European Cup winners in action [...] their performance which mixed traditional English style with continental dash, showed English football coming out of its isolation.' Another report said Anderlecht had simply been annihilated by the best team in Europe at the moment. A 10-0 win of any sort is an achievement, but Anderlecht were not Real Madrid, Honvéd, Athletic Bilbao or Fiorentina. Bigger challenges would be ahead of Manchester United.

It is often forgotten that European action involving English teams was going on before United made their bow in the European Cup. The Inter-Cities Fairs Cup was a peculiar competition, mostly because it was not a UEFA-run event and, secondly, because it had a strange 'one-city, one-team' ruling. The idea had emerged from discussions involving FIFA representatives but was essentially aimed as a football tournament between cities that had hosted trade fairs.

The initial Fairs Cup took almost three years to complete, beginning in June 1955 and finally ending in May 1958. Twelve teams entered, including a London XI and Birmingham City, but, of the 12, only ten went ahead as Cologne and Vienna both withdrew. Looking back on the competition it appears quirky, a product of its time and often rather half-baked, but the prize piece of silverware, called the Noel Beard Trophy, was a thing of beauty and eccentricity.

For Birmingham City, the Fairs Cup was an attractive interlude from everyday league competition and generated good attendances. A combined 73,000 saw them beat Zagreb and Inter Milan at St Andrew's and they won through to the semi-finals, where they were narrowly and rather unluckily beaten by Barcelona over two legs. London reached the final, drawing 2-2 with Barcelona at Stamford Bridge before losing 6-0 in the Camp Nou. The London team had little consistency about it, with only four of the first-leg line-up playing in the second. There was also almost two months between the two games. Notably, a young Jimmy Greaves of Chelsea, who was in his first season, played and scored in the first leg.

The European Cup in 1956 was certainly growing in stature and was well received by the football public in Manchester. Matt Busby recognised that the games played so far were adrenaline-inducing for his players. United, having beaten Anderlecht, were paired with Borussia Dortmund, the West German champions. This was an older team than Busby's 'Babes', and their best players were very experienced. For example, Max Michallek was 34 and Alfred Preissler 35. Half the team was, in fact, over 30 years of age. Most of the players were part-time professionals who could earn as little as £27 per month.

Despite their status as German champions, Dortmund were reputedly inferior to United's vibrant young side. Nevertheless, nobody was taking anything for granted. Some sections of the press had accused United of being too 'cocky', but Busby was always quick to discourage complacency even if his response to critics was that he wanted his players to demonstrate confidence and arrogance. Dortmund arrived in Manchester with specially designed shorts for floodlit football, a shiny, almost fluorescent material that had been manufactured by Umbro.

The game at Maine Road drew a crowd of over 75,000. By half-time, United were 3-0 ahead, with two goals coming from Viollet and one from David Pegg. Dortmund came back strongly in the second period, with Roger Byrne, a player much criticised by England fans, gifting a goal for Helmut Kapitulski. Alfred Schmidt scored a second for the visitors, but United hung on, despite being made to look very inexperienced by Dortmund. Interestingly, just a few days before the 17 October match, a young Bobby Charlton made his debut for United.

The second leg was a very delicate affair, with Dortmund confident they could knock out their English visitors. United adopted a safety-first approach and tried to protect goalkeeper Ray Wood at all times. Byrne, Bill Foulkes and Mark Jones all had excellent games and, up front, Tommy Taylor worked hard as a one-man forward line. The press reported that the Germans 'had to resort to "Big Bertha" tactics', in other words, fire in long-range shots just as they had in the First World War with their huge howitzer. If nothing else, this comment from the *Daily Herald* indicated that the rivalry with Germany went far deeper than a mere football match. The game ended goalless and sent United into the last eight, along with Athletic Bilbao, Fiorentina, Real Madrid, Red Star Belgrade, Nice, CDNA Sofia and Grasshopper Zürich. Busby knew that sooner or later his team would have to face Real Madrid, the team that was the benchmark for all others in Europe. But this time they had to encounter the team that had actually won the Spanish league in 1956, Bilbao from the Basque country.

Most of the Bilbao side were Spanish internationals and, unlike Dortmund, were in their prime. Although they did not retain the title they won in 1956, they were a tough and skilful team. They had beaten Porto and Honvéd, including Ferenc Puskás, in the competition so far. United had to travel to Bilbao for the first leg on 16 January at the iconic San Mamés stadium. This was no

Spanish holiday, however, for the weather resembled a typically seasonal day in Manchester: cold, damp and, to cap it all, snow. The team trained on a Garellano field in Bilbao but found the Spanish food a challenge. The Spanish press agency, *Alfil*, reported: 'A curious fact is that they [the United players] asked for dishes cooked without oil and if possible, from tins.'

The game itself was a hard one. In front of a Basque beret-clad crowd of 36,000, with umbrellas the order of the day, United were 3-0 down at half-time. It took only 90 seconds for Ignacio Uribe to open the scoring for Bilbao and, for a long time, the pitch and conditions seemed to upset the English champions. Tommy Taylor and Dennis Viollet reduced the deficit within ten minutes of the restart but Bilbao added two more goals before Billy Whelan scored what would prove to be the vital third.

United had given themselves a lifeline, but they struggled to get home from Spain as there was ice and snow on the wings of the aeroplane, an ominous preface to the tragedy that was to follow in 1958. Busby was anxious for nothing to delay their return in order to demonstrate to the Football League that midweek trips to Europe would not impede the fixture programme. He engaged his players, urging them to grab brooms to clear the plane as there simply was no local labour available. They eventually left two hours later than planned, but some supporters that flew to Spain went as far as returning to Manchester overland.

The press thought United had been given a hiding, but nobody doubted they would still win through. Busby told the media: 'We are still in with a good chance. We shall not give so many goals away again.' Despite the disappointing scoreline, the quality of the attacking football by both sides could not be faulted, but when Bilbao arrived in Manchester they were greeted by a city that anticipated a great football match. The *Manchester Evening News* had a message in Spanish on its front page and felt that rarely had a game in Britain attracted so much attention. A full house at Maine Road was expected, with a gate of £11,000, which would take United's proceeds from three home ties up to £27,000.

They put on another excellent display against Bilbao, leading newspapers to claim, 'El Magnifico, Manchester United!' Bilbao, with their 'abominable snowman' Jésus Garay in defence, were swamped by United's attacking prowess. Viollet scored four minutes from the interval, Taylor netted a second with 20 minutes to go and then Johnny Berry, one of the more experienced United hands, grabbed the vital third with five minutes to go. The Bilbao supporters still managed to enjoy their time in Manchester: 'We gave our best and in the process, I believe we made many, many friends,' said Joma of the *Gaceta del Norte*. United also remarked on how sporting Bilbao had been, especially Garay, their giant defender. If there was a single tie that sparked off the British appetite for European competition, it may well have been the two games between United and Bilbao. Certainly there seemed to be great excitement in Manchester after Busby's 'babes' had overcome a very good Bilbao side.

United were delighted with having slalomed their way through three rounds and awaited the draw for the semi-finals, which took place at the end of February 1957. In Cologne's Excelsior Hotel, UEFA pulled the teams out of an ice bucket and Busby got his wish. Manchester United versus Real Madrid or Nice. 'We realise we have stern opposition, but we think we have a good chance of qualifying for the final,' said Busby. He went off to France to watch Real and Nice meet in a third game after the two legs had failed to produce a winner. Nice had already met British opposition in the form of Rangers and had to play three games to get past the Scottish champions. This time, they found Real Madrid too strong and Alfredo Di Stéfano's two second-half goals were enough to seal a 3-2 win for the holders.

Real Madrid had wasted no time in strengthening their team after their successful 1955/56 European Cup campaign. They had been impressed by Stade de Reims' performance in the final and in particular the French forward Raymond Kopa. But they could not play Kopa until Di Stéfano's Spanish citizenship was effective. Real were heading for the Spanish league title, but United were also poised to win their second successive league championship. In addition, United had reached the FA Cup Final and they were now up against possibly the best club team in the world. Both sides were on the brink of achieving unprecedented success and they represented the future of the game in different ways. Real had the financial clout to sign whoever they wanted, and United were building a new model that English football had not seen before.

Real warmed up for the semi-final with a 5-1 away win at Las Palmas, with Di Stéfano scoring four times, while United were held at home 0-0 by Tottenham Hotspur. Real's form had been patchy, however, with four defeats in nine games, but their eyes were certainly on retaining the European Cup. But they had been made to work for their victories so far, with both Rapid Vienna and Nice taking them to a play-off after the two legs.

There was a sense of curiosity about United's first European campaign, especially the away games, which were seen as a great adventure. While the travelling support was not comparable to modern times, those that did make the journey to Belgium, West Germany and

Spain could well have been making their first overseas trips. News bulletins from Madrid gave strange details of the United party, such as the meal involving both teams. On 10 April, they sat down to 'beefsteak dinners'. With the United lads enjoying fried potatoes, fruit and wine. The Spaniards had a wine ration of one and a half pints for every four players and instead of potatoes they had mixed vegetables and scrambled eggs. After dinner, Busby and Jimmy Murphy led their players out for a stroll around the chilly city. As the tension built up around the tie, Busby was able to tell the team they would receive £50 per man as a bonus if they won the competition. But despite urging Busby to let them go to a bullfight, the patriarchal manager insisted they turn in for an early night.

Real received a blow before the game when defender Ángel Atienza was ruled out. On the plus side, Héctor Rial was fit again after being on the sidelines for seven months with a leg injury. Busby came back from the Nice play-off singing the praises of the Real team. He was particularly enthused about Paco Gento, whom he claimed was the fastest player he had ever seen. It was said the Real forward line, which included Di Stéfano, Mateos, Rial and the diminutive Kopa, was worth a quarter of a million pounds. Every single member of the team seemed to be a ball artist and was 'as clever as Stanley Matthews', according to one newspaper reporter.

The first game in the Bernabéu stadium also demonstrated that Real Madrid's artistic side was matched by a certain physical determination. The popular view of foreign footballers in Britain was that they applied some of the darker arts of the game in a very sly, underhand way. 'Far too often, [referee] Leo Horn let the old continental custom of bodychecking and shirt-tugging go unpunished,' claimed the *Daily Herald*. There were 37 fouls during the game, which was considered extreme at the time. The first half was goalless, despite United's promise that they would launch an all-out attack on the cup holders. But as the game hit the hour mark, Real took control, scoring twice in a three-minute spell through a Rial header and a dash and finish from Di Stéfano. Tommy Taylor, who bravely led the line for United, pulled a goal back eight minutes from time, scrambling home the ball, but with the Real supporters chanting '*Otro, otro, otro*', meaning 'another, another', they scored almost immediately through Enrique Mateos.

The headlines in the newspapers let everyone know that United had been the victims in a bruising game. Real won 3-1 and, according to most reporters, 'got away with murder', and United were 'hacked, kicked, slashed and wrestled'. Even the great Alfredo Di Stéfano came in for criticism after he kicked Jackie Blanchflower, so much so that the neutral view was that he should have been sent off. Moreover, Real defender Marquitos had apparently lived up to his reputation as the 'champion clogger of Spain'. United had been outplayed at times and were exhausted at the final whistle. The players had rarely been hit by such pace or a team that worked so much like a unit. Roger Byrne told the media that he had never seen such a brilliant team, while others were taken aback by the noise at the Bernabéu – 125,000 people paying £55,000 – and the sight of thousands of fans waving white handkerchiefs. While Real's coach, Jose Villalonga, felt United were a great team, it was apparent the home side could have won more handsomely. United had turned around a similar situation in the quarter-final against Bilbao, but this was different. In some ways, Busby's 'babes' had got away with a result that gave them a chance of saving the tie, but deep down not many felt Real Madrid could be beaten.

In between meeting Real twice, United clinched the Football League championship for the second year running, beating Sunderland 4-0 on 20 April at Old Trafford. In March, the club inaugurated its new £40,000 floodlights, so the second leg would be played at United's own ground rather than Maine Road. Real arrived in England and watched a weakened United beat Burnley 2-0 on 22 April. United were taken to Blackpool for some rest and recuperation. Busby ordered the Old Trafford ground staff to saturate the pitch as it was popularly thought Spanish teams did not play well on wet surfaces. Byrne, in his newspaper column, said rather foolishly that the club's secret weapon, the sprinklers, had come into operation, but also revealed that United did not like wet pitches either. Real, upon hearing of this admission, complained and the not-so-secret weapon was turned off.

The game at Old Trafford was something of an eye-opener. Nobody doubted Real's ability, but the fact was they made United look quite cumbersome. While the Spaniards' ball skills and passing were often elaborate and creative, United's long passing was quite ineffective. As one report said, 'The old comparison of a crude battle-axe against a Toledo blade was never more apt.' Real went into a two-goal lead, with Kopa and Rial scoring after 25 and 33 minutes, and more or less killed off the home side. At times, things got quite heated and United seemed to lose their cool. Duncan Edwards was involved in a skirmish when he, along with some team-mates, dragged Torres off the pitch because he was injured and seemingly delaying proceedings, and, generally, too many fouls punctuated the action.

United came back to level the scores, with Taylor netting after 62 minutes and Charlton adding the equaliser with five minutes to go. It ended 2-2 and Real were delighted to get past their hosts, celebrating with a victory jig that was jeered by the Manchester crowd. The *Daily Herald* was not impressed, accusing the supporters of 'one-eyed partisanship, a public display of bad manners that made me ashamed to be English'. When Real's players took corners, they were often bombarded with apple cores and orange peel. United's crowd had been myopic and closed their eyes to the sheer brilliance of Di Stéfano, Gento and others. One scribe called the fans hooligans and said not only football had been disgraced, but also Britain as a whole.

There was some criticism of the game from some quarters, who felt the 'greatest match of the season' was in fact a flop. Byrne, ever the spokesperson for the United team, commented: 'We have learned a lot. I think these two games against Real have shown every ingenious device to prevent a team playing football.' Others called some of Real's antics 'prima-donna tactics' as they lay on the ground feigning injury, and some even dismissed European football as a whole. In the cold light of day, however, it was noted that the so-called 'Continental' methods of shirt-pulling, bodychecking and sly, off-the-ball fouls were not exclusive to the visitors.

It was clearly a lesson for Busby and his young players but English football did not really take note of how the best team in the Football League was brushed aside by Real Madrid. There was an element of their play that made United feel very uncomfortable. Perhaps it was simply that Real were more savvy than United's home-grown products, or that the Spaniards had a more professional element to their play. Despite concerns about the many stoppages and obstructions originating from Real's players, Busby praised them and had no complaints about the actual result. Over the coming years, English teams often felt hard done by and treated badly by opponents, referees and crowds. In the period between 1957 and 1968, when United finally won the competition, England's champions were beaten by teams from Italy, West Germany, Spain, Netherlands, Portugal and Yugoslavia. Often defeat was accompanied by complaints of rough play, cheating and corruption.

United had already qualified for the following season's competition, but they were denied the first 'double' of the 20th century by a robust Aston Villa side at Wembley. However, they had enjoyed a great season and had excited many people. The 1957/58 European Cup would include United and Rangers, Real Madrid, Red Star Belgrade, AC Milan, Vasas Budapest, Rapid Vienna, Benfica and Sevilla, among others. The draw for the preliminary round was made in Paris in July and United were paired with Dublin's Shamrock Rovers. Little did anyone know at that stage that the club's much-loved young team would not complete another European campaign.

The tragedy that engulfed Manchester United's young team on 6 February 1958 is one of football's saddest landmarks. It sits alongside the Superga disaster overlooking the city of Turin that destroyed the great Torino team of the 1940s and other disasters that have mostly affected supporters rather than teams and players. There is little doubt that the shape of English football may have been very different had United's young players not perished in the snow at Munich airport. The impact at the time was so far-reaching, so deeply felt across the country, that one can only presume the modern practice of tragedy abuse reflects changes in human behaviour of the worst kind.

There are countless myths in football and, like in many walks of life, there is always much discussion over 'what might have been'. The Busby Babes were England's top team when Munich happened. Some claim they had not reached their peak, but their results in 1957/58 suggest they were not quite as potent as they had been in 1956/57 and even 1955/56. United's last game before flying out to meet Red Star Belgrade was a 5-4 win at Highbury against mid-table Arsenal. They were third in the league, six points behind leaders Wolves, and they had already lost seven of their 28 games. In the two previous, championship-winning campaigns, United had lost seven and six games, respectively. On paper, it looked as though they were less effective than in the two previous campaigns. Perhaps they were concentrating on the European Cup, realising that the attritional nature of a 42-game programme hampered their chances of overcoming the likes of Real Madrid.

The fact is, the Busby Babes were not invincible. They were dynamic, fit, skilful and had a youthful effervescence that was simply too much for many opponents in England. Between 1955/56 and the 28 matches up to 1 February, 1958, United had a win rate of 60 per cent and they scored 259 goals in 112 games. United also provided the England squad with several players: the trio of Byrne, Edwards and Taylor frequently lined up, and on one occasion there was a fourth in Johnny Berry. And then along came Bobby Charlton. It was widely believed that United's youngsters would be the heart of the England team in the years ahead. Byrne and Taylor were both in the 1954 World Cup squad, and four years later Charlton, Colman, Mark Jones and Viollet may all have featured in the squad.

The 1957/58 league season began well for United, five wins in six and 22 goals scored against five conceded, but then something seemed to go wrong. United were thrashed 4-0 at Bolton's Burnden Park, a ground where they had not much success in recent years. More worrying was a home defeat at the hands of a Blackpool team that that did not include Stanley Matthews.

The European Cup came around and United travelled to meet Shamrock Rovers, the League of Ireland champions. The gap between English and Irish football was very significant, so United were expected to run up a healthy score in Dublin. Shamrock had some good players, including leading scorer Tommy Hamilton, winger Maxie McCann and the tough Liam Hennessy. United won 6-0, with five netted in the second half. The 45,000 spectators were thrilled to be watching the best team in England. Ironically, the best performer on the pitch was United's Dublin-born Billy Whelan. The second leg came after United, who had been hit by an outbreak of influenza, had lost their third game in four, against Wolverhampton Wanderers at Molineux. What concerned many people was United's defence, which had now conceded 11 goals in four league fixtures.

They won the second leg against Shamrock 3-2 and were rewarded with a first-round tie against Dukla Prague, a talented team from Czechoslovakia that formed the backbone of the national team. The first leg was scheduled for the second week in November, but the death of the Czech president, Antonín Zápotocky, delayed the game. When Dukla turned up, their side was packed with quality, including defenders Ladislav Novák, Svatopluk Pluskal and František Šafránek, midfielders Jiří Čadek and Josef Masopust, and forwards Milan Dvorák and Jaroslav Borovička. United had to wait until the second half at Old Trafford to prise open the Dukla defence. Colin Webster, Taylor and Pegg scored the three goals that gave them a 3-0 win to take to Prague. In the windy and snowy Czech capital, United were beaten by a single goal but then faced an arduous journey home that eventually included a plane, a boat and train, hence United arrived back in Manchester exhausted.

United made some changes, including the acquisition of a new goalkeeper in Doncaster Rovers' Harry Gregg, and maintained their position near the top of the league, but it was clear that they had stiff competition in Wolves, whose speed and muscle was the new game in town. United's next European tie, the quarter-final, was against Yugoslavia's Red Star Belgrade.

Both teams had reached the semi-final in 1957/58, United losing to Real Madrid and Red Star to Fiorentina, so they were already building a European pedigree. Neither team were at their best, however, particularly in attack. From the side that had won the league so impressively in 1957, United had just half a dozen who were now regulars. As well as Gregg, who had replaced Ray Wood in goal, Morgans, Charlton and Albert Scanlon were now installed in the line-up, replacing Johnny Berry, Whelan and Pegg. Jackie Blanchflower had also lost his place to Jones. With the exception of Bosnian-born Ranko Borozan, the Red Star team had all been capped by Yugoslavia. Their goalkeeper, Vladimir Beara, was considered to be an athletic and very graceful custodian who would win 59 caps for his country. They also had a young midfielder called Dragoslav Šekularac, who was destined for great things. The team was renowned for being 'ball-players' that relied on guile and skill rather than blood and thunder.

Manchester put on its best show – rain and cold wind – for the arrival of Red Star and 60,000 packed into Old Trafford. For the first 20 minutes, United bombarded the Red Star defence, but it was the visitors that took the lead after 35 minutes when Lazar Tasić, taking advantage of Gregg straying off his line, sent a 25-yard shot into the top corner of the net. United responded well, with Charlton in excellent form. It was the future England legend that levelled the score on 65 minutes before Colman grabbed the winner with nine minutes remaining. It was a hard-earned victory but the margin was narrow and United had to go to Belgrade, an intimidating place for any visiting football team.

There was nothing wrong with United's attack in the two league games played between the two meetings with Red Star. Four days after the first leg, they thrashed Bolton Wanderers 7-2 at Old Trafford, with Charlton continuing his rich vein of form with a hat-trick. A week later, United won 2-0 in the FA Cup against Ipswich Town and Charlton added another two goals to his tally. The last league game before Belgrade was at Highbury and became a nine-goal thriller in which United went 3-0 up by half-time, saw Arsenal completely erode their lead by the 61st minute but eventually ran out 5-4 winners. It was riveting stuff, but United were conceding too many goals. Red Star, meanwhile, were still on a domestic mid-winter break.

On 5 February 1958, Manchester United played Red Star in bitterly cold Belgrade where there was six inches of snow on the ground. United knew they had to be cautious and resist their natural instinct to attack. Red Star had the players to take advantage of any big gaps at the back. Just as they did at Highbury, United went into a 3-0 lead thanks to goals by Taylor and Charlton (2). Bora Kostić scored Red Star's first in the 47th minute, Tasić added another eight minutes later and finally, in the 90th minute, Kostić netted with a free kick to make the score 3-3. It had been another edge-of-the-seat game, but United were through to the semi-finals. And then, at München-Riem airport, an accident occurred that would change the football world.

It was an accident, one that rightly refuses to be forgotten. If anyone wanted evidence of the role football plays in society, how it captures the hearts and minds of people, the Munich air crash on 6 February 1958 provides just that. The details have been recorded in fine detail in countless publications, the story has been told many times over. Families, friends and fans have spent decades trying to understand what, how and why. Any visit to Munich invariably has people wondering where. There are no witnesses left from that terrible day when United's first flush of nurtured youth perished in the snow and ice. The dead included Roger Byrne, Eddie Colman, Mark Jones, Duncan Edwards, Tommy Taylor, David Pegg, Geoff Bent and Billy Whelan. Their surviving team-mates probably remembered them every single day for the rest of their lives.

A nation mourned the loss of these vital young men and this arguably helped to make United the most popular and loved club in the country. The tragedy made followers out of so many people who had only a passing interest in football – hence, United's fanbase spread right across the UK and beyond. It was a reaction that combined sympathy, empathy and deep respect, as if people wanted to make the act of mass mourning a little easier for those most affected by the loss. While the badly wounded Matt Busby had his own battle for life to deal with, his number two, Jimmy Murphy, had to get the club through a major catastrophe. United regrouped, drafted in players, lost their now quite meaningless European Cup semi-final and rebuilt. Somehow, United also reached the FA Cup Final for the second successive season. They lost to Bolton Wanderers, but they would soon be back at the top. However, it would be a much-changed Manchester United, one with very different players, that ascended the mountain once more.

Would the so-called 'Busby Babes' have won the European Cup? They would have to be Football League champions to qualify, and in 1957/58 Wolves were certainly the best team. And there were other rising teams such as Burnley and Tottenham Hotspur. History has a habit of being skewed by tragic events, but there is no doubt United would have been contenders for the league title and the European Cup. Real Madrid continued to have the upper hand until 1960, so if United were going to be the champions they would have had to beat the ultimate European experts on the way at some point. We shall never know what might have been.

3

Fairs, Please

THE INTER-CITIES Fairs Cup was not especially high on anyone's agenda during the first editions of the competition, but Barcelona's success added to the growing fascination with Spanish football that was building around Europe. Barcelona had finished third in La Liga in both 1956/57 and 1957/58 and then won the title in 1959. The use of representative sides in the Fairs Cup was not a wholly satisfactory format, and for the second edition London opted to invite one team to play on behalf of the city. In this case it was Chelsea, making their European bow some three years after losing their place in the Champion Clubs' Cup. Others persisted with the 'XI' format, including Zagreb, Belgrade, Leipzig, Cologne and Basel.

Chelsea were drawn against a Copenhagen XI, otherwise known as Stævnet, and built around the Frem BK club. They won 7-2 on aggregate, displaying a rather casual attitude in the second leg at Stamford Bridge, but their European run ended in the next round against Belgrade. England's other representative was Birmingham City, who had enjoyed their first foray into Europe. They disposed of Cologne, Zagreb and the Brussels-based team Union Saint-Gilloise to reach the final, where they faced the team that beat them in the semi-final in 1958, Barcelona.

Birmingham, managed by former Arsenal and England winger Pat Beasley, were not having a good season in the league and eventually finished 19th in 1959/60. In the final, they were up against Barcelona's 'United Nations' forward line that included Zoltán Czibor, a member of the Hungarian team that had demolished England in two games in 1953 and 1954, and László Kubala. Birmingham refused to be overawed by the all-star line-up of the Spaniards and drew 0-0 at St Andrew's, but in the second leg in the Camp Nou they were easily beaten 4-1, with Czibor scoring twice. Birmingham were back in the next Fairs Cup in 1960/61, the first to be staged over a single season, and this time Britain also had Hibernian, returning after their European adventure in 1955/56.

Hibs had a bye through the first round as Lausanne-Sports withdrew, so they went straight into the quarter-finals, where they met Barcelona, a tie they were expected to lose. They were originally due to play at Easter Road, but the game was cancelled due to fog. In the Camp Nou, the home side were shocked by the Scottish visitors going 2-0 ahead, Joe Baker and John MacLeod the scorers. Barcelona came back to level the score, with Sándor Kocsis, another refugee from the Hungarian revolution, netting twice. Hibs found a second wind and went into a 4-2 lead, Baker and Tom Preston scoring within three minutes of each other. Barça, by now enduring howls of disapproval from their fans, kept going and Kocsis and Evaristo scored in the final seven minutes to earn a 4-4 draw. Although Barça had shown great character in coming back from the dead, Hibernian were certainly the moral victors of the first leg and were given a great ovation from the 60,000 crowd.

The second leg provided fuel for the critics who felt the roughness of Continental teams was something British football just did not need. Part of this was xenophobia, part was the fear that England was losing its place at the forefront of the game, and there was also an underlying feeling that while Britain pursued the virtues of sportsmanship, the foreigner just did not much care how success was achieved.

The game became known as the 'Battle of Easter Road' and produced scenes British stadiums were simply not accustomed to. Baker, who had apparently caused the Spanish more anguish than anyone since 'Sir Francis Drake sunk the Armada', gave Hibs the lead in the tenth minute, but Paraguayan-born striker Eulogio Martínez equalised, and by half-time Kocsis had given Barça a 2-1 lead. In the second half, Hibs levelled through Preston, and then the game exploded. With five minutes remaining, referee Johannes Malka awarded Hibs a penalty. The Barça players were incensed, chasing the tall German official all over the pitch. He was tripped and knocked to the ground, sustaining a leg injury. The game was delayed as chaos broke out, with the police protecting Malka. After a seven-minute break to calm things down, Hibs' Bobby Kinloch scored from the spot, a goal that proved to be the winner. As the final whistle blew, Malka, who had edged closer to the touchline to make a quick exit, was escorted off by the police. Those that had attended the second leg called for Barcelona to be severely disciplined, but few thought the Spanish club would actually be censured by UEFA.

Hibernian's next opponents were Roma, the first leg of which came at a time when the terrace talk was all about the future of Joe Baker, who had caught the eye of numerous Italian clubs. Hibs had come to the conclusion they could not keep their England international centre-forward, but the money his sale could earn the club would be useful. The first game at Easter Road was another bruising, bad-tempered encounter and, once again, the referee came under fire. Roma's Francisco Lojacono swung a boot at Mr Mellet and several times players had to be pulled apart. The first leg ended all-square at 2-2, Lojacono putting Roma in front twice, but Baker and MacLeod equalising to give Hibs hope for the second meeting. There were skirmishes near the end and the friendly handshakes were not the most sincere gestures of the season, according to the esteemed journalist Hugh McIlvanney.

In Rome at the end of April 1961, the second leg was played against a backdrop of zig-zag lightning and a fierce thunderstorm. Baker, who now looked bound for Italy, scored twice as Hibs went into a 3-1 lead with 27 minutes to go. Roma saved the day to take the tie to a third meeting, which, after much negotiation, was to be played in the same Stadio Olimpico in Rome. Hibernian had nothing much left in the tank by the time the next meeting came around and were beaten 6-0 in the play-off, with Argentine striker Pedro Manfredi scoring four times. The next day, Baker agreed to join Torino for £65,000.

While Hibernian had shown Europe what they were capable of, Birmingham had certainly impressed those that had often written them off as 'Brummie bashers', a nickname earned by their no-nonsense, robust approach. In the 1960/61 Fairs Cup, they had comfortably got past KB Copenhagen and Újpest of Hungary. The big test was the semi-final against Inter Milan, a club known for its extravagant spending habits and ability to sign big-name players. They had former Charlton forward Eddie Firmani in their ranks and he got on the scoresheet against Birmingham in Milan. But the Blues from St Andrew's netted twice, through Jimmy Harris and Mike Hellawell, names that Inter had probably never heard of. Both goals were created by teenage defender Terry Hennessey, a player who would go on to win 39 caps for Wales and play for

Nottingham Forest and Derby County, where he would win a league title medal in 1972.

Before meeting Inter in the second leg, Birmingham had signed Bertie Auld from Celtic, and he made an instant impact on the left wing. Inter were beaten 2-1 again, with Harris scoring two more goals, to send Gil Merrick's men through to the final to meet Roma in September 1961. Birmingham again showed their character in the first leg at home, but once again the football was overshadowed by overcommitted opponents. A disappointing crowd of 21,000 saw Roma go into a 2-0 lead through Manfredi. Mike Hellawell and Bryan Orritt scored in an eight-minute spell to earn a 2-2 draw. Birmingham, perhaps learning from the Inter games and Hibernian's meeting with Roma, were quite well prepared, adopting a more aggressive approach. In fact, Roma might have lost had it not been for their goalkeeper, Fabio Cudicini, the father of future Chelsea and Tottenham keeper Carlo.

The second leg was supposed to be a floodlit game, but it was switched to an October afternoon in Rome. The home side were rough, using bodychecks and obstructive tactics whenever they could. Two second-half goals gave Roma the cup, but at times the atmosphere was heated. Birmingham manager Gil Merrick and his Roma counterpart, Luis Carniglia, had something of a touchline tussle after the latter ran on to the pitch following a Trevor Smith tackle. Merrick thought Carniglia was about to strike a Birmingham player and had followed him to ensure his men were safe. There were other moments when skirmishes broke out, notably involving Lojacono, who even jostled the referee. The Italian capital became notorious for having very aggressive, cut-throat teams such as Roma and Lazio. While the European journey had largely been a good one for Birmingham, the ways of foreign players made for an uncomfortable experience for many people. It did not come without a cost, for Birmingham gained a reputation themselves among foreign opponents for being over-zealous, as evidenced by a string of sending-offs.

Birmingham were back in 1961/62 and there were two other English clubs, Sheffield Wednesday and Nottingham Forest, along with the Edinburgh pair, Heart of Midlothian and Hibernian, involved. Wednesday finished runners-up to double-winners Tottenham Hotspur in the league in 1961, while Forest were below mid-table. Forest were drawn to meet Valencia, who had finished fifth in La Liga in 1961. Forest were out of their depth and failed to respond to Valencia's 'on the carpet' football. The first leg ended 2-0 in the Mestalla, Valencia's iconic stadium, but it could have been worse if goalkeeper Peter Grummitt had not had such an inspired evening. In the second leg, Valencia tore Forest apart and won 5-1 at the City Ground, with the Uruguayan forward Héctor Núñez scoring three times to consign Forest to their first defeat under their new floodlights.

Sheffield Wednesday were beaten 4-2 in Lyon in the first round but came back to win 7-6 on aggregate. In the next round, they were up against a Roma side that applied some of the dark arts to their tactics and they also could not keep quiet on the field. The Italians were beaten 4-0 at Hillsborough, with Alan Young scoring a hat-trick for the home team. There was brawling, dissent and off-the-ball fouling, but this approach worked against Roma, who had Lojacono sent off. The second leg was a 1-0 win for Roma, thanks to an own goal by Peter Swan. FIFA had a watchful eye on the poor reputation of the Fairs Cup and announced that it would stamp out the fighting and general rough play that had characterised the competition. Wednesday were now in the semi-finals and up against Barcelona, who were not in good form and had lost four games in a row before facing a team that had seemingly discovered how to be successful in Europe. Wednesday shocked their visitors, with John Fantham scoring twice in a 3-2 win. In the return game, Barcelona won 2-0 and could have inflicted upon the Yorkshiremen a far heavier defeat but for the form of Swan and goalkeeper Ron Springett.

Birmingham's European run also ended at the hands of a Spanish side. They went ahead through Jimmy Bloomfield against Espanyol of Barcelona but were beaten 5-2. Although they won 1-0 at home in the second leg, it was not enough.

Edinburgh provided some of the most intriguing games involving British clubs in 1961/62. Both won through the first round of the Fairs Cup, with Hearts winning 5-1 on aggregate against Union Saint-Gilloise of Belgium, with a 40-strong party of National Servicemen arriving from Cologne to cheer them on. Hibernian beat Portuguese club Belenenses 6-4. Both recorded impressive away victories by three goals to one, with the press in Lisbon particularly enthused by Hibs: 'The Scots leave the best of impressions here as to their style of play […] it was a well-won victory.' Both teams went out in the second round, Hibernian losing 4-0 against Red Star Belgrade in the army stadium. This was another untidy game, with Jim Easton sent off after he retaliated to a series of kicks and punches from Dragoslav Šekularec. The game was held up due to floodlight failure and Hibernian's 4-2-4 formation was cruelly exposed by Red Star in both legs, the second of which was also lost.

Hearts also lost their tie with Inter Milan by 5-0. Hearts were cast in the role of pupils, with Inter very much the masters. 'If this is an example of what a common soccer market can bring, then it must be heavily underlined that Scottish football lags far behind.' Inter's players commented that 'Hearts are a nice side, but too slow, too cumbersome in their moves'.

Scotland had three teams in the Fairs Cup in 1962/63, but too often they were muscled out of contention by Valencia, who beat all of the Caledonian entrants. Everton, who would win the Football League that season, faced a Dunfermline team managed by future Celtic boss Jock Stein. Everton won the first leg of their first-round tie by a single goal, but Stein's side won 2-0 in the second game to go through. Celtic lost to Valencia 4-2 in Spain and drew 2-2 in Glasgow, with future Manchester United midfielder Paddy Crerand scoring one of the goals. Valencia then faced Dunfermline in the second round, and in the Mestalla it was a rough game that saw Stein admonished by the referee along with the two team captains. The Fifers were beaten 4-0, with their goalkeeper, Jim Herriot, struggling and the Dunfermline defence unable to deal with Valencia's Brazilian player, Waldo, who was given the nickname 'the Brazilian flash' by the Scottish contingent in the stadium. Dunfermline looked dead and buried, but on an icy East End Park pitch, Valencia struggled to deal with a home team that adopted a pragmatic strategy on a difficult surface – long, high balls. The local press was less than complimentary about their visitors: 'Valencia, like the prima donnas they have been built up to be, waltzed onto the park to deliver the coup de grace with elegance and ease.' The game proved to be a dramatic evening, with Dunfermline 5-1 ahead by half-time and totally retrieving the deficit. Two goals came from winger Jackie Sinclair, who would move to England later in the 1960s, where he played for Leicester City, Newcastle United and Sheffield Wednesday. The final score was 6-2, making the aggregate 6-6 to take the tie to a play-off in Lisbon. Valencia won 1-0 and were paired with Hibernian in the quarter-finals.

Valencia scored four times in the first half against Hibs and won 5-0 to make the second leg in Edinburgh a formality. Only 4,000 people were attracted to Easter Road, but Hibs, who were fighting against relegation from the Scottish top flight, achieved some form of honourable exit from the competition. They avoided the drop, while Valencia went on to win the Fairs Cup for the second successive season.

The 1963/64 season saw Arsenal make their bow in European football. They had, of course, played abroad frequently in friendlies and had built a relationship with France's Racing Club Paris in the inter-war years. But Arsenal's light had faded in the 1950s and early 1960s and they were struggling to regain their place at the summit of English football. Their lack of experience of competitive football in Europe showed when they began their campaign, notably when they were beaten in the second leg of the first-round tie with a Copenhagen XI. Although they won 7-1 in the Danish capital, with Joe Baker and Geoff Strong both scoring hat-tricks, they made hard work of the ill-attended second game at Highbury and were surprisingly beaten 3-2. Arsenal were jeered off the pitch by the 13,000 crowd.

In the second round, they were up against Belgium's RFC Liège, a team that had finished around mid-table in the Belgian first division in 1962/63. They flew into London just a few hours before kick-off and took an early lead at Highbury through Sebastièn Kilola, a 26-year-old winger from the Congo, who celebrated in flamboyant fashion, performing some somersaults for the crowd. Arsenal equalised through Terry Anderson, a young forward, but they looked like 'raw recruits to the Continental game' to quote one report. There were still hopes that Arsenal would win through as Liège would have to come out of their shell at home rather than defend in depth. On a snow-covered pitch, it was a different story, however, and Arsenal's goalkeeper, Jim Furnell, had a nightmare second leg as the Londoners lost 3-1.

All the British sides were out by the second round. Sheffield Wednesday, after disposing of Utrecht, were beaten by Köln, Hearts went out in the first round to Lausanne-Sports, and Partick Thistle, the other Scottish entrant, lost in muddy Brno to Spartak after beating Glentoran of Northern Ireland. The cup stayed in Spain as Real Zaragoza beat Valencia in the final.

England had strong representation in the 1964/65 Fairs Cup, with the 1963 league champions Everton and a Manchester United side that would win the title that season. This was the United of George Best, Bobby Charlton and Denis Law, and they were very goal-happy in their Fairs Cup run. In the first round they beat Djurgårdenn of Sweden 7-2 on aggregate before thrashing Borussia Dortmund 10-1, with a particularly stunning 6-1 victory in the Ruhr. The experts quickly proclaimed United, who were league leaders in England, as favourites to win the competition. While young Best was winning plaudits for his intrinsic skill, Charlton was enjoying a rich vein of form, confounding opponents with his body swerves and terrifying defenders with his powerful shooting. Interestingly, after beating Dortmund at Old Trafford, United's guests at the post-match banquet included none other than Alan Hardaker, who had been so opposed to English clubs entering European competition.

Everton, meanwhile, had won through against Norwegian side Vålerenga and Kilmarnock with very little trouble. The Scots did not have a successful year in the Fairs Cup, Celtic knocked out by Barcelona in round two and Dunfermline finding Athletic Bilbao too tough in a third round play-off. Everton then came face to face with Manchester United in the third round, opponents they probably did not want to meet at this stage. Everton attempted to thwart United's exciting forwards and employed Colin Harvey and Dennis Stevens in containing roles. Fred Pickering, an old-fashioned forward, good in the air, gave Everton an early lead but John Connelly, who would play in the 1966 World Cup for England, levelled before half-time. The second leg was tight but United edged home by 2-1, with Connelly and David Herd scoring the goals.

United eased past Strasbourg 5-0 on aggregate to claim a semi-final place, where they were drawn to play Hungary's Ferencváros. In a strange six-team quarter-final, Atlético Madrid and Juventus received byes to the last four. United's clash was another of those brutal, uncompromising ties that gave the Fairs Cup a bad name. United won 3-2 in Manchester in a game spoiled by a bureaucratic referee who made some bizarre decisions. United were a goal down and then 3-1 ahead before Gyuli Rákosi scored to make the home team's advantage look very fragile. In Budapest's famed Népstadion, United and Ferencváros literally battled away. Pat Crerand of United and Fradi's Pal Orosz were both sent off after a series of skirmishes and the game was constantly punctuated by incidents involving violent play. United were beaten by a first-half penalty from Deszö Novák, which meant the two teams would have to meet again. United lost the toss to determine the venue and were then escorted out of the Nép by armed police. Finally, the semi-final was decided on 16 June, with Ferencváros winning 2-1. United, who had been sent out on to the Nép turf with a very clear message from Matt Busby, 'Keep it clean, keep your heads, play attacking football,' were praised for the quality of their football.

Two ambitious teams renowned for their precocious approach were extremely anxious to show Continental Europe that English football was on the brink of a new era in 1965/66. Leeds United, managed by Don Revie, and Tommy Docherty's Chelsea had squads of young players who were rich in promise. Both were drawn against Italian sides, Leeds with Torino and Chelsea with Roma. Both ties were completed with no small amount of controversy, but it was Chelsea's games with Roma that made all the wrong headlines.

Leeds won their first leg at Elland Road by 2-1, a narrow victory that most people expected to be inadequate for them to go through. The second game in Turin ended goalless, which was enough to secure the tie, but Leeds lost Bobby Collins to a badly broken thigh, an injury due to what Billy Bremner said was the worst foul he had ever seen and one that effectively ended the player's career.

Chelsea hosted Roma in their first game and eventually won by 4-1, with Terry Venables scoring a hat-trick. It was, according to eye-witnesses, a savage and ugly game, which moved some scribes to conclude that violence was rapidly becoming part and parcel of continental combat. Chelsea were continually punched, bodychecked and aggressively tackled, and it was inevitable that somebody would retaliate. Eddie McCreadie, who was Scotland's left-back, was that person, punching Lamberto Leonardi to the ground and earning an early trip to the dressing room.

In Italy's capital, the pre-match talk around the second leg was all about Roma gaining revenge. Docherty told his players that self-control was needed in what was going to be an intimidating atmosphere. 'We must keep our heads. We have a good lead and I think we can contain Roma. But most important of all, we must keep calm.' Docherty's young team was severely tested. As soon as they went on to the pitch to inspect the playing surface, they were showered with bottles, stones, saliva and other small missiles. During the game, balloons filled with urine were thrown at the Chelsea bench and Venables was fortunate not to be injured when a sharp metal object was hurled at him. The game ended goalless, but Chelsea had to leave Rome under police escort as their motor coach was stoned by dozens of Roma fans. In the days following the game, Chelsea chairman Joe Mears protested about the disgusting scenes, but the Italian press played the victim. The daily newspaper, *Il Tempo*, searched for conspiracies: 'The British press, in a bloc, continue to vomit the worst insults not only on Rome and its public, but on all our soccer world and – was there any doubt? – on Italians as a whole.'

The general consensus was that Italian football teams were so focused on avoiding defeat that everything else was secondary. The reaction from Britain was one of mild horror, and leading journalist, Sam Leitch, felt that there was only so much English football should tolerate: 'If there are to be any future repeats of the Rome-Chelsea violence, then we are better out of Europe.'

If the game between Roma and Chelsea shocked English football, then the Leeds United versus Valencia tie disgusted those who saw the 1-1 draw at Elland Road. Leeds had followed their win against Torino with two snowy games with Leipzig before being drawn against Fairs Cup experts Valencia in the third round. It was a tense and tough evening and fighting broke out among the two teams. The referee, Leo Horn, was an experienced official, but he appeared to lose control of the game. He took the teams off the pitch for ten minutes to try to defuse the situation, but when they returned two players were missing: Jack Charlton of Leeds and Francisco Vidagany of Valencia. An off-the-ball incident involving the pair saw the latter kick the England centre-half, who may have responded. Vidagany had actually hidden behind his team-mates, so the accusation that Charlton had struck the Spanish defender were far from credible. The press were outraged about the behaviour of the teams, the 'wildest scenes to disgrace an English soccer ground for years'. The referee came in for some heavy criticism, but he responded to accusations that he had handled the game poorly: 'I saw things in the eyes of men at Leeds on Wednesday that frightened me. This is my last season in football. I shall be glad to go. I am sick of what I see, sick of what referees are having to cope with.'

With the Roma-Chelsea game still very fresh in the memory – the Italians were banned for three years following an enquiry – the antics of Leeds and Valencia added fuel to the fire that was burning underneath the Fairs Cup. Neither club was penalised for the roughhouse that was the first leg, and Leeds pulled off an impressive 1-0 win in the Mestalla, with Mike O'Grady scoring the decisive goal.

Chelsea, meanwhile, had beaten Wiener Sports Club in the second round, coming from 1-0 down in Vienna to win 2-0 in London. Their third-round opponents were AC Milan, who had won the European Cup in 1963 and were one of the chief exponents of the dreaded *catenaccio*. There were only 11,000 people in the San Siro for the first meeting, won 2-1 by the home side. Chelsea scored twice in 18 minutes in the second leg to take control, but Milan pulled one back just before half-time. The tie went to a play-off, which was to be held in Milan. It ended in a 1-1 draw and the only solution was to toss a coin to determine the winner. Ron Harris and Cesare Maldini (father of Paolo) gathered with the referee, and Harris called correctly. It was a wholly unsatisfactory way to end a 300-minute cup tie but UEFA had yet to discover away goals or penalties.

Two of the three English sides that entered the Fairs Cup were in the last eight. Everton, who had travelled to Budapest to play Újpest earlier in the competition, had got their tactics wrong and saw their man-for-man marking system torn apart in the Népstadion. Újpest were drawn against Leeds and were not overjoyed: 'We would have been happier to play some Spanish team or even Milan. The Leeds team is reputed to be too tough.' Chelsea were up against TSV Munich 1860, who had reached the European Cup Winners' Cup Final in 1964/65, losing to West Ham United. The tie was attractive, so much so that Chelsea, controversially, hiked up their ticket prices. In Munich's Grünwalder stadium, the game was drawn 2-2 and a single late goal from a young and emerging Peter Osgood in London was enough to send Chelsea into the semi-finals. Leeds easily disposed of Újpest, racing into a 4-0 lead by half-time at Elland Road. The final score was 4-1 and the second game in Budapest was a formality, but that did not stop the players from brawling on the banks of the Danube at the after-match banquet.

Chelsea and Leeds met very formidable teams in the semi-finals. Real Zaragoza, Leeds' opponents, had some exceptional forwards known as the 'magnificent five', which would test the Leeds defence. Revie's men lost 1-0 in Spain and then put on a superb performance at home to win 2-1. A third game was needed and Leeds won the toss to host it. Revie tried a little gamesmanship in instructing the local fire brigade to flood the pitch as the word was that Zaragoza did not like heavy conditions. It was something of a misconception as they appeared to relish the muddy surface. Zaragoza were 3-0 ahead by half-time and won 3-1 to end Leeds' European hopes.

It had been an invaluable and eye-opening experience for a young team. Leeds were certainly a 'together' side, but Chelsea's nearly men were imploding. Players like Peter Bonetti, Bobby Tambling and Bert Murray had asked for a transfer, Tommy Docherty had more or less decided that Terry Venables was surplus to requirements and Barry Bridges had been sold. He signed a Scottish winger, Charlie Cooke, from Dundee and brought back Allan Harris to the club.

Chelsea's semi-final with Barcelona was, like Leeds' games with Zaragoza, a three-match saga. Barcelona won 2-0 in the Camp Nou, but in the return Docherty also engaged the local fire services to make the Stamford Bridge pitch a little wetter, despite a downpour of rain in London. Chelsea won 2-0 but, once more, the game was punctuated with sly fouls, brutal challenges and petty violence. Chelsea lost their composure and were more guilty than the visitors. The play-off was in Barcelona and Chelsea had clearly lost their momentum; Barça won 5-0 and Docherty's side left the field humiliated. They had lost both the FA Cup and Fairs Cup semi-finals, which was a bitter blow to Docherty and the players. It was arguably the end of a precocious young team, but the Londoners would eventually taste European glory.

4

Cup of Cups

THE APPETITE for pan-European competition was growing, and with the Champion Clubs' Cup established and gaining positive momentum and the Fairs Cup creating a slightly ugly image, another idea came to the fore. As with the Fairs Cup, UEFA was not fully involved, in fact, they sat back and waited to see how this new concept was received. The European Cup Winners' Cup was a competition for the domestic cup winners across the continent. The inaugural tournament, in 1960/61, was effectively managed by the organising committee of the Mitropa Cup.

For English clubs, the FA Cup was, to a certain degree, the most glamorous part of the domestic campaign. Football's league games were considered to be the 'bread and butter', the everyday football that you could afford to lose at occasionally. If a team lost in the league it was not the end of the world, indeed the philosophy was that another game would come along soon for the team to redeem itself. This frame of mind does not exist in the modern football industry and each defeat is treated as a minor catastrophe. The important stuff was the FA Cup. Lose in that and your hopes were dashed for another year. Cup ties were seen as 'money-spinners', 'plum ties' and 'crowd-pullers'. Nobody ever called a league game a 'money-spinner'.

The FA Cup became part of the social calendar, not as much as Wimbledon, the Ashes or the Boat Race, but along with the Derby and Grand National, the cup final was an occasion for the working man and woman, certainly up until the 1980s. The country almost came to a standstill on FA Cup Final day with all-day coverage of every aspect of the match. Not many European countries had the same feeling about their domestic cup competitions, at least that was the popular view in Britain. Hence, the European Cup Winners' Cup, while officially considered as the second most important of the three UEFA competitions that eventually emerged, often had weak fields and appeared easier to win than, for example, the UEFA Cup.

The first Cup Winners' Cup comprised just 11 teams, seven of which had won their national cup competition in 1959/60. These included Wolverhampton Wanderers, FA Cup winners against Blackburn Rovers, and Rangers. West Germany were represented by Borussia Mönchengladbach, the DFB Pokal winners, while East Germany's standard-bearers were ASK Vorwärts, the army-backed side that had been runners-up in the DDR-Oberliga in 1959. Fiorentina were Italy's entrant, although they had been runners-up in the Coppa Italia to Juventus, who had also won Serie A.

It was a pocket-sized competition in 1960/61, with just 18 games played. It kicked off in August with Vorwärts going out to Red Star Brno of Czechoslovakia 3-2 on aggregate. Rangers also had to play in the preliminary round, against the much-fancied Hungarians, Ferencváros, who had a very exciting young player in Flórián Albert, seen by many pundits as a natural successor to Ferenc Puskás. The predictions about his future proved to be quite accurate, because Albert went on to win the Ballon d'Or in 1967. Fradi also had the experienced veterinary surgeon

Máté Fenyvesi in their ranks, so Rangers expected a hard game at Ibrox Park.

It was a turbulent evening and the Hungarians silenced the crowd by taking the lead. Rangers came back to win 4-2, but the press called it an 'inglorious hour and a half' owing to the violent play and bad sportsmanship. This time it was not the foreigners who were to blame, as Rangers were also far from angelic, and players such as Jimmy Millar and Jim Baxter got caught up in the turmoil. The second leg in Budapest was played after heavy rain, and the pitch was heavy and far from ideal. The myth that overseas teams did not like playing on muddy pitches was rolled out again but Ferencváros won 2-1, which meant Rangers scraped through 5-4 on aggregate.

Wolves had a bye to the quarter-finals of the competition and were also sent to Central Europe, to meet FK Austria in the famous Prater stadium. The home side won 2-0 but Wolves were confident of turning the tie around. The Austrians were made welcome when they arrived in England. Training facilities were made available for them at the Aldersley Stadium in Wolverhampton, a new facility built in 1956 that included athletic tracks and a cycle track. They were received at Wolverhampton town hall by Mayor Harold Marsh and were also guests at a boxing match. It was not unusual for English clubs to unfurl the red carpet for their foreign visitors, making the game something of a diplomatic exercise. Wolves won 5-0 with an exhilarating display of speed, efficiency and power to clinch a semi-final place. Rangers came through their quarter-final with ease, beating Borussia Mönchengladbach 11-0 across their two meetings.

The semi-final draw paired the two British sides and, naturally, national fervour came to the surface. Wolves had been Football League champions in 1958 and 1959 and had won the FA Cup in 1960. They were one of the pioneers when it came to staging games with foreign teams. Rangers wanted nothing more than to beat Wolves to show England that Scottish football was superior. Needless to say, demand for tickets for the first leg at Ibrox Park was very high. They went on sale at 9.30am on 20 March and within three hours the 'sold out' signs were put up at Ibrox. Rangers, who were weakened by injuries, won comfortably by 2-0 in the first game nine days later. Almost 80,000 were packed into the stadium and they saw an heroic display by Rangers, capped by goals from Alex Scott and Ralph Brand.

Wolves had three weeks to regroup but they still could not match Rangers in the second leg. Wolverhampton was besieged by 5,000 Rangers fans who were in a very boisterous mood, ringing bells and waving wooden rattles. The local police were nervous, and during the game, beer bottles were thrown from the end where the Rangers fans had gathered. Their team took the lead through Scott and it was not until the hour mark had passed that Wolves finally equalised. With a 3-1 aggregate victory, Rangers were extremely satisfied that they had beaten one of England's top teams. Their opponents in the final would be Fiorentina, who had disposed of Dinamo Zagreb in the other semi-final.

Scottish football was in need of a boost as Rangers prepared for the two-legged final. Earlier in the spring, the national team had been humbled 9-3 by England at Wembley, with young goalkeeper Frank Haffey of Celtic making his second and final appearance for Scotland. With the World Cup only a year away, Scotland were trying to qualify for Chile 1962, but they suffered a 4-0 defeat in Bratislava with a team that included half a dozen Rangers players. Scotland would eventually fail to qualify after a play-off against the Czechs.

Rangers were the best team in Scotland and were champions in 1961, finishing one point ahead of Kilmarnock, who they also beat in the Scottish League Cup Final. Fiorentina had ended their Serie A campaign and won the Coppa Italia. They had some outstanding players in their line-up, including the Swedish forward Kurt Hamrin. Nobody seemed to know too much about Fiorentina, but their coach was Nándor Hidegkuti, a member of the Hungarian team that had thrashed England twice in the early 1950s. He was the legendary 'deep-lying centre-forward' that England just could not deal with, but he remained very respectful of British football: 'Our players have a high regard for Rangers. We do not imagine for a minute it will be an easy game at Ibrox on Wednesday night.'

Fiorentina had played five games in 14 days before meeting Rangers, but they were fit and their training methods were well advanced of British clubs. They arrived in Glasgow with a 15-man squad. The Ibrox Park crowd was partisan and tried to intimidate their Florentine visitors. The game was rough at times and players from both sides were involved in scuffles. The tension spilled over on to the terraces, with bottles and cans thrown on to the pitch. Fiorentina's Luigi Milan scored after 12 minutes but five minutes later Rangers had the chance to equalise when they were awarded a penalty. Fiorentina's goalkeeper, Enrico Albertosi, who would later play for Italy and feature in the famous 1970 World Cup Final, did his best to distract Rangers' penalty-taker, Eric Caldow, and it worked – the defender missed the spot-kick. Milan scored a second goal with two minutes remaining to win 2-0, and the very unhappy home crowd was quick to show its feelings. They jeered, hurled objects and tried to tear down the Italian flag that was flying from the stand. The police rushed to save *Il Tricolore* from being damaged and made around a dozen arrests.

There was an air of disappointment as a two-goal deficit from the home game was a bitter blow to Rangers' hopes. The second leg at the end of May was not a foregone conclusion, but the task was onerous. The local police in Florence made their presence felt in large numbers. The stadium was unlike British arenas, with tall wire fences and iron spikes to deter pitch invasions. Rangers' fans made plenty of noise, singing 'Follow, Follow', their club song, but within 12 minutes Fiorentina had made the aggregate score 3-0 as Milan netted his third of the tie. Alex Scott equalised after 59 minutes with a low shot, but seven minutes from the end Hamrin lifted the ball over Rangers' goalkeeper Billy Ritchie after dashing through the middle. That killed the game and capped a fine season for the Italians. Rangers, who had put up a brave fight in Italy, could look forward to European Cup football in 1961/62.

Scotland's representatives in the Cup Winners' Cup that season were Dunfermline Athletic, who were managed by Jock Stein. They had won the Scottish Cup in 1961 against a Celtic team that included members of Stein's 1967 Lisbon Lions, notably Billy McNeill and Steve Chalmers. While England's Leicester City went out in the first round to Atlético Madrid after beating Glenavon in the preliminaries, Dunfermline got past St Patrick's Athletic and FK Vardar of Yugoslavia. They then faced Hungarian side Újpest, one of Budapest's most storied clubs, and the club of the Ministry of the Interior. They embarked on a 44-day tour of South and Central America before facing Dunfermline and arrived back just before their scheduled quarter-final tie.

Journalists were of the opinion that Újpest were a strong team, but the game itself demonstrated that the teams were evenly matched. Dunfermline took the lead through Alex Smith after only 40 seconds, but 17-year-old rising star Ferenc Bene equalised almost immediately. Tommy McDonald made it 2-1 for the Scots within six minutes, only for Sándor Lenkei to level once more. Goals from Ernö Solymosi and János Göröcs gave Újpest a 4-2 lead before McDonald reduced the deficit to one goal with five minutes to go. Stein was proud of his players for their performance in the Nép stadium in driving rain and was confident Dunfermline could retrieve the tie at East End Park.

Újpest took 47 hours to get to Scotland for the second leg, but it did not appear to affect their players, who needed just 30 minutes of training ahead of the game. Their coach was Dr Geza Kalocsai, a much-travelled and respected football figure. The game ended 1-0 to Újpest, with another goal from Bene, a disappointment for Stein and Dunfermline. But for the club's manager, European triumph was just a few years away.

The first British success in Europe arrived in 1962/63 with Tottenham Hotspur lifting the Cup Winners' Cup. But before Spurs entered the competition, British clubs experienced mixed fortunes. Bangor City of the Cheshire League had gained entry by surprisingly winning the Welsh Cup and they pulled off one of the big shocks of European football that season. Up against a Napoli team that had created history by becoming the first Serie B side to win the Coppa Italia, Bangor were given no chance at all. Napoli also won promotion in 1962 and had strengthened their team in the close season. Bangor beat Napoli 2-0, with goals from former Manchester City player Roy Matthews, and Ken Birch, the latter a penalty. The game was punctuated by pitch invasions that prompted an abandonment threat from the referee.

Bangor were a part-time club who paid their players £8 per week, while Napoli had several highly paid individuals. Humberto Rosa, for example, had been signed for £75,000 from Juventus following Napoli's promotion. Bangor's manager, the former Wales international Tommy Jones, was proud of his team: 'We've done better than anyone could have hoped for. The knives may be out in Naples for the game on September 26, but who cares? What about their blanket defence now?' Bangor had been advised by John Charles, the legendary Welsh player about the Italian style and what they might expect from Napoli in that first leg.

The Italians were stunned, but their coach, Eraldo Monzeglia, promised a warm reception for Bangor in the second leg. 'In Naples, it will be a different story, for every Neapolitan has Vesuvius in his blood.' He was not wrong, for Naples won 3-1 to level the tie 3-3 on aggregate. A third game was required and scheduled for Arsenal's Highbury stadium, where 22,000 people turned up to see the plucky giantkillers of Europe. Napoli were not going to be caught again, and Rosa scored twice to give them a 2-1 win, the decisive goal coming six minutes from the end.

Meanwhile, Rangers came through a difficult preliminary round meeting with Sevilla, another tie that provided ammunition for those that felt pan-European football was tantamount to warfare. The first meeting in Glasgow saw Rangers win 4-0, with Jimmy Millar scoring a hat-trick. Their performance earned great praise from the Spanish media. Their speed and ability to shrug aside challenges from the Sevilla players impressed journalists and visiting fans alike. Although four goals was a huge margin for Sevilla to make up, they did beat Rangers 2-0 in Spain. But the game got very heated at times, so much so that the police had to enter the field of play.

Northern Ireland's representatives, Portadown, suffered a crushing 5-1 defeat in their first-round match with OFK Belgrade and, despite winning the return in Ireland, they went out 7-4 to the Yugoslavs. Rangers were then drawn to meet England's Tottenham Hotspur in the first round, who had won the FA Cup for two consecutive years. This tie excited football fans all over London, and the first leg at White Hart Lane saw the stadium besieged by ticket touts, or 'spivs' to use the popular expression of the time. Hundreds of Rangers fans travelled down from Glasgow by special train to London Euston, and by the time the game kicked off, there were 10,000 Scotsmen inside the ground.

Rangers had great respect for Spurs, notably manager Scot Symon, who had watched them play Manchester United and came away describing their performance as 'wonderful'. The Scottish press called Spurs the 'mightiest team in England' and Symon added that, from what he had seen, Bill Nicholson's side were better than any European opponent they had faced in recent years. Rangers trained at White Hart Lane, where the pitch had been covered with transparent plastic sheeting to protect it from the elements, a somewhat innovative idea in 1962.

The game was exhilarating, with Spurs' speed and precision proving to be too much for Rangers. It took them just four minutes to go ahead when John White headed home a Jimmy Greaves corner. Throughout the evening, Rangers' defence struggled with Greaves' kicks, and Spurs carved out three goals from corners. Spurs went in at half-time 4-2 in front and it was a Maurice Norman goal with 12 minutes remaining that left the final score 5-2, a formidable margin to take to Scotland for the second leg. Although Spurs were the better team by a distance, Rangers refused to buckle and continued to fight for opportunities.

But their fans left London just before midnight, knowing a three-goal deficit was almost impossible to retrieve against a top-class team like Tottenham.

And so it proved in December, some 41 days after the first leg. By this time, Spurs had lost some of their firepower and had struggled to score goals. They also had injuries, with Cliff Jones a big worry for the game at Ibrox Park. In the end, thanks to trainer Cecil Poynton, Jones was passed fit and Nicholson decided to make one important change in restoring Bobby Smith to his team in the place of Les Allen. It worked a treat as Smith scored two goals, including the 89th-minute strike that gave Spurs a 3-2 win in front of 80,000 people. The Spurs manager was delighted: 'I wish our boys would play like they did tonight in the league. Then we'd walk the championship.' At the time, Spurs were in third place, three points behind leaders Everton. And for all the talk of them being goal-shy, Spurs had netted 62 goals in 21 games, the highest in the division by some distance.

Through to the last eight, Spurs were drawn to meet Slovan Bratislava of Czechoslovakia, who won the Czechoslovak Cup in 1962 and 1963. Czechoslovakia, although considered a country from behind the Iron Curtain, had come to the fore in the 1962 World Cup and had surprisingly reached the final. Some of Slovan's players were well known to Western audiences, such as goalkeeper Villiam Schrojf, defender Ján Popluhár and striker Pavol Molnár. Schrojf, especially, had an excellent World Cup and was named by many judges as the best keeper of the tournament. He also featured in several all-star XIs and received several votes in the 1962 Ballon d'Or. Schrojf was a popular figure and had several nicknames, including 'rubber man' and 'the tiger with the bald head'.

As Spurs made their way to Bratislava, Slovan's fans were feverishly clearing the pitch at the Tehelné Pole stadium of snow and ice for three days. Spurs were well known in Czechoslovakia and regarded as a great team, but during a tortuous 90 minutes they rarely looked like the all-conquering side that had won the double in 1961. Bill Brown, their understated goalkeeper, saved them from a very heavy defeat. As it was, it was 2-0, with goals coming from Ľudovít Cvetler and Anton Moravčik. Brown repeatedly dived at the feet of Slovan forwards and earned himself several cuts and bruises, not to mention a gashed nose. Nicholson was incensed by his team's performance: 'We have never played so badly. They have let us off the hook, giving us a chance we should never have had.'

Spurs had just one game between the two legs against Slovan, but they won 2-0 away at Manchester United. When the day came, Spurs were clearly highly motivated and looked confident of saving the situation. Dave Mackay scored the first goal after 31 minutes, and by half-time they were 3-2 ahead on aggregate, with goals from Greaves and Smith. The 60,000 crowd were singing the famous 'Glory, Glory Hallelujah' song that became so associated with Spurs in the 1960s. Three more goals came in the second half, from Greaves, Jones and White, and Slovan were completely crushed. Their coach, Anton Bulla, a wily veteran, admitted he had underestimated the power of the crowd, claiming the White Hart Lane hordes had been worth two goals. Peter Lorenzo of the *Daily Herald* summed up what many people leaving the stadium felt: 'Surely Spurs will one day, perhaps next season, be hailed as champions of Europe.'

For the time being, it was the Cup Winners' Cup and not the European Cup that concerned Spurs. It says a lot about how brilliant they were in the 1960–1962 period that 1962/63 was laden with relative disappointment for Bill Nicholson. The press also expected a lot of them and were quick to underline how lacklustre they were at times. Between beating Slovan Bratislava and taking on their semi-final opponents, OFK Belgrade, Spurs had been beaten by Sheffield Wednesday, Liverpool and Everton. At the same time, they had thrashed Liverpool 7-2 at home and, in total, they had scored 102 goals in 37 games.

Nicholson drilled his players hard in sun-baked Belgrade ahead of the first leg. Spurs had seemed to lack fire and creativity in recent weeks and away from home they appeared less determined than when on their own turf. OFK had two outstanding wingers in Spasoje Samardžic, a Serb, and the Croatian Josip Skoblar, but they were not title contenders in Yugoslavia and eventually finished in fifth place, some 12 points behind champions and neighbours Partizan.

Spurs had some walking wounded ahead of the first meeting in Mackay, Danny Blanchflower, Cliff Jones and Norman. There was, however, a degree of kidology involved in pre-match team news when it came to European games. Spurs won 2-1 in Belgrade, thanks to a late winner from the quick-thinking Terry Dyson, who had whipped the ball off the foot of Miroslav Milovanović before scoring. There was a setback when Greaves, playing in an unfamiliar right-wing role, was sent off early in the second half. Nobody was absolutely sure why the 22-year-old goal machine had been dismissed at the time, but the referee, one Lajos Aranyosi from Hungary, explained that Greaves had taken a kick at OFK's Blagomir Krivokuća.

OFK's management were anxious about the effect of the big London crowd on their players in the second leg. 'The Spurs fans are feared throughout Europe,' said one club official. The game itself was bad-tempered and the two teams seemed more preoccupied with agitating each other than playing the ball. Some Spurs players lost their composure and it needed an old head, 37-year-old Blanchflower, to provide the necessary inspiration. He created two goals, makeshift inside-left Mackay's 23rd-minute opener and Jones' effort that put Spurs 2-1 ahead just before half-time. Smith, who had been labelled 'the Ox' by the Yugoslavs, had the final say with a beautiful diving header. Spurs were constantly provoked as OFK lived up to their reputation of being 'Belgrade bodycheckers' and were often barracked by the White Hart Lane crowd with chants of 'off, off, off' in response to their brutish challenges. The 3-1 victory sent Spurs through to the final, where they would meet Atlético Madrid, the holders of the Cup Winners' Cup, in Rotterdam.

Many commentators felt that Spurs were the underdogs, that their team was ageing and past its best. It could not be denied that five of the regular line-up were over 30 years of age, with Blanchflower now 37 and struggling with a suspect knee. Moreover, Mackay, who was 28, had a troublesome stomach injury that was very debilitating. He was very doubtful for the final, claiming it would need a miracle for him to be fit enough to play against Atlético Madrid. Spurs' opponents were considered to be a very decent team with some outstanding players. Feliciano Rivilla was a highly regarded defender, while Adelardo Rodríguez was a dangerous forward. Enrique Collar, a fast and tricky left-winger, was another player Spurs had to look out for. Nine of the team that won the competition in 1962 against Fiorentina would line up against Spurs in the De Kuip stadium, the home of Feyenoord.

Spurs and Atlético Madrid both finished runners-up in their respective leagues in 1962/63, although Atlético were 12 points behind their rivals, Real Madrid. The

Spanish side had beaten Hibernians of Malta, Bulgarians Botev Plovdiv, and West Germany's Nürnberg on their way to the final. Even the most patriotic English journalist doubted whether a tired and out-of-touch Spurs team could beat one of Spain's best. But they need not have worried, for Nicholson's team put on a dazzling show in Rotterdam. Greaves gave them the lead on 16 minutes and John White made it 2-0 a quarter of an hour later. A penalty by Collar gave Atlético some hope, but Dyson, who had an outstanding game, restored the two-goal advantage. There was more to come as Greaves added a fourth ten minutes from time before Dyson completed the scoring with five minutes to go. Apart from a spell just after half-time, Spurs never looked in danger from Atlético's efforts. A 5-1 victory gave Spurs the Cup Winners' Cup, the first British team to win a major European trophy. 'In the main, the match was extremely clean. I thoroughly enjoyed it,' said Greaves after the final. The well-known referee, Leo Horn, who watched the game from the sidelines, was very impressed: 'This was the best performance I have ever seen from an English club. Why doesn't your national team play like this?'

The truth was that Tottenham's double-winners of 1961 had reached the end of their road. As thousands of fans welcomed the team back to North London, Nicholson and the Tottenham board were planning an overhaul of the club's playing resources. Names like Jim Baxter of Rangers and Southampton's Terry Paine were linked to Tottenham, but the only immediate acquisition was St Mirren's Jimmy Robertson. A year later, Spurs would add significant strength to their squad in the form of Pat Jennings, Alan Gilzean, Alan Mullery and Cyril Knowles, all of whom would enjoy European success with the club. One era was ending for Spurs, but another was not too far away.

5

Hard Luck and Hard Tackles

WHEN WOLVERHAMPTON Wanderers claimed they were champions of the world after hosting and winning a succession of floodlit friendlies, it proved to be the catalyst for the creation of a football competition between Europe's domestic champions. There was a certain degree of arrogance in claiming superior status, especially as English clubs had not tested themselves on a competitive basis, despite the underlying feeling there was little that 'johnny foreigner' could teach the cradle of the game.

Wolves were a fine side in the mid-to-late 1950s and they became the leading team in England after the young side fashioned by Matt Busby had died in such tragic circumstances. Wolves had been pushed into United's shadow in 1956 and 1957 but in 1957/58, they were leading the way and had comprehensively beaten United 3-1 at Molineux. On the eve of United's ill-fated trip to Belgrade in the European Cup, Wolves were league leaders and had a six-point advantage over third-placed United.

Wolves went on to win the title and were set to make their bow in Europe in 1958/59. Their opponents in the second round (Wolves had a bye in the first round) were West German champions Schalke 04. These were the days of regional football in post-war Germany and the

Bundesliga was still some way off, so Schalke had to first play in the Oberliga West before meeting the other winners. They won their regional league by a single point ahead of Köln, and then met Karlsruher, Eintracht Braunschweig and Tennis Borussia Berlin in their group. They finished with a 100 per cent record and a goal difference of 16-1. Their opponents in the final in Hannover were Hamburg, who had the 21-year-old Uwe Seeler, who had played for West Germany in the 1958 World Cup, in their line-up. They won 3-0 to become champions.

Wolves were confident going into the first game at Molineux; they were, after all, leading the Football League and playing well. But Schalke were a hard side, not as calculating as some English clubs' opponents had been in the early European ties, but physically tough. Günter Siebert demonstrated that West German teams lacked nothing in guile when he body-swerved around three defenders before scoring for Schalke in the 23rd minute. Peter Broadbent levelled three minutes into the second half despite protests from the visitors that he was offside. He headed his second goal in the 66th minute and Wolves looked poised to finish the game 2-1 winners, but, with time running out, Willi Koslowski equalised.

Six days later, Wolves travelled to Gelsenkirchen for the second leg knowing they faced an uphill struggle to go through. By half-time, Schalke looked as good as through as they led 2-0 thanks to goals from Heinz Kördell and Siebert. Wolves started to adopt a more robust style and the crowd whistled and jeered as the home team's popular defender Otto Laszig was stretchered off after clashing with Eddie Clamp. It was desperate measures really, because the real damage had been done at Molineux. It was a disappointing debut for Wolves, but they were bound for a second successive league title, which meant an immediate return to the European Cup.

Although Wolves were clearly the best team in the Football League, the early years of the European Cup suggested that English clubs were not as progressive as some of the leading sides of Spain, Portugal and Italy. Perhaps it was the last vestiges of the concept of British fair play that restricted teams from competing with ultra-professional Continental opponents, but it would take some time for England's best clubs to learn how best to deal with teams that had a 'win-at-all-costs' approach.

Wolves drew German opposition again at the start of their campaign in 1959/60, but this time it was from the German Democratic Republic, which was about to celebrate its tenth anniversary. Vorwärts of Berlin were a team named after one of the guiding principles of East Germany – 'looking forward' – and were the de facto club of the army. They had won the Oberliga with an unblemished home record but when Wolves arrived in East Berlin the experts were predicting an easy victory for the English champions. It did not work out that way, for Wolves were beaten 2-1. They took the lead after 15 minutes through Broadbent, but two goals in five minutes turned the game around for Vorwärts. The crowd of 60,000 included 600 British servicemen who had hopped over the border from West Berlin to cheer Wolves on.

The general feeling was that the current Wolves side was way behind the one that had beaten clubs such as Honvéd, Real Madrid, Spartak and Dynamo Moscow. Wolves won 2-0 in the second leg and *The Times* captured the very obvious suspicion of anything from across the channel. 'Wolves maintained their unbeaten record against the foreign invader under the floodlights of Molineux.' Vorwärts had what the experts were calling an 'interlocking defence' and a 'close-weaving attack', but on the night Wolves were too powerful, despite fine performances by the East German goalkeeper, Karl-Heinz Spickenagel, a product of Weimar Berlin, and Jürgen Nöldner, the son of a famed resistance fighter who was killed by the Nazis. Nöldner also went on to become editor of the renowned German football publication, *Kicker*.

Wolves' next opponents, Red Star Belgrade, promised to be a tougher proposition. Red Star had won the Yugoslav league in 1959, finishing ahead of their fierce rivals, Partizan, on goal difference. Yugoslavia had shown how good they could be when they beat England 5-0 in the JNA stadium, the home of Partizan. That Yugoslav side included three Red Star players who would appear against Wolves: goalkeeper Vladimir Beara, Dragoslav Šekularec and Branko Zebec, who was playing for Partizan at the time. Beara was considered to be one of the best goalkeepers in Europe and was so agile that he was known as 'the ballet dancer with the hands of steel'. Šekularec, a quick and skilful forward, had run England ragged in Belgrade, while Zebec captained Yugoslavia in the 1958 World Cup and went on to become a successful coach in Germany, winning the Bundesliga and taking Hamburg to the 1980 European Cup Final. There were other players, such as Bora Kostić, a prolific striker, and Vladimir Popović, who also had a varied and colourful managerial career.

Wolves travelled to Belgrade accompanied by Mayor Norman Bagley, the town clerk and a Viscount aircraft full of supporters, journalists and a TV crew. Manager Stan Cullis had attempted to watch Red Star in Titograd, but due to fog he had not been able to get to the game, so Wolves did not have much information ahead of the game aside from what they already knew from the England game in 1958. The first leg was rough, but Wolves were every bit as guilty as the home side. In fact, Wolves' 'heavy' style was considered to be in stark contrast to Manchester United's more purist approach. It ended 1-1 in Belgrade but still the British media felt that there was something more 'honest' in the traditional qualities of the game in England, which involved hard tackles and shoulder charges, rather than the blindside obstructions adopted by 'the Continentals'. The tackling of Wolves did not go down well with the locals, notably the Red Star president. 'We have learnt some things we shall put to good use in the return match,' he said in the banquet after the game.

At Molineux, the battle was red-blooded and not a place for shrinking violets. The teams appeared to forget about the ball and were too concerned with each other. There were almost 40 fouls in the game, with 25 committed by the home team. Wolves' power was too much for Red Star and, after an early goal from Jimmy Murray, two very late efforts from Bobby Mason clinched a three-nil victory and sent them into the last eight.

Whoever Wolves met, the quality of the competition meant it would be a hurdle, but Barcelona was a severe and daunting task. Barça had already won the Inter-Cities Fairs Cup and would retain the trophy in late March 1960, and had clearly embraced the concept of European combat. The club had, like Real Madrid, started trawling the world for fresh talent and their squad to face Wolves included Hungarians, a Uruguayan and a Brazilian. There was something very cosmopolitan and modern about building teams across borders, a practice that English clubs could not do until the 1980s. Furthermore, the mere sight of Barcelona's Camp Nou stadium was awe-inspiring for Wolves and their supporters. Equipped with a fully stocked hospital, a chapel and tiers of spectators, the stadium was intimidating even when it was empty. One journalist was so astounded by the Camp Nou that he proclaimed such football arenas made England's grounds look like hen coops.

Once the football got underway, Barcelona were so advanced that Wolves could not match the invention of the Spaniards or South Americans. English football was made to look hard, formal and unimaginative, while Barcelona were clever and had intricate skill in abundance. By half-time, it was 2-0, with goals coming from Ramón Vallaverde and László Kubala. Evaristo and Villaverde added two more in the second half, sending Wolves home with their European Cup run effectively over.

The return offered no encouragement for Wolves. Sándor Kocsis, a member of the Hungarian team that dismantled England at Wembley and in Budapest in 1953 and 1954, respectively, scored four goals as Barcelona won 5-1 at Molineux. *The Times* said that the scoreline confirmed it as a case of workmen facing artists and magicians and added a postscript to the final score: 'We may salute the past, but our footballers are now the victims of a system.' That system, built around traditional football qualities of hard work, aggression and power, looked suddenly very dated – courage and stamina were no longer enough.

Similar sentiments were expressed when Rangers were trounced twice by Eintracht Frankfurt in the semi-finals of the competition. The Gers had enjoyed an incident-packed run to the last four, beginning in the preliminary round against Belgian champions Anderlecht. They won 5-2 in the first leg after scoring twice in the first two minutes and then finished their opponents off with a 2-0 win in Brussels. Then they faced Czechoslovakian side Červená Hviezda, the team that would evolve into Inter Bratislava, beating them 5-4 over two legs.

Rangers were severely tested by their next opponents, Sparta Rotterdam, who took them to three games. Rangers won in the Dutch port by 3-2, so when the second leg at Ibrox Park came around, they were confident, but a late goal by Tonny van Ede levelled the scores. A third meeting was staged at Highbury, home of Arsenal, the first European Cup tie to be held at their stadium. There were plenty of goals on a pitch that resembled a beach at low tide, but two of Rangers' three were own goals and one of Sparta's was a penalty. Rangers went through by 3-2, but it was, to quote one report, 'Straightforward and not highly intelligent.' Their semi-final opponents were Eintracht Frankfurt and there was no shortage of motivation to win through to the final, for it was to be held at Hampden Park. What better way to remind Rangers' Glasgow rivals of their superiority than winning the European Cup in their home city?

But it was not to be. The first leg finished any aspirations Rangers had of winning through to Hampden. Both teams supposedly had injury problems, including Rangers' goalkeeper George Niven, and Alex Scott, but unsurprisingly all the so-called casualties played in both games. Rangers flew to Frankfurt, taking 30 fans, 19 players and half a dozen club officials. Frankfurt was expecting an 80,000 crowd, so security was stepped up with police introducing some 'special precautions'. Rangers' manager Scot Symon was full of respect for Eintracht and called them a well-balanced side. They had five internationals, including defender Friedel Lutz, winger Richard Kree and strikers Erwin Stein and Alfred Pfaff. They had beaten Young Boys Bern and Wiener Sport-Club on their way to the semi-final and had benefitted from a walkover in the preliminary round.

Dieter Stinka opened the scoring for Eintracht in the 29th minute but within two minutes, Eric Caldow equalised from the penalty spot. If Rangers felt they had matched the Germans for 45 minutes, they had a rude awakening in the second period. Frankfurt scored five times, with Pfaff and Dieter Lindner both netting twice and Stein rounding the scoring off in the 86th minute to give them a 6-1 advantage. It was one of the biggest setbacks Rangers had ever experienced at that point in their history. Symon was devastated: 'I was very disappointed in our display. We missed two good chances in the second half and then appeared to become unsure of ourselves. But, all credit to Eintracht.'

It was, of course, an impossible task for Rangers, but that did not stop 69,000 turning up at Ibrox Park to see if the Gers could pull off something remarkable in the return. In between the two legs, Rangers had won the Scottish Cup, beating Kilmarnock 2-0 at Hampden. Twenty-four hours before the game, Poland had beaten a Scotland team that included Denis Law, Dave Mackay and Ian St John 3-2. The second leg provided no solace for Scottish football fans. Frankfurt won 6-3 to run up an impressive and shocking 12-4 aggregate scoreline. Hugh McIlvanney of *The Scotsman* painted a grim picture: 'Rangers hopes of success in the European Cup were buried last night after the abject poverty of Scottish football had been exposed.' Frankfurt were faster, had better ball control and quickly destroyed Rangers' confidence. They went on to play Real Madrid in one of the most memorable European Cup finals, losing 7-3 in Glasgow.

Fellow Scots Heart of Midlothian, who won the Scottish League in 1960, were beaten in the preliminary round of the 1960/61 competition by the rising stars of Benfica. English champions Burnley received a bye to round one and were drawn to meet Stade Reims, a club that had played in two of the first four European Cup finals. They were widely acknowledged to be the best team outside the two Spanish giants, Real Madrid and Barcelona. They had two stars who had already made their mark on European football, Raymond Kopa and Just Fontaine. Kopa had returned to Reims after playing for Real Madrid, while Fontaine, who had topped the scoring charts in the 1958 World Cup with 13 goals, remained in France.

Burnley produced a very impressive performance to beat Reims 2-0 at Turf Moor, both goals coming early in the game from Jimmy Robson and Jimmy McIlroy. There was no guarantee that a two-goal margin would be enough, however. Kopa was injured and missed the second leg in Paris, but Fontaine, who was troubled by a leg injury in the 1960/61 season, was restored to the team. Burnley added to their two goals to lead 1-0 at half-time – scorer Robson – against a backdrop of a fierce crowd singing 'Allez Reims' all evening, not to mention firing rockets into the sky. Reims led 2-1 but were immediately pegged back by a John Connelly goal. Bruno Rodzik scored a third for Reims, but it was not enough. It was a landmark victory, not just for Burnley, but also English football.

Hamburg were next, including Uwe Seeler, who was now recognised as one of the best centre-forwards in Europe. Indeed, a poll conducted by a magazine in 1960 revealed that there were only two better forwards, Luis Suárez of Barcelona and Ferenc Puskás of Real Madrid. As Burnley prepared for the game, there were discussions in progress about player transfers that could have resulted in a strike. The point of contention was, among other things, the practice of selling players without their approval. Jimmy Hill, later of TV fame, was chair of the Professional Footballers' Association and, with a walkout looking imminent, forced an agreement with the Football League.

This was not just Burnley versus Hamburg, this was also England against Germany, and the media could not resist a few references to the Second World War. The German spectators were not just capable of cheering and applauding, according to reports, they produced a 'Germanic roar' as they enjoyed a 'resurgence of power'. Furthermore, the wooden rattles of the Lancastrian crowd produced a noise that was likened to machine-gun fire. If the game had been between representatives of any other nation, such comments would not have been made.

Burnley won 3-1 with two fine goals from Brian Pilkington and one from Jimmy Robson. Gert Dörfel responded for Hamburg and gave them hope for the second leg. That game did not take place until mid-March, by which time Burnley were chasing a treble of league, FA Cup and European Cup. The game at the rebuilt Volkspark stadium was sold out weeks in advance. Hamburg were powerful and confident and undeterred by having to retrieve a two-goal deficit. They did just that in the first half with goals from Klaus Stürmer and Seeler. When Gordon Harris scored in the 55th minute, Burnley fans were so excited that they ran on to the pitch, but Dörfal scored almost immediately and swung the game Hamburg's way again. With 15 minutes remaining Seeler netted once more and the rout was completed. Hamburg had pulled off the type of determined comeback that one day would be seen as a strong characteristic of German teams at both club and national level.

Despite producing some very strong and functional champions, there was clearly something missing from England's representatives in the European Cup. Of course, the nation still mourned Manchester United's Busby Babes, who many felt were destined to be European champions, but when Tottenham Hotspur won the double in 1960/61, there was a feeling that this team could more than hold its own against Europe's finest.

Bill Nicholson was of the opinion that Real Madrid were not the force they were in 1960, and in 1961 they had been beaten by Barcelona, who themselves had lost in the final to Portugal's Benfica. The 1961/62 field was formidable, with Real back in the competition along with Benfica, Juventus, Sporting Clube de Portugal and Partizan Belgrade, not to mention Rangers. Benfica had discovered a new star in 19-year-old striker Eusébio, who was from Mozambique and possessed power, speed and phenomenal shooting ability. Tottenham would soon learn all about the likeable lad from one of Portugal's colonies.

But Spurs were about to enter unknown territory in their first European Cup campaign. Górnik Zabrze, the champions of Poland, had a prolific forward called Ernest Pol in their line-up. He averaged almost a goal a game and was top scorer in Poland in 1960/61. A trip behind the Iron Curtain was a journey into the unknown for English clubs and the players were shocked by some of the things they witnessed. Danny Blanchflower and his team-mates spoke of prisoners digging holes in the streets, women cutting grass in the parks with scissors and armed guards standing over them. Blanchflower also recalled being asked to exchange fundamental items like razor blades with eager fans of English football. The press pack that followed Spurs to Katowice was also heavily policed and anyone taking unlicensed photographs was whisked away for questioning.

Nicholson went to Poland ahead of the tie to investigate training facilities and hotels. In Katowice and Chorzów, nothing met his requirements. When the teams met, Spurs took time to settle and Górnik were 4-0 ahead before they started to play. 'I was bloody upset, we showed no determination or discipline,' recalled Nicholson. Luckily, despite the screeching and partisan 90,000 crowd, goals from Cliff Jones and Terry Dyson in the last quarter of an hour made the scoreline more respectable at 4-2. The Polish media warned their team that the game in London would test the Górnik team: 'The Cockerels may have been more like hens in Katowice, but we must not underestimate them. Before their own crowd, they may do better than they did in the last 20 minutes in Poland.'

Turning the tie around was still a formidable task, but Spurs were confident. In the first leg there were some accusations that they had resorted to rough tactics when they were behind and this irked some of their fans. Górnik were without two of their key players, Kowalski and Musiałek, both of whom had injuries from that first game. The White Hart Lane crowd played their part, producing a crescendo of noise that seemed to unsettle the Poles. Furthermore, a group of fans dressed all in white with wings, in response to claims that Spurs had been 'no angels' in Poland. It took the team only 20 minutes to make it 4-4 on aggregate and at half-time Spurs were 7-5 up and Jones had scored a hat-trick. Three more goals came in the second period as Nicholson's team won 8-1 and 10-5 on aggregate. The 'angels' came on to the pitch with a placard reading, 'Rejoice. This is the hour of Revenge'.

The next round's opponents were a little more accessible. Feyenoord of Rotterdam were within easy reach. The club's De Kuip stadium, in the Dutch city's hinterland, was renowned as a raucous venue and with 60,000-plus inside was an intimidating atmosphere. The team was considered to be methodical, no more than that, but on their home turf could be a difficult proposition. Spurs overcame the noise, which was boosted by a cacophony of sirens from passing ships along the waterfront, and won 3-1.

They had to field two young players in Eddie Clayton and 18-year-old Frank Saul from Canvey Island. Saul scored twice in the second half after Dyson had put Spurs ahead four minutes from half-time. Two weeks later, Feyenoord put on a stubborn performance at White Hart Lane in an untidy contest that ended 1-1. Spurs were through but the competition was now getting interesting and had been narrowed down to the stronger survivors. Nicholson knew he needed to add to his double-winning team and started to track Jimmy Greaves, the former Chelsea forward who was looking to leave AC Milan in Italy. Greaves was eventually signed for close to £100,000, but he was ineligible to play in the European Cup until the semi-final round.

Spurs had to get past Dukla Prague before they could think of the last four, a team that was packed with Czechoslovakian internationals. Dukla were the club of the Czech army and could handpick the players they required, which did not make them especially popular. Despite their famous name, Dukla were one of the worst-supported teams in the top division with crowds that were around a third of Sparta Prague's usual attendance. And yet they had seven players in the 1962 World Cup squad a few months later, including the great Josef Masopust, who would go on to be named European Footballer of the Year. Spurs were not at their best when they flew out to Prague, as their title bid was faltering a little after some careless draws and the championship race was rapidly becoming a battle between Burnley, Spurs and Ipswich Town.

The weather in the Czech capital was poor, howling wind and rain, and the pitch was a sea of mud. Nicholson adopted a patient approach with a solid defence and, although they were beaten 1-0 by a goal from Rudolf Kučera, a player who was repeatedly being called 'the Greaves of Czechoslovakia', Spurs flew home believing they had gained the upper hand from a tactical perspective. The British media, while acknowledging Dukla's team of artists and ball-players, felt Spurs would summon up another great European night and come through the test. Jaroslav Vejvoda, Dukla's coach, expressed some caution when he arrived in London, insisting his team would not play a defensive game but would vary its tactics to the state of the match.

Before the game, the Tottenham angels were back again, with a new placard: 'Rejoice ye mortals in the coming triumph'. Dukla did not have much time to settle at White Hart Lane thanks to two early goals from Bobby Smith and Dave Mackay. Josef Jelínek pulled one back for Dukla before the same two Spurs men scored again to make the 4-1 scoreline look quite emphatic. The crowd were ecstatic as they reached the semi-final, singing, 'The Spurs go marching on'. Nicholson's team now had the final in their sights.

Benfica were the holders of the European Cup and their reputation was such that there was no small amount of fascination about them. Certainly, no London fixture had attracted so much attention since the famous Hungarians trounced England in November 1953. Every member of Benfica's regular XI was a Portuguese international, and their manager, Béla Guttmann, was well known and someone who had lived a turbulent history. Guttmann was a Holocaust survivor and had spent time in a concentration camp but escaped before he could be sent to Auschwitz. Guttmann was a figure that divided opinion to some extent, but in some ways he was ahead of his time.

His Benfica team was strong, powerful and skilful. Eusébio was their crown jewel, but they also had Mário Coluna, António Simões, José Augusto and José Águas in their line-up. Eusébio confirmed his arrival on the international scene in October 1961 at Wembley when Portugal were beaten 2-0 by England in a World Cup qualifier. The youngster rattled the England crossbar twice in the closing stages of the match and generally impressed the crowd with his shooting ability.

Spurs had their own trump card in Greaves, who had already made his mark since joining the club from AC Milan. He could play in the semi-final after being ineligible since arriving back in England. Nicholson was confident that the winners of the Benfica-Spurs tie would go on to lift the European Cup, and so it would prove, but the trophy would not end up in the hands of his team. Spurs went to Lisbon expecting a very difficult time but they left the Estádio da Luz feeling a sense of injustice about the way referee Daniel Mellet had officiated. Spurs were 2-0 down inside 20 minutes thanks to two untidy goals from Simões and Augusto. Smith sent a powerful header into the net in the 55th minute to give Spurs hope of recovery, but Augusto added a third nine minutes later. Greaves and Smith both had goals disallowed that would have completely changed the face of the game, but in a stadium of deafening sound they did well to keep the tie alive, even though Nicholson complained that his team had made some 'stupid mistakes'.

Guttmann played a little psycho-game with Spurs and the media immediately after the first leg. He told reporters he was concerned about the physicality of Smith and Mackay ahead of the return at White Hart Lane, a comment that was misquoted by some newspapers and was interpreted as Guttmann putting pressure on the match referee to keep an eye on Spurs. Guttmann explained it differently, however: 'I told the journalists that I expected a bloodbath and they, in turn, went to Poulsen, the Danish referee, and told him Guttmann did not think he was strong enough to handle the match.'

In between the two games with Benfica, Spurs had beaten Everton 3-1 at home and also reached the FA Cup Final by beating Manchester United 3-1 in the semi-final at Hillsborough. Their hopes of retaining the Football League championship, with eight games to go, were fading as they were in third place and eight points behind leaders Ipswich Town. The Suffolk side, managed by Spurs' former player, Alf Ramsey, had played two games more, though.

People were clamouring to see Tottenham versus Benfica and 64,000-plus turned up to see if Spurs could achieve what some saw as the impossible. When the game came, Guttmann kept Benfica's hosts waiting as the teams entered the field. Benfica did not undergo a warm-up on the pitch because he feared the crowd would upset his players. Nothing could have been further from the truth; the Angolan-born Águas opened the scoring for Benfica in the first quarter of an hour to silence the Spurs fans and add to the tension. Greaves had a goal disallowed before Smith equalised in the 35th minute with a volley inside the penalty area. Eusébio struck the woodwork but it was Spurs who went ahead from the penalty spot just after half-time through Blanchflower. It was 2-1, but still a big ask of the Spurs players. They pressurised Benfica and, in the closing minutes, Mackay headed against the crossbar. That third goal never came and Benfica won through to the final. They went on to beat Real Madrid 5-3 in Amsterdam. As for Spurs, this was their last European Cup match until the Champions League expanded to include non-champions. There was still some mileage left in their double-winners, but one of British football's finest post-war sides would soon start to break up.

The Manchester United side that drew 3-3 in Belgrade against Red Star on 5 February 1958. Twenty-four hours later, many perished on a Munich runway.

Tottenham clash with Benfica in the 1961/62 European Cup at White Hart Lane. Dave Mackay makes his point.

*A year later, Spurs lifted Britain's first
European trophy, beating Atlético Madrid
in the European Cup-Winners' Cup Final
in Rotterdam.*

Alan Sealey, Bobby Moore and Martin Peters enjoy West Ham's 1965 triumph in the European Cup-Winners' Cup Final. Sealey scored both goals in the Hammers' 2-0 win over Munich 1860.

Rangers fans in Nuremberg for the 1967 Cup-Winners' Cup Final against Bayern Munich. Franz Beckenbauer scored the only goal of the game for the Germans.

Celtic's Jimmy Johnstone in action against Inter Milan in the 1967 European Cup Final in Lisbon. Celtic made history in becoming the first British club to win the coveted trophy.

Billy Bremner, captain of Leeds United, at Manchester airport, full of admiration for the Fairs Cup his team had just won in Budapest in September 1968.

Bobby Charlton, Brian Kidd and Paddy Crerand congratulate Matt Busby at the final whistle of the European Cup Final, May 1968.

The appeal of Newcastle versus Rangers in the Fairs Cup semi-final in 1969 is encapsulated by daring fans scaling the floodlights at Ibrox.

Arsenal ended a barren spell in their history by winning the Fairs Cup in 1970. Charlie George, a mercurial figure, played his part in the Gunners' victory in the final against Anderlecht.

Celtic and Leeds met in the European Cup semi-final in 1970. Two titanic battles, billed as England v Scotland, ended with more heartbreak for Leeds.

The trendy Chelsea players celebrate with thousands after winning the European Cup-Winners' Cup in 1971, beating Real Madrid.

Alan Mullery returned to Tottenham from a loan spell with Fulham to score a spectacular goal in the UEFA Cup semi-final against AC Milan in 1972.

Ray Kennedy, Kevin Keegan and David Fairclough enjoy Liverpool's 3-1 win against Saint-Étienne in the European Cup quarter-final in 1977.

Nottingham Forest's 1979 European champions, moulded by Brian Clough and Peter Taylor, after beating Malmo 1-0 in Munich.

Alan Kennedy, Liverpool's unsung hero, scores the only goal of a lack-lustre European Cup Final in 1981.

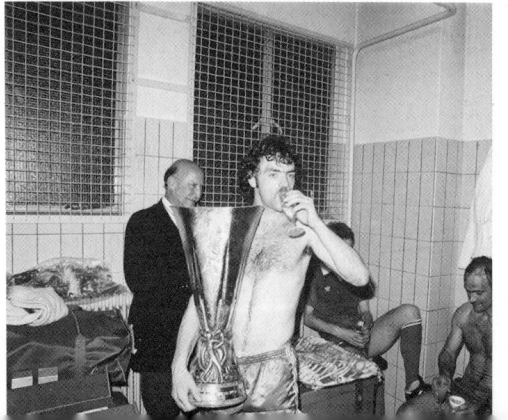

John Wark, who scored 14 goals in the 1980/81 UEFA Cup for Ipswich Town, holds the silverware after beating AZ Alkmaar 5-4 on aggregate.

Aston Villa's Peter Withe scores the winning goal against Bayern Munich in the 1982 European Cup Final in Rotterdam.

Everton's players celebrate a goal in the 1985 Cup-Winners' Cup Final against Rapid Vienna. The last success by an English club until 1991 …

… and this was why. The Heysel Stadium disaster in Brussels, the European Cup Final 1985 between Liverpool and Juventus.

6

If I Had a Hammer

WEST HAM United's manager, Ron Greenwood, was a big advocate of European football competitions. When the Hungarians of 1953 dismantled England at Wembley and cast huge doubts about the country's position in the game, he was in awe. Watching Puskás and his team-mates play football from a different planet left an impact on Greenwood, who was a Chelsea player at the time. His first steps into management started at Eastbourne United and then as a coach with Oxford University. It was at Oxford that he came to the attention of Harold Thompson, who became the chairman of the FA. Greenwood was later involved with England's youth and under-23 set-ups and in 1957 he joined Arsenal as assistant manager to George Swindin.

When West Ham were looking for a replacement for manager Ted Fenton, they approached Arsenal to seek permission to talk to Greenwood. Arsenal did not stand in his way and Reg Pratt, chairman of the Hammers, was immediately impressed. It did not take long for a deal to be agreed but Pratt was very clear that Greenwood would be a very modern appointment. 'Ron isn't coming to us in the old-fashioned idea of a manager. His duties will be confined to picking the team, coaching and reporting to the board. He is entirely in agreement with this,' said Pratt.

West Ham became something of an academy for would-be coaches and managers, and several former players from the post-war years went on to make their mark in management. Players such as Dave Sexton, Malcolm Allison, John Bond, Frank O'Farrell and Noel Cantwell were all influenced by West Ham. Greenwood added his own style to the club and encouraged players to develop an understanding of coaching. Quite a few of his proteges went on to have respectable careers in management, although some of his players have highlighted a certain 'coldness' when dealing with the man. Often, his ideas, drawn from an encyclopaedic mind, were too complex for the players at his disposal.

But the club, for many years, acquired a reputation for playing good, thoughtful football, which won plenty of plaudits but was not especially successful. But then West Ham were not a club that had the sort of financial backing enjoyed by London neighbours Arsenal and Tottenham Hotspur. They were not a knee-jerk club that did not give employees time to develop something long-term; before Greenwood, there had only been three managers of the Hammers.

There was an element of prophecy about Greenwood's views on the game. He could see the way the industry was developing and felt exposure to foreign football would not only test his own players, but ultimately benefit their technique. In 1963, the Hammers played a summer competition in the US called the International Soccer League and won the trophy by beating Poland's Górnik Zabrze 2-1 on aggregate over two games in New York. Bobby Moore won the Eisenhower Trophy as Most Valuable Player and Geoff Hurst was leading scorer with eight goals. It may not have been of the highest quality, but West Ham's young side had exposure to teams from Italy, Scotland, Brazil, Germany, Mexico, Poland and France.

The first real piece of silverware won by the Hammers was the FA Cup in 1963/64. They had surprisingly beaten holders Manchester United in the semi-final by 3-1 and faced Second Division Preston North End in the final. They were firm favourites to win, with many hoping their cultured style would show others that teams could win with something other than power and pace.

With English clubs struggling to succeed in Europe, there was a growing feeling that the traditional ways of football in Britain were simply not good enough to combat skilful and cunning sides from Spain, Italy and Portugal. Among the tactics that Greenwood 'borrowed' from the Hungarians and others was the use of near-post corners and crosses, which became something of a West Ham trademark that was also adopted by England. Respected journalist Ken Jones felt that Wembley would be the ideal canvas for West Ham to display their 'intelligent application of skill and effort'.

And so it proved. It was a classic FA Cup Final and Preston North End refused to be overawed. They fielded 17-year-old Howard Kendall, a midfielder who would go on to enjoy an outstanding career with Everton and also a successful managerial career. For decades, he was thought to be the best player never to win a cap for England.

Preston led twice but West Ham finally won 3-2, with a 90th-minute header from Ronnie Boyce. Interestingly, Boyce was one of nine players, including Bobby Moore, Geoff Hurst and John Sissons, who had come through the club's youth system. West Ham's commitment to development of young players was much envied and not only delivered success for the club, but also the national team. As well as Moore and Hurst, Martin Peters would become part of the England side that won the World Cup in 1966.

Victory in the FA Cup gave West Ham entry to the European Cup Winners' Cup in 1964/65. Again, the general consensus was that West Ham's approach might be more successful than some of the teams that had carried the flag for the English game before them. Only Spurs, winners of the Cup Winners' Cup in 1963 and semi-finalists in the European Cup a year earlier, had convincingly picked up the baton since the tragic demise of the Busby Babes in 1958.

The Cup Winners' Cup had some formidable participants in 1964/65: Real Zaragoza of Spain and Torino of Italy were the teams to avoid in the draw; Portugal's Sporting [Lisbon] were also tipped as potential winners. West Ham were drawn to play Gent of Belgium, also known as *La Gantoise*. Aside from the excitement and curiosity of playing in Europe for the first time – tours and friendlies aside – West Ham's biggest concern was how to cope with possible match congestion now the Football League Cup was also on the fixture calendar.

West Ham's league displays placed them very much in the mid-table area in the early weeks of the 1964/65 season. They had drawn 2-2 with Liverpool, the 1964 league champions, in the FA Charity Shield, a game that promised much for the weeks ahead, but lost five in seven before their European programme got underway. The trip to Gent offered the chance for fans to travel across the channel to Belgium at a reasonable price. Around 1,000 Hammers supporters took the train to Dover and then the ferry across to Ostend, where the team was staying. The city of Gent made them welcome and there was a carnival atmosphere that included parading bands and a fairground. Greenwood took 16 players to Belgium and insisted on some hard training to prepare them for a robust home team. The game was to be played at the Jules Otten Stadion, a multipurpose arena that was used in the 1920 Olympics.

West Ham pulled off a 1-0 victory, thanks to a 52nd-minute header from FA Cup hero Boyce from Alan Sealey's corner. It was not a riveting game, but most people felt it would be enough for the second leg at Upton Park, especially as West Ham had a decent home record. Results between the two legs were mixed: Sheffield United were beaten 3-1 at the Boleyn Ground, but Sunderland thrashed Greenwood's team 4-1 in the Football League Cup. Just ahead of the game in London, West Ham drew 1-1 at Everton and were only denied victory in the closing seconds.

They were equally frustrated by the Belgians in the second leg. The 24,000 crowd was expecting a leisurely 90 minutes but a 32nd-minute own goal by Peters levelled the aggregate scores. Even though the visitors had one player exiled to the flank due to a pronounced limp, *La Gantoise* were stubbornly resistant. Johnny Byrne scored just before the half-time break and that was the way the game ended, 1-1. Greenwood was a little relieved but was unhappy with the way by which West Ham got through.

Also through to round two were some teams that had inflicted heavy defeats on their less-equipped opponents: Sparta Prague won 16-0 on aggregate against Cypriots Anorthosis Famagusta, Real Zaragoza won 8-1 against Maltese side Valletta, and TSV 1860 Munich hit ten past Union Sportive Luxembourg. Interestingly, all three would play West Ham in the competition. If *La Gantoise* were tricky, there were more difficult fish swimming in the Cup Winners' Cup pond.

Sparta Prague, or to use their name at the time, Spartak Praha Sokolovo, had a reputation for being a very fit and ultra-efficient team. They also had players who had experienced international football such as the Olympics and World Cup. Ivan Mráz, for example, had scored five in the first leg of their tie with Anorthosis Famagusta and had netted five times in the 1964 Olympics in Tokyo. Václav Mašek was also a prolific scorer and had represented Czechoslovakia in the 1962 World Cup. Another forward, Andrej Kvašňák, went on to win 47 caps and was included in the 1962 and 1965 Ballon d'Or voting.

Sparta entered the arena at Upton Park 15 minutes before the teams were due to run out, in order to become accustomed with the floodlights. Despite their obvious firepower, Sparta opted for a very cautious, blanket defence to thwart the enthusiasm of the home team. Within the first 20 minutes, their safety-first defensive work saw them kick the ball out of the stadium three times. John Bond, whose career at West Ham was coming to an end, scored a notable goal in the 59th minute and Sealey prodded home an important second with eight minutes to go. West Ham were, at this time, without Moore, who was in hospital. Only many years later was it revealed that the club's talismanic leader was having treatment for testicular cancer. A two-goal lead was enough to give the Hammers confidence for the second leg in Prague, but Greenwood was being quite secretive about his team selection. 'This will be a test of character,' he insisted, but felt that recent away form, notably at Chelsea and Arsenal, was very encouraging.

The second leg, with 100 West Ham fans making the relatively long journey to Czechoslovakia, was not easy at all as Sparta's tough tackling, along with some very bizarre refereeing decisions, made for a testing 90 minutes. John

Sissons, who was earmarked as a danger man after the first leg, was repeatedly fouled and Alan Sealey ended the game with a gashed leg requiring four stitches. Sparta won 2-1 with two late goals in response to one from Sissons, but West Ham crept through by 3-2.

The quarter-final draw paired West Ham with Lausanne-Sports, a team destined to become Swiss champions in 1965. They were coached by Karl Rappan, an Austrian from Vienna who spent most of his managerial career in Switzerland. Rappan was credited with influencing the development of a system called 'the bolt' or the 'Swiss bolt' that evolved into *catenaccio* and became the property of Italian teams in the 1960s. *Catenaccio* was notorious for producing dull, defensive games in which teams sat back in defence and waited for opponents to attack. At its most effective, it included swift counter-attacking, an approach adopted by AC Milan and Inter Milan, among others, in the 1960s.

Rappan was appointed coach of Lausanne in 1964 and was really coming to the end of his career. His club played at the Stade Olympique de la Pontaise, which was not far from Lake Geneva. The pitch had been like a skating rink only a week before West Ham arrived in Lausanne, but had since become a muddy morass, a surface that Swiss journalists felt might suit the Hammers better. While Greenwood openly said he would gladly accept a draw, Rappan believed Lausanne could win, but made it clear that winning the Swiss league was more important.

West Ham had to field 21-year-old reserve striker Brian Dear, and he made an immediate impact with a goal in the 21st minute. Johnny Byrne extended their lead after going on a solo run that saw him evade two tackles. Lausanne scored near the end through Swiss international Robert

Hosp, but West Ham went home with a very credible 2-1 victory, making them favourites to reach the penultimate stage. In between the two games, a slightly changed West Ham side were beaten 4-0 away at Blackburn Rovers, their third consecutive league defeat. When Lausanne arrived at Upton Park for the second leg, the two teams already knew who they would face in the semi-final. Real Zaragoza had beaten Cardiff City in February. The Welsh Cup holders had earlier beaten holders Sporting Lisbon thanks to a memorable 2-1 win in the Portuguese capital. Cardiff would return to the Cup Winners' Cup in 1965/66 after retaining the Welsh Cup.

Lausanne shocked the 32,000 crowd by taking the lead in the 37th minute through Dutch international Pierre Kerkhoffs. But within five minutes an own goal levelled the scores. Seconds later, Dear put West Ham 2-1 ahead. Lausanne were not daunted and equalised just three minutes into the second half. Peters restored the Hammers' advantage but yet again the Swiss came back with a spectacular overhead kick by Norbert Eschmann. Finally, with a minute remaining, Dear scored his second goal to give West Ham a 4-3 victory on the night and a 6-4 aggregate win over the two games. The spectators clearly enjoyed what was a superb display of attacking football and gave both sides a standing ovation at the end. The biggest cheer of the evening had, interestingly, come after Eschmann's outstanding finish!

Real Zaragoza were reputed to be one of the best teams in Spain and were, apparently, pushing Real Madrid all the way in the Spanish league title race. They had in their ranks a forward line that was feared throughout Spain, comprising the Brazilian Canário, Carlos Lapetra, Marcelino, Eleuterio Santos and Juan Manuel Villa. Zaragoza's frontmen were known as '*Los cincos magnifico*'.

They also had an accomplished defender in Severino Reija, who would feature in Spain's 1966 World Cup side.

This was, without doubt, West Ham's toughest tie so far, but they started spectacularly at home in the semi-final first leg. Man of the moment Dear scored after nine minutes and Byrne added another a quarter of an hour later. They played some spectacular football in the first half but there was a lack of urgency about them. Their Spanish opponents were very relaxed and refused to panic, and it paid off – in the second half Canário made it 2-1 and that was the way it ended. There was an underlying feeling West Ham had not done enough, so Zaragoza would retrieve the deficit and win.

The second leg proved to be a hard evening for nervous fans. Lapetra put the home team ahead to level the aggregate but, in the 54th minute, Sissons scored a solo goal, restoring West Ham's advantage. Greenwood's side, which had an emphasis on defence, was marvellously organised by Moore, who had an excellent 90 minutes. Moreover, the Hammers kept Zaragoza on their toes by launching swift counter-attacks. The 3-2 victory took them into the final where they would meet TSV 1860 Munich, who won through a week later via a play-off against Torino.

The final at Wembley was billed as the biggest night-time event to take place at the 'Empire Stadium'. The public were warned to get to the ground early as rush-hour traffic had the potential to cause chaos in the Wembley neighbourhood. German fans were heading to London en masse via boats from Hook of Holland to Harwich and by around a dozen specially chartered aircraft. There was an air of great excitement about the final as England needed to remind the Continent that it was the home of football. Munich 1860 were a good side, however, and just a year later would win the Bundesliga. Seven of their starting line-up were internationals, but none of Munich 1860's five West German caps, including goal machine Rudolf Brunnenmeier, made the final squad for the 1966 World Cup. They also had two Yugoslav internationals in goalkeeper Petar Radenković and midfielder Stevan Bena.

West Ham's league season had ended on 23 April and their last game had been on 28 April against Zaragoza. Twenty-one days later, the Hammers were at Wembley for the final. Munich's Bundesliga programme ended on 15 May, just four days before their date in London. Coach Max Merkel fielded the team that would line up against West Ham, but they were beaten 3-0 by Meidericher. Nobody was too fooled by this result but West Ham's Greenwood was very upbeat: 'Of course I am optimistic. One has to go into a match of this sort with a spirit of optimism. Here we have two good sides and no doubt they will serve up a brand of football worthy of the occasion.'

They did indeed, for the 1965 European Cup Winners' Cup Final became one of the defining moments of English football in the 1960s. West Ham played football that was a great advertisement for Greenwood's philosophy. Those that witnessed the game recall the skilful, swift and exciting performance by the Hammers. Munich, a powerful unit, frustrated them in the first half, but midway through the second period the game was won. The first goal came in the 69th minute, Ron Boyce surging forward, feeding Sealey, whose shot went high into the net past Radenković. Sealey, who earlier had punched the ball into the net when he could not quite reach a cross, somersaulted and leapt like a salmon. Munich did not have time to reflect, for Sealey did it again less than two minutes later. A free kick from Moore ricocheted off Peters and Sealey prodded the ball home.

It was no more than West Ham deserved and, as they received the trophy, the club's famed anthem, 'I'm Forever Blowing Bubbles', echoed around the stadium. Munich were sporting in defeat, Merkel congratulating West Ham and saying it had been a privilege to have taken part in such a fine match. Two hours after the game, Greenwood and his men finally got back to Upton Park to be greeted by hysterical fans. West Ham had shown the world football could be played beautifully and in doing so, added to the expectation building up for the 1966 World Cup.

European football had arguably acted as the ideal preparation for West Ham's younger players with ambitions of appearing in the World Cup. Moore, of course, had established himself as an England regular and was now captain, a role he had filled on and off since May 1963. Hurst (24), who would become the hat-trick hero in the 1966 World Cup Final against West Germany, made his debut against the same opposition in February 1966, while in May, Peters (22) made his England bow against Yugoslavia.

The 1965/66 European Cup Winners' Cup had two representatives from England: West Ham, the holders, and Liverpool, who had won the FA Cup in 1965 against a precocious Leeds United. Bill Shankly's team had participated in the European Cup in 1964/65 and had experienced the brutal and shady side of the game during that run. In 1965/66, they won the Football League again, while West Ham's inconsistency meant they hovered around mid-table. Although they were lacklustre in the league, West Ham were becoming known as a cup team, hence they reached the final of the Football League Cup, losing to West Bromwich Albion, and also enjoyed another engaging European campaign.

They were assisted by their first-round opponents, Poland's Czarni Żagań, withdrawing from the competition.

They were from the third tier of Polish football and had reached the Polish cup final in 1965 and lost to Górnik Zabrze, who had also won the league title. Czarni, a club formed the Polish army's Żagań Garrison, were unable to play due to military obligations.

The second round paired West Ham with Olympiacos of Greece, a team with a reputation for adopting aggressive tactics. They were run by two Hungarians, Márton Bucovi and Mihály Lantos, but their team bore little of their country's football heritage and was very workmanlike. On a muddy Upton Park surface, West Ham won 4-0 in the first leg, while Olympiacos were unluckily hit by injuries to two players, Sideris and Paulidis. Despite the four-goal margin, some commentators felt the Hammers would have an unenviable challenge in Athens. A week later, West Ham had to endure taunts, insults, smoke bombs and some violent tackling. Peters scored twice in a 2-2 draw and was carried off with a leg injury. For all the intimidation and verbal threats, West Ham were applauded off by sections of the Athens crowd.

There was an air of mystery about the Hammers' next opponents, East Germany's SC Aufbau Magdeburg, who were going through a reorganisation that would rename them as 1. FC Magdeburg. They arrived in London with a clear mission to avoid defeat and to keep their defence tight.

West Ham played badly, notably in their finishing, which was described as atrocious. Magdeburg brought 200 fans with them, but they went home disappointed as Byrne scored the only goal just after half-time. Was it enough? Many people felt it was too narrow a margin to take to East Germany, although Magdeburg were not a strong team in the DDR-Oberliga, in fact they suffered relegation at the end of 1965/66.

Although they averaged only 7,700 at their home games in the Oberliga, there were 35,000 at Magdeburg's Ernst Grube Stadium. West Ham played in an uncharacteristic defensive style and frustrated the East Germans. The game ended 1-1 with Sissons equalising just 45 seconds after Joachim Walter had given the home side the lead. Greenwood clearly had a plan: 'We contained Magdeburg to only two clear-cut chances in the first half. You can't do much better than that.'

West Ham had sneaked through to the semi-finals 2-1 on aggregate. There were, quite astonishingly, two other British teams in the last four: Celtic and Liverpool had beaten Dynamo Kiev and Honvéd, respectively. Greenwood wanted to avoid Liverpool in the draw and that is exactly what happened – Jock Stein and Bill Shankly, compatriots from the same part of Scotland, would send their teams, Celtic and Liverpool, into battle, while West Ham would face Borussia Dortmund.

Ironically, West Ham and Borussia Dortmund would provide three players apiece for the England and West Germany sides in the World Cup Final later in the summer of 1966. Goalkeeper Hans Tilkowski was named German footballer of the year in 1965 and had won his first cap for West Germany in 1957. Lothar Emmerich, the son of a miner, was a talented winger who was the Bundesliga's top scorer in both 1966 and 1967. He scored 45 times in all competitions in 1965/66. Emmerich and Siggi Held formed a partnership that was so compelling that they were nicknamed 'the terrible twins' by opponents.

West Ham had something of a dark shadow hanging over their preparations for the semi-final. Captain Moore had revealed he was not going to renew his contract with the club when it expired at the end of the season. Greenwood reacted by stripping Moore of the captaincy and claimed that the England star had said he did not want to play for West Ham. There was no shortage of interested parties and stories began to surface that Tottenham were particularly keen and would offer their goalkeeper Pat Jennings as a possible exchange deal. Moore would command a big fee, but Greenwood commented: 'If people are willing to pay the money, then he can go.' The stand-off between Moore and West Ham and Greenwood had a negative effect on the dressing room, and when the teams were announced before the Dortmund game at Upton Park, Moore's name was jeered. The player himself insisted he did not say he never wanted to play for the club. Obviously, it was in West Ham's interest to keep Moore, but the potential fee of around £100,000 must have been a temptation.

The Hammers were up against a very skilled side on a rain-soaked pitch. Peters cleverly opened the scoring on 52 minutes and it looked as though West Ham would hang on to claim a slim victory. But with five minutes remaining, Emmerich scored an equaliser, shooting home from 15 yards to silence the home crowd. Within seconds, the scoreline changed again as Held dashed down the left flank, crossed to the far post and Emmerich turned the ball into the net. West Ham were stunned and the tie had been turned on its head.

If Greenwood's side were to overcome the deficit in Dortmund, in front of a partisan audience, a good start was imperative, but it could not have been worse. With the Ruhr crowd fringing the pitch, Dortmund went 1-0 up after 90 seconds through Emmerich, who struck the bar with a shot inside the area and followed up to head into the net. Emmerich did it again on the half-hour, shooting a free kick low past the Hammers' wall. Byrne, who had assumed the captaincy from Moore, headed them back into the game just before half-time, but in the final exchanges

Gerd Cyliax's shot deflected its way past Jim Standen to make the result safe.

Dortmund's aggregate win (5-2) was deserved and highlighted some of West Ham's shortcomings. Dortmund, meanwhile, would go on to win the European Cup Winners' Cup, beating Liverpool 2-1 in Glasgow after extra time. It would be another decade until West Ham tasted European football again.

7

The Bastard *Catenaccio*

OPPONENTS HATED *catenaccio*, fans disliked its sterility, journalists despaired of it and the football purists spat on the ground at the mere mention of it, but coaches, especially from Italy in the 1960s, saw it as a way to get results and to preserve their jobs. British football followers were deeply suspicious of Italian football; it was supposedly, 'dirty', 'sly', 'boring' and 'cynical'. At the same time, it was glamorous, wealthy, very technical and ultra-professional. There were times in the 1960s and early 1970s when the Italian football results read like binary computing language: 0 – 1 – 0 – 0 – 1 – 1 and so on. Moreover, English players found it hard to assimilate in Italy due to its highly disciplined approach and the lack of goalscoring opportunities. Very few British players stayed in Italy, despite its glossy footballing veneer.

It was very clear that England's best teams found their Italian counterparts simply infuriating to play against. There was a history of stormy co-existence between the two nations when it came to football. The infamous 'Battle of Highbury' in 1934, England's 3-2 win over world champions Italy, was just one example of how combat could become very real on the pitch. England was always slow to learn football lessons, but while the Hungarians of 1953 hinted that things needed to change, they were, at least, showing a direction for positive transformation. The arrival of *catenaccio*, driven by chief exponents Inter Milan and AC Milan, suggested a darker, more sinister style was becoming the new modus operandi for modern football. Some called it anti-football, but for a few years it became very successful while the rest of Europe tried to work out a formula to counter the spoiling tactics from Italy and other countries. What made it worse was that *catenaccio*, with all its stifling efficiency, bored the life out of two fine, footballing teams in Benfica in 1964 and Real Madrid a year later. What chance did England's champions have against this system?

Ipswich Town, the surprise league champions from Suffolk, were the first to come up against *catenaccio*. Defending their title was never going to be easy for them and they had started 1962/63 poorly. The European Cup was a distraction from the mediocrity, and a tie with Maltese champions Floriana was just what they needed to get some confidence back. But the conditions were hot and sticky with a very humid wind, and the pitch at the Empire Stadium was sandy and devoid of grass. Malta was known as a charming little island that had won the George Cross for its valiant efforts during the Second World War. There were no floodlights, so the game was played at 4.30pm. Ipswich won 4-1 and then took Floriana back to England for a 10-0 drubbing, with Ray Crawford netting five times.

By the time Ipswich prepared to meet AC Milan, Alf Ramsey had agreed to become England manager. He was taking up his new position at the end of the season, but Ipswich were not in good shape, and their players were burnt-out after the monumental effort of winning the championship as a team of underdogs. The San Siro pitch resembled a rich plum pudding with pools of water across its surface. Their team included the 19-year-old Gianni Rivera, who was the so-called 'golden boy' of Italian football. Despite the presence of clever players like Rivera, they were also arch-exponents of *catenaccio*, adopting a seven-man 'chainmail defence' to stifle the opposition.

Milan won the first leg 3-0 but Ipswich clinched the second game 2-1 with two late goals. With the European Cup now out of the way, Ipswich could concentrate on improving their deteriorating league position. At the end of the season, they finished just two points off relegation, a disastrous defence of the title. The other Milan side, Inter, met the 1963 English champions Everton in the first round of the European Cup. Inter were seen as more cynical in their approach than Milan, with their coach, Helenio Herrera, a strict disciplinarian who did not suffer fools gladly. Blanket defence was their forte, but they were also capable of swift and skilful counter-attacks. There was plenty of money in Italian football as evidenced by Inter's signing of Spanish midfielder Luis Suárez for 25 million Spanish pesetas (£152,000) in 1961. This was the famed *Grande Inter* team that dominated Europe for the next two years.

Everton struggled to get to grips with Inter and a defence organised by Giacinto Facchetti. The game at Goodison Park ended 0-0 and was bad-tempered. Everton had expected a very defensive display from Inter after Herrera had promised a cautious approach. Anticipating a bruising battle, Everton themselves were quite ruthless, but the crowd was treated to some very sophisticated football from the visitors, who were well-drilled and precise. They also adopted man-to-man marking and had a defence that was 'slotted, tongued and grooved', according to contemporary reports. Everton tried, industriously, to prise open that defence and simply lacked the ingenuity to threaten their goal. Indeed, *The Times* noted that Everton may have learned that 'physical challenges and sheer horse power will never win this big prize'.

The second leg was always going to be an uphill battle for Everton, but they were ill-prepared for the way in which Inter and their crowd would try to influence the game. Harry Catterick was without Scottish wing-half Jimmy Gabriel and opted to blood 18-year-old Colin Harvey for his debut. Catterick's strategy was to defend deep and frustrate Inter, much as Herrera's team had done to Everton at Goodison. The crowd became more and more angry and the tension spilled over on to the pitch. After a goalless first half, Inter scored through their speedy winger Jair, who was seen as a successor to Garrincha in the Brazilian national team. His shot struck the crossbar and nestled into the back of Gordon West's net. The game was ruined in the latter stages by flying fists and feet, and the *Liverpool Echo* came to this conclusion: 'The trouble is what is allowed in Britain is not, inevitably, allowed in Italy and vice versa, and while the rewards in a tournament of this kind are enormous, every game must come close to being something of a pitch battle.' Everton's first foray into Europe was over, but Inter would be back in Liverpool very soon.

Liverpool under Bill Shankly were in full stride by 1964. They had won the Football League in 1963/64, their second season after promotion from the Second Division. They had developed the knack of using very few players and their line-up was settled from the first game. They used just 17 players, of which ten made more than 30 league appearances. It would not be the last season that Shankly would operate with a minimalist squad. Defending their league title was a challenge; Manchester United's second great team under Matt Busby was maturing, with the holy trinity of Best, Charlton and Law functioning well, Leeds

United's tenacious machine built by Don Revie had arrived and were upsetting a few people, and Tommy Docherty's Chelsea, all energy and speed, had their eyes on winning a trophy. Liverpool lost some of their consistency, but they had their target set on the European Cup and FA Cup.

When they began their European trail, their league form was poor. They managed to find their shooting boots against KR Reykjavík, scoring 11 times and conceding once. But immediately after winning 6-1 at home in the second game, they were beaten 4-0 by Everton at Anfield and sat 17th in the table. Anderlecht were beaten comfortably in the next round and then Liverpool and Köln took three games to decide a difficult encounter, with the play-off in Rotterdam decided on the toss of a gambler's chip, a wholly unsatisfactory way to decide deadlock between two teams. The Köln team included two players, Wolfgang Weber and Wolfgang Overath, who would play against England in the 1966 World Cup Final. Liverpool skipper Ron Yeats called correctly and Liverpool went through to the semi-finals.

Inter were as uncompromising as they had been in the past two seasons, on the road to a second successive European Cup. They had lost the league title in 1963/64 via a play-off with Bologna after the two teams had ended level on points, but they regained their crown in 1965, finishing three points ahead of AC Milan. Winning the 1964 European Cup enabled them to return as holders. Inter had already experienced a British crowd in the competition in the form of Glasgow Rangers. Rangers were beaten 3-1 in the San Siro and were determined to put Inter under pressure in the second leg. Jim Forrest scored early on but, no matter how hard they tried to break down the Inter defence, Rangers could not score again. How they would have liked to have taken on Liverpool in the semi-final.

Liverpool knew they faced arguably Europe's meanest team when Inter arrived at Anfield, just three days after Shankly's side had won the FA Cup at Wembley against Leeds United. It had been a tiring, extremely physical contest that went to extra time, but Ian St John headed the winner to enable Liverpool to lift the cup for the first time. Gordon Milne and Gerry Byrne, who were both sidelined through injury, paraded the FA Cup before the crowd at the Inter match to add to the fever-pitch atmosphere at Anfield. They sang 'Go home to Italy' to the Inter players but they showed no sign of being intimidated, such was the intense nature of Italian football.

It took just three minutes for Liverpool to score, Roger Hunt volleying on the turn after good work by Tommy Smith, Geoff Strong and Ian Callaghan. Inter responded with a tenth-minute goal from Sandro Mazzola, but half an hour later Callaghan, after a good one-two with Ian St John, scored Liverpool's second. It was almost 3-1 by half-time when Chris Lawler unleashed a fierce left-foot drive after beating no less than three Inter players, sparking off celebrations described as a 'cacophony of noise, of Bedlam, almost animalistic in its sound', but it was to no avail, for the referee disallowed the goal. The third goal did come with 15 minutes remaining, St John netting after Hunt's shot was parried by Inter goalkeeper Giuliano Sarti.

The Italian media was impressed. The *Corriere Della Sera* said: 'Inter were dazed. We lift our hats to Liverpool, they are a marvellous team. We expected a Liverpool exhausted by its efforts, satisfied of its ambitions. Liverpool gave an exemplary demonstration of athletic vitality, a surprising show of moral force, an unusual exhibition of robust and practical teamwork.' Meanwhile, *La Gazzette Dello Sport* added: 'The dream of an English team winning in Europe is no longer absurd.' There was a problem, though. Liverpool had to go to the San Siro, where more than 60,000 people, almost all of them Inter disciples, would make life as uncomfortable as possible for the English champions. Reporters compared the atmosphere to 'Dante's inferno', with giant flags, klaxons, chants and singing and a barrage of insults greeting the Liverpool team. Shankly took his team to Lake Como to relax and to train for the game. It was a calming environment, but the local church bells ringing regularly kept the players awake. Shankly, needless to say, spoke to the priest, whom he described as a 'nice man, but he couldn't stop the bell'. The Italian fans knew how to create a hostile backdrop, painting slogans on the roadside that translated as 'Inter will massacre Liverpool', while in and around the stadium, they chanted 'brutal savages'.

Shankly and his players expected an evening of controversy and they were right in their assumption. Within ten minutes, Inter had completely wiped out Liverpool's two-goal advantage. The first blow came in the eighth minute when the referee awarded Inter a rather dubious free kick after Willie Stevenson had fouled Mario Corso. He took the free kick himself and sent the ball over Tommy Lawrence and into the net. Shankly was insistent that the free kick was indirect and therefore the goal should have been ruled out.

Liverpool could not settle due to the deafening noise. Two minutes after Corso's goal came an even more debatable incident. As Lawrence gathered the ball from an attack, he bounced it a few times and Joaquín Peiró, who had come from behind the keeper, cunningly connected with the ball in mid-bounce. Peiró simply curled his shot into the net as Liverpool's players, notably Ron Yeats and Tommy Smith, pursued the referee to protest. Was it a fair goal? Looking closely at the incident, some referees in the modern game would give it, but analysis by technology might not. Shankly was incensed, but a goal it was.

The third and decisive goal came in the 62nd minute from Facchetti, who fired home a low effort after finding himself free on the edge of the penalty area. The *Liverpool Echo* felt the locals had overdone their celebrations: 'The citizens [of Milan] have greeted the 3-0 victory by which Inter Milan knocked Liverpool out of the European Cup as if they personally had won world war three.'

But they were also subtle about the way Inter played in a feral atmosphere that was positively gladiatorial. 'It only needed some animals to perform tricks – there were plenty of human animals going through their acts.' Liverpool fans told the media of their experiences. One told the *Liverpool Echo*: 'We couldn't understand what they [Inter fans] were saying but the crowds were trying to take the micky. It was peaceful enough, however, no punch-ups followed the game.'

The Liverpool capitulation may have been the result of fatigue after a long season, the bear-pit vibe of the San Siro and Inter's determination to win the tie at all costs. Many believed it was unjust, that Liverpool had fallen victim to the gamesmanship of the Inter team, which included time-wasting, shamming injury and continual back-passing. It felt harsh and not within the spirit of the game. It would not be long, however, before English teams were also adopting some of the dark arts that upset them so much in the early years of pan-European competition. Inter won the 1965 European Cup, using *catenaccio* to good effect against an exciting Benfica team, winning 1-0 in their own stadium. Liverpool would be back in the European Cup in 1966/67 and would eventually learn multiple lessons from a team from another part of Europe.

Liverpool had a very fruitful European Cup Winners' Cup campaign in 1965/66, one that led them to the final. It was a season that saw them win the league title in England for the second time in three years. In Europe, they came up against some very accomplished teams, including Juventus, Standard Liège and Honvéd, in the days when Hungarian club teams could still compete with elite clubs. Their semi-final opponents were none other than Celtic, who were also on the brink of a golden season at home and abroad. Celtic won the Scottish championship, the Scottish League Cup and were finalists in the Scottish Cup. Jock Stein, their manager, had moulded together a side that was mostly drawn from the Glasgow area, playing a brand of attacking football that delighted their supporters.

Liverpool took a big following to Glasgow and the local police seemed to be anticipating some trouble. Celtic won 1-0 and after the game Liverpool's fans were confronted by locals throwing bottles and other missiles, but the message from the police was that the visiting fans had behaved impeccably. The Scottish newspapers were not enthused about Liverpool's style of football, which they dismissed as boring: 'The ballyhooed English league leaders are not supermen.' The second leg was a different story. Liverpool won 2-0 to clinch a place in the final, thanks to goals from Tommy Smith and Geoff Strong. At the end of the game, Celtic fans tried to invade the pitch as objects rained down on them from the stand. There was a certain intensity at any 'battle of Britain' game involving the champions of England and Scotland. Liverpool returned to Glasgow for the Cup Winners' Cup Final against Borussia Dortmund. This time it was Hampden Park, where less than 42,000 people were attracted to the huge rainswept bowl. Ken Jones of the *Daily Mirror* was adamant TV was to blame: 'Hampden Park looked more than half empty and the picture underlined the lunacy of live television of football.'

Dortmund took the lead through Siggi Held and Liverpool's equaliser came from Roger Hunt, a controversial goal that many felt should not have been allowed. The game went to extra time and Reinhard Libuda saw his 107th-minute shot strike the crossbar and rebound off Ron Yeats before entering the net. Shankly was a bitter loser on this occasion. 'We were beaten by a team of frightened men,' he insisted. 'I am quite sincere when I say they were the worst team we met in the competition this season.' This sort of comment was classic Shankly but at the same time was a combination of kidology, denial and motivational speech. Celtic, meanwhile, were anticipating their first European Cup campaign in 1966/67. Liverpool would also be returning to the competition as champions of England.

Shankly was in a similar defiant mood when Liverpool tumbled out of the competition in December 1966, surprisingly beaten by Ajax, 7-3 on aggregate. The first leg in Amsterdam was played in thick fog, which made visibility difficult. But the real source of angst for Liverpool was a young Dutchman called Johan Cruyff, who tore the English champions apart. A 5-1 defeat was a huge shock for Liverpool and English football, but Shankly blamed the weather. 'They are used to playing in fog,' was one of his throwaway comments.

Yet both Ajax and Liverpool had wanted the game to go ahead – the Reds had a big game against Manchester United the following weekend and wanted to get this clash out of the way. 'I wasn't too impressed with Ajax [...] they got lucky. They played defensive football on their own ground. Next week in Liverpool we will beat them 7-0,' insisted Shankly. Cruyff summed it up in his posthumous biography: 'In a technical sense, the English champions were blown away.' If the Anfield fans thought that Shankly's prediction of a seven-goal win was credible, they were soon put right. The return leg ended 2-2, with Cruyff scoring both goals for the Dutch side. The press said that Liverpool were beaten over the two games because 'they ran into their superiors'. Shankly was now very graceful in defeat, visiting the Ajax dressing room afterwards and congratulating each and every player.

Celtic began their European Cup programme with a tie against Switzerland's FC Zürich. Stein's team had a compelling mix of youth and experience, the classic ingredients for success. Two members of the regular line-up were over 30, the veteran Ronnie Simpson who had enjoyed success with Newcastle United a decade earlier, and Steve Chalmers. Eight of the squad would form the heart of the team for the next few years, including Tommy Gemmell, Billy McNeill, Bobby Lennox and Jimmy Johnstone. And then there was Bertie Auld, who had European experience with Birmingham City in the early years of the Inter-Cities Fairs Cup. Celtic liked to play attacking football, but they also had a tough edge and an inspirational captain in McNeill.

Zürich gave Celtic a hard game at Parkhead, but goals from Joe McBride and Gemmell were enough to win the first leg 2-0. The second game was easier, a 3-0 victory that took them through to the second round to meet Nantes. Two assured performances against the French team both ended with 3-1 wins for Celtic and allowed Stein to put the European Cup aside until the new year. Celtic had already won the Scottish League Cup, beating Rangers 1-0, and had begun their Scottish Cup campaign. They had lost just once in the league but they had scored 30 goals in seven games prior to meeting Vojvodina from Novi Sad, in the quarter-final. The Yugoslav champions were an ambitious outfit and had installed new floodlights at their ground. Although they had lost star man, Silvester Takač, to Rennes during the winter break, they still had some excellent players.

Vojvodina won 1-0 in the first leg, but the return in Glasgow was played to a soundtrack of 69,000 noisy Celtic fans urging their team on. The home team attacked relentlessly and, unlike so many games involving British and Continental sides, the emphasis was on playing the game and not the man. Celtic went ahead through Steve Chalmers and, suddenly, Vojvodina found themselves like 'a nut between the crackers', to quote one Scottish journalist. The game was drifting towards extra time when Billy McNeill headed Celtic's second goal to win the tie 2-1 on aggregate.

Almost a fortnight after beating the Yugoslavians, Celtic were drawn to meet Dukla Prague. In doing so, they avoided the favourites and holders, Inter Milan, who would play CSKA Sofia. 'That suits us fine,' said Stein. 'It will be hard, of course, but it is a good draw for us.' Inter were obviously equally pleased to dodge Celtic, and the club's secretary-general, Mr Italo Adoli, said Inter versus Celtic would make for a fantastic final. Celtic first had to get past a difficult Dukla Prague side that had won the double of league and cup in 1965/66. Their team included the excellent goalkeeper Ivo Viktor, who was rated one of the best in the world. They also had Josef Masopust and Ján Geleta, a midfielder who was named Czechoslovak footballer of the year in 1967. Celtic were in excellent form in the first leg, winning 3-1. Johnstone, who ended the game limping and was rated doubtful for the forthcoming England versus Scotland clash at Wembley, scored the first goal, and although Dukla responded just before half-time, two goals from Willie Wallace settled the match. Celtic's pace, fitness and intensity was just too much for Dukla and left Stein confident of success: 'It takes three goals to beat us in Prague. I think we can reach the final. They'll have to go some to beat us.'

Stein was absolutely right, for Celtic tightened up and went to Prague to stifle Dukla. Geoffrey Green, the famous *Times* journalist, warned it would not be a simple task, describing Dukla as 'a talented, dangerous collection of technicians, cleverly led by their ringmaster, the wily but ageing Masopust'. It was a poor, goalless game, one that certainly failed to live up to the frenzy of the game in Glasgow. 'We came here to do a job and I'm delighted with the way we did it, once we settled down after that uneasy start,' beamed Stein. Just ten days earlier, Scotland had beaten world champions England at Wembley by 3-2, with four Celtic players – Simpson, Gemmell, Wallace and Lennox – in the team. Rangers were also going well in the European Cup Winners' Cup and had just won their semi-final first leg against Slavia Sofia, a tie they would clinch at Ibrox Park to secure a place in the final. These were good days for Scottish football.

Inter Milan, who were top of Italy's Serie A, won through to the final after a play-off against CSKA Sofia, but there were some clouds hanging over Helenio Herrera's side because of injuries to key players. Both Luis Suárez and Jair would miss the European Cup Final against Celtic, which was good news for Stein. Regardless of these setbacks for Inter, they were considered the most professional, battle-hardened team in Europe and they had beaten Real Madrid, the holders, on their way to the final. Herrera was a little downbeat when he was interviewed prior to the game: 'This will be a difficult game without Suárez and Jair, but the greatest obstacle is Celtic.'

Inter's form was not good. They had not won for five games and Juventus were breathing down their neck at the top of the table. Celtic had won everything on the domestic front and, to add to the discomfort of Rangers, they had clinched the Scottish League on 6 May at Ibrox Park in a 2-2 draw.

Celtic were taking no chances for their trip to Lisbon and took their own supplies with them. The inventory was impressive if you were a carnivore: 70 Aberdeen Angus steaks, 30 spring lamb chops from Perthshire, 10lb of Ayrshire bacon, 10lb of gammon and 10lb of sausages. If nothing else, Celtic would not lack protein. Hundreds of cars made their way across Europe, the so-called 'Celticade' snaking its way into the Portuguese capital in the dead of night. The police and the locals were nervous about a Scottish invasion due to stories of trouble at past events involving football fans from Glasgow. However, the Celtic fans were aware that Portuguese law and order meant that any drunks would be arrested and placed in jail overnight. But the people of Lisbon were on their side, as they had not liked Inter's tactics against Benfica in the 1965 final of the competition and also the way the Italians had refused to shift that game from the San Siro (their home stadium).

For some reason, Inter's players, officials and management were very glum when they arrived for the final. Herrera had continually played the absent Suárez card, but the plain truth was the 32-year-old Spanish midfielder had not been in great form in 1966/67. Celtic were clearly feared by Inter, but it may have been because there was a realisation that the days of *Grande Inter* were coming to an end. A year earlier in England, four of the current Inter side had featured in the humiliation of Ayresome Park, where North Korea beat Italy 1-0 in the World Cup group stage, sending the *Azzurri* home to a barrage of tomatoes and abuse. That defeat did have something of a debilitating effect on Italian football for a while.

At the end of May 1967, Inter's form suggested they had lost some of their mojo. Within 12 months, Helenio Herrera, who had been coach since July 1960, had departed and Inter were never quite as great again. But they had a very good chance of a third European Cup in four years and they were top of Serie A with one game to go. No crisis yet, Suárez or not, but Inter were destined to end the season without a trophy. Celtic were being heralded as the most stylish and modernist team in Europe. They were renowned for their whirlwind approach right from kick-off and many experts felt this would overcome Inter early in the game. One French football journalist had a word for it – *L'orage*, the storm.

The signs seemed to have been misread in the very early exchanges of the game. In the seventh minute, Jim Craig clumsily brought down Renato Cappellini, who only had Simpson to beat, and Sandro Mazzola scored from the penalty spot. This did not deter Celtic for too long and was the signal for Inter to fall back into their customary packed defence. In effect, they exposed themselves to the full power of Celtic's 'hurricane'. Inter were thankful for the form of veteran goalkeeper Giuliano Sarti and the woodwork, which was struck by Bertie Auld and Tommy Gemmell. It was Gemmell that finally equalised for Celtic with ten minutes remaining in the Lisbon sunshine. Craig pulled the ball back from the flank and the full-back hit a fierce shot through the Inter defence. Celtic continued in search of the winner and in the 85th minute Gemmell repeated Craig's trick, and Bobby Murdoch's shot was touched home by Steve Chalmers. The final whistle was greeted by a pitch invasion with hundreds of supporters in green kneeling on the pitch, kissing the turf. There was a sense of disbelief about it, but scarcely had the European Cup seen a more one-sided final. The 11 players who won British football's first European Cup became known as 'the Lisbon Lions' and all have been granted legendary status.

Stein was jubilant after the match: 'This was a triumph for attacking football methods. This victory will be good for the game because attacking football is what the fans want.' Herrera was generous in defeat: 'It was impossible to stop the Celtic onslaught. The better team won. That's all there is to say.' Another Inter reaction from Mazzola suggested a little bitterness: 'Whenever we clashed with a Celtic man, we were liable to get hurt.' Celtic have never won the trophy again, but at the time they were one of Europe's top sides. Between 1967 and 1974, they reached two finals, two semi-finals and two quarter-finals. In 1967, they were, without doubt, the team of the year.

8

1968 and All That …

THE 1966/67 season could have been an even more glorious campaign than Celtic's ground-breaking triumph against Inter Milan suggested. British teams reached all three finals, including Celtic's Old Firm rivals Rangers in the European Cup Winners' Cup and Leeds United in the Inter-Cities Fairs Cup. Rangers had the daunting task of playing their final against Bayern Munich just two days after Glasgow celebrated the return of Celtic. Leeds United's two-legged final with Dinamo Zagreb was delayed until the start of 1967/68.

Rangers' run in Europe had been overshadowed by Celtic's progress, but they had beaten some very tricky opponents on the way to the Nuremberg final. Borussia Dortmund, who had won the Cup Winners' Cup in 1966, were overcome 2-1 on aggregate, and the tie with Real Zaragoza was so tight that each side beat each other 2-0 on their own ground. Rangers were fortunate to go through on the toss of a coin. The semi-final was against Slavia Sofia, who had beaten their better-known local rivals, CSKA in the Bulgarian cup final in 1966.

The final with Bayern Munich was always going to be a substantial challenge; this was a team that included Sepp Maier, Franz Beckenbauer and Gerd Müller. They were an emerging force and within a few years would dominate Europe as well as West German football. The Städtisches Stadion in Nuremberg, as well as being relatively close to Munich, was also near the site of infamous Nazi rallies in the 1930s. Bayern had finished sixth in the Bundesliga and Müller was joint-top scorer with 28 goals. There were some doubts about his fitness, though, given he had fractured two bones in an arm playing for the national team in Belgrade. Unsurprisingly, Müller lined up to face Rangers.

The game was a good advertisement for attacking football, but the two teams cancelled each other out in 90 minutes, so extra time was needed. It was finally settled in the 109th minute when a long ball from Rainer Olhauser caught the Rangers defence napping and Franz Roth volleyed past goalkeeper Norrie Martin. It was an important victory for Bayern, their first major European prize, but Rangers would finally lift the Cup Winners' Cup in 1972.

The Fairs Cup Final of 1966/67 was not played until the end of August, with the second leg a week later on 6 September. Leeds had not started their new season well, in fact they were bottom of the First Division and had scored just once in three games. They lost the first leg against Dinamo Zagreb in Yugoslavia by 2-0, so it was a significant task for Don Revie's young players. Dinamo had clearly been influenced by the school of *catenaccio* and packed their defence to allow minimal room for manoeuvre in the second leg. Leeds pumped the Zagreb back line with high balls, often aimed at the giant frame of Jack Charlton. There was a distinct lack of subtlety about their approach and Zagreb soon worked out the home team's strategy. The game ended goalless, which meant Dinamo went home with the trophy in their luggage, the first Slavic side to win the Fairs Cup. Leeds were soon back on song and challenging for everything in sight.

Celtic, who had completed a clean sweep in 1966/67, would be among the first British clubs to exit European competitions in 1967/68. They were shocked by Soviet side Dynamo Kiev, who beat the very line-up that had lifted the European Cup in May. They won 2-1 at Parkhead after silencing the home crowd with two goals inside half an hour. The scoreline was big news across Europe and in the Soviet Union, and demand for tickets for the second leg was incredible – 350,000 people applied to see the game. Celtic were a minute away from drawing 2-2 on aggregate before Anatoliy Byshovets equalised on the night in the Central Stadium in Kiev. Celtic could not quite believe what had happened to them. There had been an air of invincibility about the quadruple-winning team in green and white. But Dynamo were so impressive that the *cognoscenti* started to predict the Soviets were now serious challengers for the European Cup. There was certainly something different about this mysterious team from behind the Iron Curtain. Their coach, Viktor Maslov, was very innovative, an early adopter of 4-4-2 and an advocate of playing football at considerable speed. It caught Celtic out and ended their reign as European champions. But these methods did not work too well against their next opponents, Górnik Zabrze, who beat them 3-2 on aggregate.

Manchester United were England's hopes in the European Cup in 1967/68 after they had won their second league title in three seasons. Matt Busby, a close friend of Stein, was inspired by his Celtic counterpart and remained obsessed with winning the competition. Busby could still call on Best, Charlton and Law, and in 1966/67 the trio had netted almost 50 goals between them. Law would suffer from injuries in 1967/68, Charlton was almost 30, but Best, supposedly, was some way off his prime.

United started the season slowly, losing at Everton and picking up eight points out of a possible 14. Best did not get on the scoresheet until mid-September but the 1967/68 season would prove to be the peak of his career – by the end of 1968 he was named European Footballer of the Year, following in the footsteps of his team-mates Charlton (1966) and Law (1964).

The competition was packed with big names, with Real Madrid, Benfica, Juventus, Celtic and Ajax among the contenders. United, one of the favourites, had what many assumed would be an easy draw in the preliminary round, the Maltese side Floriana. However, it was not noticed until the following day that Floriana, as Malta's cup winners, had been placed in the wrong competition, while Hibernians, the actual league champions, had been included in the Cup Winners' Cup. An embarrassment for UEFA, but it also demonstrated that very few people had deep knowledge of the European game at that time. So United's opponents were changed to Hibernians, arguably no stronger or weaker than their compatriots, Floriana.

As expected, they easily beat Hibernians 4-0 in the first leg of their tie, with in-form David Sadler, who was being tipped for England honours, and Denis Law scoring two apiece. The return was something of a culture shock as the pitch in Valletta was barely playable. It was a curious surface of hard, baked ash and made for a poor exhibition that ended 0-0. Matt Busby had prepared his team by training on a similar pitch in Manchester. Regardless, United were warmly welcomed in Malta, with local supporters' clubs greeting them at the airport.

The next round was altogether more unfriendly. Sarajevo, the old capital of Bosnia & Herzegovina was a mysterious place for United and the journalists travelling to what was then part of Yugoslavia. The hacks painted a very patronising and primitive picture of the country, talking of 'men who live among the mountains', 'ploughmen watching airplanes' and 'an unusual mixture of the oriental and the modern'. It was also a city with a brutal history, notably the location that sparked the First World War with the assassination of Archduke Ferdinand in 1914. Played in a rather tense and inhospitable atmosphere, United came away from Sarajevo with another 0-0 draw. United kept their head, however, and Busby expressed his pride in his players. 'This Sarajevo team gave the most disgraceful exhibition of vicious tackling I have ever known,' he said.

The Sarajevo players were offered a bonus of £500 per man to win the tie, which was an astronomical figure for players accustomed to earning £20 a week in a country where the working man's wage totalled £8 per week. Perhaps this explained why there was no shortage of drama in the second leg at Old Trafford. United were winning 2-0 thanks to goals from John Aston and George Best, who was harassed all night by the Sarajevo defenders. In fact, one of them, Fahrudin Prljača, was sent off for a particularly nasty tackle on the Northern Ireland international. There was more aggression when Busby appeared to be struck by goalkeeper Refik Muftić, although the United manager played it down, describing it as a 'wee bit of a skirmish'. Sarajevo netted a consolation towards the end, but United were relieved to get off the pitch and into the quarter-finals.

The violence was not confined to Old Trafford on the night of 29 November; Tottenham had a bruising 90 minutes with French cup holders Lyon, which saw Alan Mullery dismissed and manager Bill Nicholson punched in the head. Tottenham went out of the European Cup Winners' Cup, but United would soon find out their opponents in the last eight of the European Cup – Polish champions Górnik Zabrze.

There was an assumption that Górnik, being a steely team from the east, would be a major hurdle, especially as they had beaten Dynamo Kyiv, conquerors of the holders, Celtic. If nothing else, the weather would be an added challenge as Poland was likely to be under a blanket of snow in late February. It was important for Manchester United to get a good result before heading east. There was great respect for United from the Górnik camp, most notably from their Hungarian trainer, Dr Geza Kalocsai, who had been involved with the famous Mighty Magyars in 1953. His praise was specifically for young Best: 'He could have played at any time in any of the world's great teams. He is the best winger in the world and will be difficult to contain. He does not need room to work, he is a good dribbler and has a very sharp shot with either foot.'

Górnik had their own star in Włodzimierz Lubański, a 21-year-old forward who was the leading goalscorer in Poland in 1966 and 1967 and would also top the list in 1968 and 1969. United had been warned about the Poles by none other than the Soviet striker Byshovets, who called them 'powerful physically and technically' when he played at Wembley for the USSR against England. They had visited the UK before, in 1961/62, when they were beaten 8-1 by Tottenham in the European Cup.

Busby was adamant his team should ensure no tension crept into the game as the previous round against Sarajevo had resulted in two edgy affairs. It was not an easy 90 minutes and Górnik were difficult to break down, but once United settled, the visiting goalkeeper, Hubert Kostka, prevented them from running up a healthy scoreline. Eventually, United opened the scoring with an own goal by Stefan Florenski on the hour and a 90th-minute strike from

Brian Kidd. The biggest cheer from the Old Trafford crowd at the end was not for their own players but for Kostka, who had been like a 'man inspired on a flying trapeze.'

United were without Law, who watched his team-mates from his bed with the swollen knee that would plague his 1967/68 season. He was not available for the second leg, either, which was to be played in Chorzów. Zabrze was a city close to Katowice, deep in the heart of the Silesian industrial heartland. Snow, as expected, was falling when United landed in Poland, but it did not worry the home team's officials. The president of Górnik, Fran Tiz Gladwyc, told the press: 'We shall sweep the pitch and put some salt on it. It may not be perfect, but it will be playable.'

There were other important events happening in Poland as the teams prepared. It was the year of protests around Europe, with Polish students demanding freedom of speech, among other rights. This sparked off some very violent riots in Warsaw, Kraków and also in Chorzów. The stadium, which could hold 100,000 people, was well known for its intense atmosphere. The local population predominantly comprised miners and other industrial workers with a reputation for toughness. There were almost 78,000 people in the vast bowl of a ground that exposed almost everyone to the blizzard of snow. In some corners of the arena, fans lit small bonfires to keep warm.

Górnik won 1-0 with a goal from Lubański and United relied on a containing approach that involved putting five men behind the ball. It was enough for Busby's men to win through to the semi-final, a considerable achievement. The draw in Prague a week or so later involved four very strong teams, so there would be no easy route to the final. Benfica were drawn to meet Juventus and United's prize was another clash with Real Madrid.

United's league form had become a little patchy. Since beating Górnik, they had lost three league games, including two home defeats at the hands of title-chasers Manchester City and Liverpool, and had drawn with Southampton. Law had returned to the team but his fitness was unreliable, and other players were struggling with injuries. There was an underlying feeling that Charlton and Best were carrying the team to some extent.

Real Madrid had last won the European Cup in 1966 but they were dominant at home and won the league in 1966/67 and 1967/68, not to mention 1968/69. This was a very different Real side from the one that stood astride Europe a few years earlier, but they had players such as Amancio, Paco Gento, Ramón Grosso, Zoco and Pirri in their ranks. They had a reasonably comfortable ride to the semi-final, beating Ajax (and Johan Cruyff), Danish champions Hvidovre from Copenhagen and Sparta Prague.

Needless to say, the first leg was a box-office attraction and 63,000 packed into Old Trafford. United were in charge for most of the 90 minutes but Real's goalkeeper, Antonio Betancort, kept them at bay from the first whistle. Paddy Crerand struck the woodwork and Kidd was only inches away from opening the scoring. The only goal of the game came from Best, who hit a first-time shot high into the roof of the net after John Aston had pulled the ball back.

For all their hard work, this was United's only goal of the game, which looked a little meagre given the quality of the Real Madrid team. Law played but his knee flared up again in the days following the match. United were not out of it, by any means, but there was a blow to their morale when they relinquished their league crown on the final day of the season to neighbours City. United lost their final game at home to, of all teams, Sunderland, who ended the league programme in 15th position.

The second leg in Madrid was on 15 May and the big talking point was Law's fitness. The Spanish press assumed Real would turn the tie around in the cauldron of the Bernabéu stadium. Madrid was a humid and sticky place after an intensely hot day. The 2,000 United fans, who had been taxied to the Spanish capital in 16 specially chartered aeroplanes, were in for a nervous night and, at one time, it looked like a lost cause. Law was not, after all, selected, but Busby pushed Sadler into a forward position and he began the game with a 5-3-2 formation. Against Real Madrid, a famously attacking side, this was inviting trouble.

The game sprung into life in the 32nd minute when a free kick by Amancio was headed home at the near post by Pirri. Nine minutes later, Gento gratefully received the ball after Shay Brennan failed to intercept and sent a left-foot shot in off Alex Stepney. United responded when Tony Dunne's high ball into the area was scythed home by defender Zoco, but Real immediately scored a third through the impressive Amancio. The Real crowd, which was way below the expected 125,000, was confident and felt their team had done enough to reach the final. But United remained dogged and kept going, and a tame, bundled goal by Sadler in the 73rd minute was followed by a simple, backpass-like effort from Bill Foulkes, a home-grown veteran of 36 and a survivor of Munich 1958. There was something surreal about both goals, but at the end there was an air of destiny about United's 4-3 aggregate victory. There was also a bottle in the air, thrown at Nobby Stiles by a Real fan who repeatedly called him an 'assassin'. By the time United arrived back in Manchester, it was smiles all round and Foulkes was being heralded as the hero of the hour. He had also been guaranteed a place in the final on 29 May at Wembley against Benfica, who had beaten Juventus 3-0 on aggregate in the other semi-final.

Manchester United versus Benfica remains one of the pivotal moments in the history of the modern game – it was certainly a high point of the 1960s, perhaps one of the final throes of British 'superiority'. United became European champions because they were destined to do so. It was described as Busby's 'Everest' and the 'crowning glory' of Charlton's career, and was a reminder of British fair play and justice. Portugal had left England in 1966 heralded as good guys who played the game the right way. Most pundits had ignored the fact that Portugal had kicked Pelé to pieces and hounded him out of that World Cup. Benfica went to London determined to maintain the positive public relations that the national team had started in 1966. Half a dozen of the Benfica side had played in the 1966 semi-final against England. They spent their time in London handing out gifts for the natives, pictures, autographs and badges, among other things. At the same time, they were nervous about the game, specifically the safety of Eusébio and the tackling of Stiles. They remembered the toothless, tenacious United player from 1966.

United were firm favourites, but it was generally believed that Busby's current team, his fourth European Cup semi-finalists, was the least powerful of the quartet. Certainly, without Law they were not as potent up front and they were carrying the pain of losing out on a second successive league title on the final day of the season. London was invaded by Mancunians, some 30,000 already with tickets, others hoping to get one before kick-off. The ticket touts were doing good business in the capital, charging £12 for a 10 shilling (50p) ticket and £18 for a £1 seat. Furthermore, 5,000 supporters in ten special trains headed for London Euston station.

Eusébio, renowned for his shooting, reminded the Wembley crowd of his World Cup days, splintering Stepney's crossbar from 28 yards. But it was not until the 52nd minute that United, dressed in unfamiliar blue, took the lead. Charlton, never known for his heading ability, got on the end of a cross by Sadler and glanced the ball home. For a long while, it looked to be enough, but with ten minutes to go José Torres 'rose like some Eiffel Tower' to head the ball on to Jaime Graça, who sent a low shot past Stepney. Charlton, who was feeling the effect of an intense and challenging game, was so deflated that he doubted he could carry on. It could have been worse, for in the 86th minute Eusébio sprinted clear of the United defence and was left with a simple one-on-one to execute. His shot, as hard as ever, was saved by Stepney, but there were no histrionics – Eusébio turned and applauded to congratulate the goalkeeper on his match-saving reaction.

When full time came, both teams slumped on to the Wembley turf, seeking inspiration. Stiles admitted: 'We were really shattered in extra time, but so were Benfica. And once we all sensed this, we really began to play.' United summoned up their last reserves of energy in the opening stages of extra time and by the halfway mark, they had secured the trophy, thanks to three goals in eight minutes.

Firstly, Best netted what has become an iconic goal two minutes into extra time. He had been shackled by Fernando Cruz, so when he raced on to Kidd's flick-on from Stepney's long ball, rounded Henrique and slipped the ball into the net, it was very satisfying. Two minutes later, Charlton's corner was met by Kidd, who was denied by Henrique but sent his second header past him for the third goal. United were not finished and, in the 99th minute, Charlton flicked the ball home from a Kidd cross. At 4-1, the game was over and everyone knew it. At the end, Busby, tears in his eyes, was elated: 'This is the most wonderful thing that has happened in my life. At the moment, I'm the proudest man in England.' His players, hearing the crowd chanting Busby's name, urged him to collect the trophy from the Royal Box, but he refused, modestly allowing his players to receive the accolades. London, as well as Europe, belonged to Manchester United, and their fans cavorted all night long in Trafalgar Square and other landmarks. For Busby and his players, this was a landmark occasion.

Second Division Cardiff City, managed by another Scot, Jimmy Scoular, went very close to adding to United's achievements in Europe, almost reaching the European Cup Winners' Cup Final. The Welsh Cup offered a relatively simple route into the competition and in 1966/67 they had won the two-legged final against Wrexham. The Bluebirds were not having a good league campaign but they seemed to raise their game and enjoyed matching themselves against overseas teams. They beat Shamrock Rovers and the Dutch side NAC Breda before a three-game saga with Torpedo Moscow. Cardiff won the first leg thanks to a Barrie Jones goal, but had to travel to Uzbekistan's Tashkent – a round trip of 8,000 miles – to play the second leg as Moscow was still in the grips of a harsh Russian winter. They lost the second meeting in the 'Cotton Pickers stadium' and a play-off was scheduled for Augsburg. Cardiff won through with a solitary goal by reserve forward Norman Dean. Their opponents in the semi-final were Hamburg, a team that had two West German internationals from the 1966 World Cup Final, Uwe Seeler and Willi Schulz. However, Seeler was missing from the game in Hamburg in the impressive Volksparkstadion. Dean was on target again but Hamburg came back to earn a 1-1 draw. Scoular was overjoyed: 'The lads were really magnificent and we are confident of winning in Cardiff.' Among those lads was one John Toshack, a tall forward who would go on to enjoy a successful career as a player and a manager.

At Ninian Park, Seeler was back for Hamburg, so the task had got a little harder. Dean did it again and put Cardiff ahead after four minutes, but Franz-Josef Hönig levelled on 15. Ten minutes into the second half, Seeler, despite not being at his best, put Hamburg in front. Cardiff refused to give in and, nine minutes from the end, Brian Harris restored parity with a header. Hamburg's fitness started to tell and right at the end a shot from Hönig was misread by goalkeeper Bob Wilson and the ball rolled over his shoulder and into the net. It was a heartbreaker of a goal but there was no time for Cardiff to come back. The consensus was that Cardiff, a Second Division side that finished 13th in 1967/68, had been on a brave and memorable run that had taken them right across Europe. They won the Welsh Cup again that season and returned to the Cup Winners' Cup with valuable experience in the bank.

Leeds United also used their experience in 1966/67, when they lost in the final of the Fairs Cup to Dinamo Zagreb, to reach the final again in 1967/68. Don Revie's tight-knit team were fighting on four fronts – the league, the League Cup, the FA Cup and the Fairs Cup. Their squad was not especially big, so the strain of chasing multiple honours proved to be their undoing. Leeds thrashed Spora Luxembourg 16-0, overcame a difficult Partizan Belgrade and then beat Scottish opposition – Hibernian, Rangers and Dundee – to reach the final against Hungary's Ferencváros.

Leeds won their first honour in the form of the Football League Cup, beating Arsenal in a bad-tempered game. They were beaten in the FA Cup semi-final by Everton and fell short in the title race by only three points.

The Fairs Cup gave them the chance to win another piece of silverware in what was a memorable season for the Yorkshire side. The two-legged final was held over to the start of 1968/69 due to fixture congestion.

Leeds were fresher than they would have been if they had played the final in the last few days of the previous season, but Ferencváros were stubborn, well marshalled and they had two outstanding players in Flórián Albert and Zoltán Varga. Leeds hosted the first game and had to contend with a tight Hungarian defence. The deciding goal came in the 41st minute when Peter Lorimer sent over a corner, Jack Charlton played the part of distractor-in-chief and Mick Jones hooked the ball into the net. Ferencváros protested, claiming Charlton had impeded their goalkeeper. A one-goal lead to take to the Nép stadium was precarious, especially as it was packed with supporters urging 'Fradi' on. Leeds packed their defence and fought out a 0-0 draw, enough to win the trophy. There could be no denying it, 1968 had been a good year for English clubs in Europe.

9

Farewell Fairs ...

IN 1968, Europe seemed a much bigger place than it is today, even though the break-up of the Soviet Union and the plethora of velvet revolutions in the USSR's countries added a large number of additional countries to UEFA's membership. Travel was not something everyone did in 1968, as the cost was prohibitive and Europe was still 'far away' for many people. Whenever there was a skirmish, military action, revolts or uprisings in another part of the world, they were considered to be too far from Britain to be a serious problem. In August 1968, the Cold War erupted when the Soviets and members of the Warsaw Pact invaded Czechoslovakia. The TV footage of tanks rolling into Prague, the sight of armed Russian troops, started to make the world nervous again. The spring of 1968 saw numerous protests in Prague and other cities about reforms and rights. UEFA had already made the draws for the first rounds of the European Cup and European Cup Winners' Cup, and the Inter-Cities Fairs Cup draw had also been made in the summer.

UEFA held an emergency meeting on 9 September following protests by Bulgaria, Hungary and Poland about its decision to pool teams from the Warsaw Pact countries so they played each other. UEFA had revised their two competitions after the initial exercise in June. Celtic, who had been paired with Ferencváros of Hungary, were now facing France's Saint-Étienne in the European Cup. Some teams withdrew after UEFA decided to stand by its decision.

The Fairs Cup saw no change other than the competition being expanded from 48 teams to 64, a decision that did not win total approval from FIFA President Sir Stanley Rous. The competition had a strict 'one-club, one-city' ruling, which meant in 1968/69 that, in England, Everton, Tottenham and Arsenal all missed out on qualification. There were four Fairs Cup places to be filled: Liverpool (third in the league in 1967/68), Leeds United (fourth), Chelsea (sixth) and Newcastle United (tenth) filled the slots. The aforementioned unlucky clubs were ineligible under Fairs Cup rules as Liverpool represented their city and finished ahead of their neighbours, Everton, and Chelsea had already claimed London's place, thereby denying their local rivals, Tottenham and Arsenal. West Bromwich Albion, who finished eighth, went into the European Cup Winners' Cup as FA Cup holders. Newcastle, one place above mid-table, were extremely lucky to be included.

There were ten British and Irish entrants in the Fairs Cup in 1968/69 and only one, Liverpool, fell at the first hurdle. They were beaten by the Basque team Athletic Bilbao on the toss of a coin after the two teams had beaten each other 2-1 in their home legs. Newcastle started their first European campaign by meeting Dutch side Feyenoord. Joe Harvey had a team that was decent at home but something of a soft touch away from St James' Park. They had some good individuals such as Bryan 'Pop' Robson, an underrated forward who scored consistently, and centre-forward Wyn Davies, a Welsh international who was exceptionally good in the air. Goalkeeper Iam McFaul was a Northern Ireland international, and skipper Bobby Moncur was something of an inspirational figure. Strength in depth was always a problem for Newcastle, so if they sustained a few injuries and suspensions, they could struggle.

Feyenoord were a hard team, and by the end of 1969/70 they would surprisingly be crowned European champions. They were, in some ways, the Dutch Rolling Stones to Ajax's Beatles, and were a more pragmatic outfit coached by Ernst Happel. Newcastle were in good form in the first leg on their own turf, winning 4-0 against a team that included Wim van Hanegem, Rinus Israël and Ove Kindvall. They could have had more goals, as they struck the woodwork three times. It was enough to see off Feyenoord, who in the second leg retrieved two of the four goals conceded in Newcastle, but went out 4-2 on aggregate.

Chelsea, who had started 1968/69 well, won through to the second round with a comfortable 9-3 aggregate win against Greenock Morton, the first leg a 5-0 thrashing at Stamford Bridge. The Scottish side from the banks of the Clyde were swept aside, proving that English football had far more depth at that time. Morton, for some strange reason, had three Danes in their team – Børge Thorup, Preben Arentoft and Bjarne Jensen. Chelsea's run would end rather shabbily in round two after two very frustrating 0-0 draws against DWS Amsterdam, who featured another Dutch notable in Robbie Rensenbrink, a member of the Netherlands' 1974 and 1978 World Cup teams. Chelsea outplayed their opponents for long spells over the two games, but the tie went beyond extra time and was settled by the toss of a coin.

Leeds United, the Fairs Cup holders, had to contend with a stubborn Standard Liège side, drawing 0-0 in

Belgium's industrial heartland before recovering from two-down to win 3-2 by virtue of a very late goal from Billy Bremner. Leeds were, generally, in outstanding form and would lose just two league games all season. Their target was the Football League title after four years of going so close, but having won their first trophies in 1967/68, they had the taste for more glory.

Their next opponents were Italy's Napoli, a team that had been involved in some very heated European ties in the recent past. They had finished runners-up in Serie A in 1967/68 and had in their ranks José Altafini, the 30-year-old Brazilian-born striker who briefly played for Italy in the World Cup. Visiting foreign sides were given a very hostile reception, including Burnley in 1967, so much so that they had to be escorted out of the stadium by armed troops and mounted police. Leeds had the chance to establish control of the tie at Elland Road and both of their goals came from the towering Jack Charlton midway through the first half. Leeds also had three goals disallowed. Don Revie, while pleased with the result, feared the second leg in Italy: 'While they played a lot of good, clean football, some of their men also resorted to moves which upset me. Some of our players had fingers poked in their eyes and Mick Jones was punched while on the grass.'

Revie asked for special observers to be present at the game, and some of Napoli's tactics left much to be desired. The crowd was not as venomous as the Leeds manager anticipated as only 15,000 turned up, although they were armed with firecrackers. Napoli had some key players sidelined but still won 2-0 to send the tie to extra time. Nothing changed, so the dreaded toss of a coin was the decider, with Bremner calling correctly.

Newcastle United, Rangers and Hibernian also won through to the third round. Rangers, who had beaten

Vojvodina in the first round, thrashed Dundalk 9-1 on aggregate, while Hibernian easily disposed of Lokomotive Leipzig 4-1 on aggregate. Newcastle's next port of call was Lisbon to play Sporting Clube de Portugal, more commonly known in Britain as Sporting Lisbon. Newcastle were enjoying Europe, despite being called 'backdoor entrants' by the cynical media. They headed for Lisbon via London with Joe Harvey claiming that he would use all 13 permitted players, which included two substitutes.

Lisbon was shrouded by bad weather and, on the day of the match, the Portuguese capital was continually drenched in rain, and a lightning storm hovered over the city at kick-off time. This kept the attendance down to around 10,000, so the terraces looked depressingly bare as Newcastle ran out to face their hosts. They adapted well and took a first-half lead through a calmly taken side-footed goal from Jim Scott. It was almost a memorable win for the Magpies but for a 90th-minute goal from winger João Morais, whose 25-yard shot went in off the crossbar past a very unhappy Iam McFaul. The home fans were not happy and sarcastically whistled at their team to show their disapproval.

Newcastle returned to England very upbeat, and three weeks later they got the chance to finish off Sporting. Robson scored early on, the goal being created by Davies, who headed a Tommy Gibb free kick across the area for Robson to jump high and volley into the net. Sporting did not impress many people; their slow, strolling style and cautious passing implied a lack of interest and ambition. Their first shot came 11 minutes from the end of the game. Robson's strike was enough to win the tie 2-1, putting Newcastle into the last 16. It was an impressive victory and one that prompted reporters to note that the team was showing a remarkable level of maturity in their debut season in Europe.

There were four British sides in the last 16, but they all avoided each other in the draw. Leeds United were paired with West Germany's Hannover, Rangers faced Chelsea's conquerors, DWS Amsterdam, and Hibernian were also up against Germans in the form of Hamburg, a particularly hard draw. Newcastle were heading back to Iberia to meet Real Zaragoza.

Strangely, the first leg was played on New Year's Day in freezing weather more associated with an English winter. Newcastle's form was typically inconsistent; since winning the tie with Sporting, they had lost heavily to Wolves, drawn with struggling Queens Park Rangers and beaten Ipswich Town and Southampton. On Boxing Day, they had lost 2-1 at Leeds United. The match in Spain was bruising, with both teams adopting a tough approach. Some members of the Newcastle team were suffering from a throat ailment, but this did not seem to stop them from competing. Twice they came back after trailing, with goals from Robson and Davies, who was a constant thorn in Zaragoza's side. Finally, Zaragoza scored a winner through Francisco Planas ten minutes into the second half. Losing 3-2 was no disaster; in fact, manager Joe Harvey was more than satisfied, having declared a one-goal deficit would be a very good result. Zaragoza's coach, César Rodríguez, a prolific goalscorer in his playing days, felt Newcastle were a very hard team.

The second leg was another intense occasion, with 56,000 people crammed into St James' Park. There was plenty of pre-match talk that Newcastle might make a bid to sign Queens Park Rangers' mercurial forward, Rodney Marsh, who had asked the London club for a transfer. They had a healthy bank balance, and they had an interest in Marsh, having failed in a previous attempt to sign him and his team-mate Roger Morgan for a fee of £100,000. Two years on, QPR had slapped a £150,000 price tag on their star man. Newcastle would not be trying to sign him; they simply did not feel such a valuation was realistic.

Once again, Robson revealed his appetite for Fairs Cup football, scoring with a 30-yard rising left-footed drive after just two minutes. The aggregate score was 3-3. On 28 minutes Tommy Gibb sent a header over the confused Zaragoza goalkeeper Manolo Nieves and his defence to swing the pendulum Newcastle's way. Just before the interval, Armando Martín pulled a goal back to increase the tension, but Newcastle held out and went through on the new rule where any goals scored away from home counted double in the event of the aggregate scores being level. Rodríguez felt his team effectively lost the game in Zaragoza by letting Newcastle off the hook. Joe Harvey commented: 'I was a little bit worried in the first half, but the second half belonged to us. I wasn't as worried as in some of the other Fairs Cup games. I only smoked nine cigarettes, which is good going for me.'

Newcastle were in the last eight, a significant achievement, to be joined by Rangers, who had overcome DWS Amsterdam, and Leeds United, who were too good for Hannover, winning 7-2 over the two meetings. There was no such joy for Hibernian, however, as they went out to Hamburg on away goals.

It was Portuguese opposition again for Newcastle, Vitória de Setúbal, who finished fifth in the Primeira Liga in 1967/68. Having beaten Feyenoord, Sporting and Zaragoza, Newcastle's momentum was good despite being dealt a string of hard draws. When Setúbal arrived in Newcastle, they were faced with some of the most brutal North East weather – a blizzard of snow and sleet and sub-zero temperatures. It did not suit the Portuguese, but it was not exactly comfortable for the home team either. But

Harvey's team had full control of the game, winning 5-1 with goals from a young Alan Foggon, Davies, Gibb and two from Robson, who seemed to excel in the competition. Setubal were so out of sorts that *The Times* concluded, 'How they must have sighed for the orange groves of home.'

Setubal's coach, Fernando Vaz, claimed his players were beaten before the game started and that they were so cold they barely had any feeling in their arms and legs. 'We've no chance now,' he conceded. Newcastle's chairman, Lord Westwood, responded: 'Setubal claimed that conditions beat them, but I reply there was also a team called Newcastle United.' While Setubal saw the weather as an obstacle, Newcastle had to deal with opponents who were still smarting from their 5-1 humbling. They wasted no time in seeking retribution in the form of harsh tackles, shin-kicking and shirt-pulling. One report called it 'savage soccer warfare'. Although the home team took the lead, Davies headed an equaliser that put out the fire for a while. Two goals in the second half gave Setubal a 3-1 win, but Newcastle had done the hard work in the first leg.

Leeds United were not able to join Newcastle in the semi-finals. They were knocked out by Újpest, the Budapest rivals of Ferencváros, who they had beaten in the 1967/68 final. The Hungarians had won 1-0 at Elland Road and survived an onslaught by Leeds that saw them strike the woodwork three times and miss a penalty. Újpest also won the second leg in Budapest, by 2-0, with the final goal a spectacular solo effort by the outstanding Ferenc Bene. Leeds were out, but they were closing in on the league title, ample consolation for their European exit. No Leeds, but Rangers had made it through to the last four after beating Athletic Bilbao 4-3 on aggregate. They won 4-1 at Ibrox, with future Manchester United manager Alex Ferguson opening the scoring, but lost 2-0 in Bilbao. The draw paired Newcastle with Rangers, a tie that promised to be a marginally diluted England versus Scotland clash.

Newcastle had just one game to go in their league programme, on 17 May, three days after their first leg with Rangers, but the Scots had completed their domestic season, finishing runners-up to Celtic and also emphatically losing the Scottish Cup Final by 4-0 against their Old Firm rivals. Rangers felt they could beat Newcastle at Ibrox in the first game, but it did not go quite as planned. They dominated most of the 90 minutes but Newcastle's defence withstood a second-half onslaught as the 75,000 crowd urged on the home team. The best chance was a penalty, which was awarded after goalkeeper McFaul had brought down Örjan Persson. Andy Penman took the kick but McFaul pulled off a fine save to help Newcastle leave Glasgow with a 0-0 draw. The fans that travelled up from Tyneside were relieved to get home – so incensed were the Rangers fans that their team had been thwarted by what the *Daily Record* called 'a good, but hardly outstanding team', that there was a certain amount of hostility shown to anyone with a black-and-white scarf.

The mood in Newcastle-upon-Tyne for the second leg was one of an invasion taking place. Around 20,000 Rangers fans descended upon the city and created an atmosphere that started out as good-natured but, after large quantities of alcohol, became rather frantic. Pubs closed early and police were on overtime. There were arrests before, during and after the match, and an entrance gate at St James' Park was even stormed by drunken fans. The game itself was hard and tense, occasionally a little too aggressive. Rangers had the better of the first half, but Newcastle opened the scoring through Jim Scott eight minutes after the interval. This triggered off a pitch invasion and some fighting that forced referee John Gow to take the teams off the field. It took

17 minutes for the game to restart against a backdrop of long lines of policemen, Aisatian dogs and supporters being escorted out of the ground. Interestingly, of the 52 arrests, 24 were Scots, so there were clearly some locals joining in with the fracas. However, Harry Cavan, the vice-president of FIFA, was in attendance and was outraged by the behaviour of the Rangers fans. 'Scottish clubs could be banned from European football after this. Something must be done to make supporters see sense,' he told the media. Rangers player Billy Mathieson was among those trying to calm the fans down and urged them to get back on to the terraces.

Newcastle scored a second goal through Jackie Sinclair to secure the tie. The match made the front pages of some newspapers, but it was not the football that grabbed the attention. The Scottish newspapers did not hold back, calling the culprits 'the animals that shame us', and their antics 'blind banditry'. For them it was a 'night of bitter shame' for Scottish football. Joe Harvey, the triumphant Newcastle manager, commented that he felt sorry for the Rangers club and their players. John Lawrence, the Rangers chairman, was horrified: 'My board of directors and I consider that the exhibition by a small percentage of Rangers supporters has brought disgrace to our grand old club.'

Little did anyone realise at St James' Park that night, but they had witnessed scenes that would appear to represent the character of British football over the course of the next two decades. The trouble at Newcastle came just after a bout of violence at the Manchester United versus AC Milan game that same week, which threw many football people into mild panic about the state of the national game. For the time being, though, Newcastle had a two-legged Fairs Cup Final to concentrate on.

Newcastle's opponents were Újpest Dózsa, who had breezed past Turkey's Göztepe Izmir in the semi-final.

But it was their two-legged victory (3-0) over Leeds that prompted people to claim Újpest were 'the best team in Europe'. A little elaborate praise, perhaps, but they were a strong outfit and almost every player was a Hungarian international. In their careers, the 11 players that appeared in both legs of the final accumulated over 300 caps, with seven winning Olympic medals between 1960 and 1968. They had Ferenc Bene, one of the successors to the Mighty Magyars of the 1950s, in their ranks, and a prolific scorer called Antal Dunai. Leeds' captain Bremner had been very impressed by them: 'They were fantastic. The ball moved around so fast it was difficult to make a tackle.' They won both the Hungarian league and Magyar Kupa in 1969.

They had also beaten Aris Salonika and Legia Warsaw on route to the final and received a bye against Union Luxembourg, a game that would surely have caused them no difficulties. Their route to the final had been somewhat easier than Newcastle's, but their coach, Lajos Baróti, one of the most celebrated coaches in Europe, was rather dismissive of the Geordies and admitted that he had a plan to keep Newcastle's main threat quiet. 'We will use a bear trap and quickly put it over Davies's head. He will not trouble us very much then.'

The St James' Park pitch was heavy, and initially Joe Harvey insisted that Újpest train on Hunters Moor, but he relented and allowed them to use the stadium, watched by a 'tiny knot of urchins', according to the *Newcastle Journal*. The Hungarians' training methods were very different to those adopted by Newcastle and, after a strenuous session, Baróti said he was comfortable with the pitch, but admitted his players were tired after a long season. The first leg at St James' Park was tight for 45 minutes, but in the early stages of the second half a free kick by Gibb was aimed at the head of Davies, who sent the ball goalwards, only for Újpest goalkeeper Antal Szentmihályi to thwart him. As the ball spun out, Moncur left-footed it just inside the post. His first goal for the club. Ten minutes later, he did it again, playing a wall pass with Danish midfielder Preben Arentoft before hitting another left-foot drive low into the net.

Newcastle scored again through Jimmy Scott, a surging run, a one-two with Arentoft and, as he squeezed past a defender, he lifted the ball over the advancing goalie. Three-nil to the good, surely Newcastle were home and dry? Chairman Lord Westwood certainly felt so, expressing his confidence in a tongue-in-cheek manner: 'It seems a waste of time to carry the cup all the way there [to Budapest] when we have to bring it back.' Joe Harvey was more cautious, but cautiously agreed that 'we must fancy our chances now'. It was June before Newcastle travelled to Hungary and they were under pressure from the kick-off in the Nép stadium. Bene, the danger man, scored after 30 minutes. Just before the interval, János Göröcs extended Újpest Dózsa's lead. By the 50th minute, however, Newcastle were level. Moncur – incredibly – scored on 46 minutes, and Arentoft, with plenty of space, provided the equaliser four minutes later. With 16 minutes remaining, substitute Foggon, a player rich in promise but ultimately falling short of fulfilling it, went on a long run, struck the crossbar and followed up to score Newcastle's third. The aggregate score was now 6-2 and the trophy was secure. 'We began as outsiders in the Fairs Cup and finished as champions,' beamed 50th birthday boy Harvey.

Around 10,000 fans welcomed them back to St James' Park, but the timing of their arrival – in the middle of the so-called 'rush hour' – meant the team could not embark on a celebratory procession of honour through the city. There were speeches and joyous scenes, and Moncur, the three-goal hero of the final, told the crowd: 'It has been the greatest day of our football lives, but there is a little touch of sorrow that we didn't win this cup in front of you all.' Nevertheless, Newcastle had their first trophy since 1955 and new heroes to look the likes of Hughie Gallacher and Jackie Milburn in the eye.

Arsenal, in 1970, were also a club whose honours list was in need of an update. They had not won anything since 1953, which was their longest stretch without a major prize. They had shown signs of resurgence in the late 1960s, reaching two successive Football League Cup finals, losing to Leeds United and, rather shockingly, Swindon Town. Arsenal had fallen behind Chelsea and Tottenham, but under Bertie Mee and his coach, Don Howe, the Gunners were starting to look like contenders again. They finished fourth in the league in 1968/69 and qualified for European competition for only the second time in their history. Mee made some changes to his squad at the start of 1969/70, letting centre-half Ian Ure, who was exposed by the Swindon defeat, go to Manchester United. His replacement was supposed to be John Roberts, signed from Northampton Town, but he failed to establish himself at Arsenal and moved to Birmingham in 1972. As the season progressed, Gunners fans also saw the last of Northern Irishman Terry Neill as a player.

The most significant player movement for Arsenal was the arrival of two youngsters, Charlie George and Ray Kennedy, both of whom were blooded during 1969/70. There was no place for striker Bobby Gould, though, and he made less than a dozen appearances before finding himself on his way out of Highbury. In the first weeks of 1970, the club attempted to add some flair to an otherwise workmanlike team, paying £100,000 for Peter Marinello, Hibernian's George Best lookalike. With his long hair, trendy clothes, model girlfriend and jinking wing play,

Marinello arrived in London on a wave of hype. 'We've just signed the nearest thing that football has to the Beatles,' said one Arsenal director. Marinello was just 19 years old and, although he scored on his debut, at Old Trafford of all places, the move to Arsenal seemed to overawe the young man from Edinburgh.

Europe provided a welcome distraction from a very average league campaign. The Fairs Cup could be an attritional competition and any team with ambitions of lifting the trophy would have to play 12 games. Glentoran of Northern Ireland were beaten 3-1 on aggregate before Sporting Lisbon were overcome 3-0. A tough tie with Rouen of France saw Jon Sammels score the only goal over the two games to squeeze Arsenal through. Dinamo Bacău were then thrashed 9-1 on aggregate before a very daunting semi-final with Ajax Amsterdam and Johan Cruyff, the clear flavour of the month in European football.

Ajax were not yet the triple-crown winners of Europe, though, which was fortunate for Arsenal. This was George's moment, for he netted twice in a 3-0 win against the Dutch. They lost the second leg 1-0 in the Netherlands, but Arsenal were through to the final. Their opponents would be Belgium's Anderlecht, who had disposed of three British clubs on the way: Coleraine, Newcastle United (the holders) and Dunfermline Athletic. They had also beaten Inter Milan in the semi-final. Furthermore, they had some genuine talent in their line-up, including Belgian international Paul Van Himst and the Dutchman Jan Mulder. It was Mulder who tormented Arsenal in Brussels in the first leg of the final. He scored twice, adding to Johan Devrint's opener, to give Anderlecht a 3-0 lead. Arsenal looked buried, but substitute Kennedy headed a consolation goal to provide the Londoners with a glimmer of hope.

The second leg, on 28 April 1970, saw Arsenal go ahead after 25 minutes through Eddie Kelly, another young player who had made his bow in 1969/70. Arsenal remained patient, although Mulder hitting the woodwork jangled Highbury nerves. It was not until the final quarter of an hour that Arsenal broke through, John Radford and Sammels scoring within a minute of each other. Arsenal had won with a miraculous comeback that had not looked possible a week earlier in the Belgian capital. The crowd streamed on to the Highbury pitch as Don Howe declared that victory was the start of a new dawn at the club. He was right, to some extent. Arsenal won the double in 1971, but that triumph signalled the peak of that team's achievement, not the beginning of a dynasty. The period between 1968 and 1970 had been the build-up, 1971 the climax. Arsenal became the second successive English club to win the Fairs Cup, following in Newcastle United's footsteps. The Magpies had lost to Anderlecht in the quarter-finals, while Southampton had earlier fallen to Newcastle, and Liverpool, who had won 14-0 on aggregate against Dundalk, went out at the second hurdle.

The British representation for the 1970/71 Fairs Cup, the final season of the competition, was very strong. England had no fewer than five teams: Arsenal (the holders), Coventry City, Leeds United, Liverpool and Newcastle United. Scotland had four teams: Dundee United, Hibernian, Kilmarnock and Rangers. Coleraine were Northern Ireland's sole flag-bearer. There was a growing feeling that matches in the Fairs Cup and indeed other European competitions were becoming unruly and violent. In the first round, those that questioned whether it was worth entering tournaments that were merely stages for foul play, cheating and antisocial behaviour were given plenty of ammunition for their argument. Arsenal were drawn to meet Italy's Lazio, a team renowned for its uncompromising style. The Gunners had started 1970/71 well and would eventually enjoy a season that would deliver more than any of the club's past achievements. The first leg in Rome was a fractious affair that ended 2-2, but only after a controversial finale in which Giorgio Chinaglia scored two goals in six minutes. His second goal, a penalty, was awarded after Arsenal's captain, Frank McLintock, headed the ball off the goal line. The referee claimed he handled the ball and awarded a penalty. Chinaglia had upset Arsenal earlier when he aimed a high kick at Eddie Kelly and then threw the ball in the player's face.

But the real drama came later that evening during a post-match social gathering. As Arsenal's players left a restaurant, several Lazio players were waiting in the street. Some insults were traded and then Ray Kennedy was attacked and Bob McNab was thrown across a parked car. There are various accounts of what actually happened, but Lazio's players had to be ferried away by coach and Arsenal were escorted to their hotel by police. Arsenal arrived home at Luton Airport the next day and Bertie Mee, their manager, refused to reveal what had happened. 'I have no comments to the press because there is nothing to comment about. We drew 2-2 and we are very happy with the result,' he said. Meanwhile, Lazio were refusing to travel to Highbury unless Arsenal's players retracted insults hurled at their team. Lazio also insisted that UEFA guarantee that Arsenal did not conduct a 'bullfight' in the second leg.

If that was not bad enough, Newcastle United had to go into battle against Inter Milan in the first round. Inter, who would win the Italian league in 1970/71, had finished runners-up to Cagliari in 1970, so they were clearly a very accomplished side, with half a dozen members of

Italy's 1970 World Cup squad. It was a daunting tie for Newcastle, but they returned home with a 1-1 draw. At St James' Park, Inter adopted a cynical approach and pushed the boundaries beyond acceptability. Bobby Moncur gave Newcastle the lead but then things started to become chaotic. Inter goalkeeper Lido Vieri punched Belgian referee Joseph Minnoy in the face, earning a red card. The police had to intervene at one stage and the game was held up as order was restored. Minnoy, a courteous and friendly fellow, was quite diplomatic. 'I have refereed Italians before and they are very excitable. Very Latin. I think it's the sun,' he said, tongue in cheek. Newcastle scored again through Wyn Davies to rubber-stamp a 2-0 victory. Afterwards, Inter failed to turn up at the post-match dinner, which gave some insight into the Italian game. 'The players cannot eat or drink anything they want. They must watch their diets,' said an Inter official. Instead, the Italians returned to their Gateshead base and flew home.

The English contingent started to fall out of contention from the second round. Coventry, who were playing in Europe for the first time, got past Bulgaria's Trakia Plovdiv with ease but were then trounced by Bayern Munich, who had already beaten Rangers. Newcastle also went out in the second round, losing to Pécsi Dózsa on penalties, and Hibernian lost to Liverpool in round three. Bill Shankly's team then beat Bayern Munich in the last eight, winning 3-0 at Anfield with a hat-trick from Alun Evans. Arsenal, who had comfortably slalomed through the challenges of Sturm Graz and Beveren, went out on away goals in the quarter-finals to Köln, leaving them to concentrate on the Football League title and FA Cup. Their title rivals, Leeds, had travelled to the far north, Central and Eastern Europe, then Portugal to reach the last four, where they would meet Liverpool.

As ever, Leeds were chasing multiple honours but Liverpool also had hopes of winning the FA Cup. Leeds had been pursued vigorously by Arsenal in the league and had slipped up in the FA Cup against Colchester United. The Fairs Cup became their best hope of silverware but Liverpool were always difficult opponents for Don Revie's team; however, they received a boost when Bremner returned from long-term injury. The flame-haired midfielder scored the only goal of the first game at Anfield, heading home from Johnny Giles's free kick. A typically tense second meeting at Elland Road ended goalless, so Leeds went through to play Juventus in the final.

Before that took place, the league title had gone to Arsenal, who had finished one point above them. Some teams would have wilted and found it hard to lift themselves, but they were determined to end the season with something to show for their consistent efforts. Leeds, however, did not need two more games to add to their schedule, let alone a further 51 minutes. Turin was under siege from the heavens as rain fell incessantly before and during the first leg. Eventually, six minutes into the second half, the referee abandoned the game at 0-0. Leeds had to stay in Turin for another two days to try again, and this time it ended 2-2, with Leeds relying on a deflected effort from Paul Madeley and a Mick Bates shot into the roof of the net. In hindsight, this proved to be a vital draw and more preferable to a goalless game.

As it was, the away goal advantage went to Leeds after a 1-1 draw at Elland Road on 3 June. Allan Clarke put Leeds in front and Juventus, who had some outstanding individuals in their line-up, including Fabio Capello, Helmut Haller, Roberto Bettega and Franco Causio, equalised through Pietro Anastasi. It was 3-3 on aggregate and enough for Leeds to win the very last Fairs Cup.

10

A Battle for Britain and Beyond

IN 1969, Leeds United and Celtic were ranked among the top three clubs in Europe. Both were champions of their respective countries and both had won European honours. They were remarkably consistent, had teams packed with internationals, and their managers, Don Revie and Jock Stein, were among the most respected in the game. Stylistically, there were big differences between the two clubs; Stein was an advocate of dynamic attacking football, while Revie had a win-at-all-costs intensity about him. Celtic were well ahead of their domestic rivals apart from Rangers, while Leeds had severe competition in the Football League from other northern clubs. In the case of Revie's team, their desire to win everything would often prove to be their downfall. Invariably, in the period 1967 to 1972, Leeds would end a season frustrated, exhausted and not always recognised for their exceptional football and burning desire to win.

It was widely believed that despite not winning the league in 1970, 1971 and 1972, Leeds were the best team in the land, but their ultra-professionalism and tough underbelly did not make them especially popular. Celtic under Stein were a much-loved side, as much a representation of Scotland as the national team. The Home

International Championships were, for most people, all about England versus Scotland. This rivalry was felt more by the Scots, who would invade Wembley Stadium every two years and light up central London, bolstered by beer, Scottish nationalism and ancient irritations. At club level, they got very little chance to prove their claim that Scottish football was superior, even though Celtic were the first British club to lift the European Cup, a trophy managers such as Sir Matt Busby, Bill Shankly and Revie had been striving to win.

Leeds had beaten a cluster of Scottish sides in their Fairs Cup runs of the 1960s – they had come up against Hibernian, Rangers, Dundee and Kilmarnock across 1966/67 and 1967/68. Celtic had met Liverpool in the European Cup Winners' Cup semi-finals in 1966 but were beaten 2-1 on aggregate. A few years earlier, Tottenham put Rangers in their place, winning 8-4 in the same competition. Although the best of Scotland – some of whom played south of the border – could match England's national team, it was generally considered that the English top flight was somewhat superior to its Scottish equivalent.

Celtic's win in 1967, which instantly passed into Scottish football folklore – the fabled Lisbon Lions – followed by Manchester United's emphatic win in 1968, suggested the wind had changed direction. For so long, British clubs had to raise their hats to the Spanish, the Italians and the Portuguese, but Inter Milan and Benfica had both been beaten and, from United's perspective, they had also overcome Real Madrid on the way to the 1968 final. In 1968/69, Manchester City flopped miserably in the European Cup, but Manchester United were beaten in the semi-final by eventual champions AC Milan. Celtic went out of the competition in the quarter-finals.

Celtic and Leeds were destined to come face to face in 1969/70, even though the European Cup cast was impressive; Real Madrid, AC Milan, Fiorentina, Bayern Munich and Benfica were all involved and then there were the relative unknowns from Eastern Europe – Legia Warsaw, Red Star Belgrade, Dynamo Kyiv, CSKA Sofia and East Germany's Vorwärts. There were several clubs who could be strong on their own ground and very stubborn away from home.

Leeds began their European season with a 10-0 win at home to Norway's champions, Lyn Oslo, while, on the same night, Celtic had a slightly uncomfortable 90 minutes in Basel, drawing 0-0 thanks to a solid performance from goalkeeper John Fallon. Leeds were relentless against the outclassed Scandinavians, with Mick Jones scoring three of eight goals that would make him the competition's top scorer for 1969/70. Celtic, though, had started to look fallible and had won just one of their four league games, losing twice. They only lost three in 34 in their league programme in 1968/69. But some reporters wondered whether Celtic's halo was starting to slip, that the air of invincibility was fading a little.

Leeds, with £165,000 new signing from Leicester City, Allan Clarke, in their forward line, had lost once in their nine league games. They had little trouble winning their second leg in Norway by 6-0, while Celtic put on a powerful show in disposing of Basel by two goals. Only Basel goalkeeper Marcel Kunz prevented Celtic from running up an emphatic scoreline from the 50 shots they had on goal. Although they were far from their best – they had just lost their third game of the season – Celtic pulled off an impressive 3-0 second-round win against a Benfica side that included Eusébio, Mário Coluna, José Augusto, António Simões and José Torres. These were all well-known figures in European football, but Coluna, Augusto and Torres were all over 30 years of age and Eusébio failed to complete the game due to injury. Celtic's three goals set them up nicely for the second leg in Lisbon, but everybody knew Benfica were very dangerous at home. They had lost just one league game in 69 on their own turf and in 1969/70 had scored 21 goals in four games without reply.

Leeds were also in good form, scoring three first-half goals against Ferencváros at a muddy Elland Road. The Hungarians were without two of their key figures, Flórián Albert, the European Footballer of the Year in 1967, and Gyula Rákosi, and were completely outplayed. They even impressed the famous 'Russian linesman', Tofiq Bahramov (from Azerbaijan) who officiated the game: 'This was the finest performance I have seen in a European Cup tie and one of the best behaved matches.' Leeds followed the first leg with another 3-0 win in Budapest, becoming the first British side to emerge victorious from the Nép stadium. Only 5,500 people were present on a rainy night in the vast concrete arena, but Leeds were praised for being 'flexible, skilful and sensible', and likely winners of the European Cup. Celtic scraped through by the toss of a coin after losing 3-0 to Benfica, who had played brilliantly to turn around the three-goal deficit. The quarter-finals beckoned and Leeds were paired with Standard Liège, while Celtic had to contend with Italian champions Fiorentina.

Leeds knew all about Standard for they had narrowly beaten them in the 1968/69 Fairs Cup. They were Belgian champions in 1968/69 and went on to win the title in 1970 and 1971. They contributed seven players to Belgium's World Cup 1970 squad, including goalkeeper Christian Piot, Wilfried Van Moer and Léon Semmeling. Leeds went out to Belgium aware of the challenge ahead of them and a very difficult playing surface that was 'scarred and ugly'. They won 1-0 in a hard-fought contest, with Peter Lorimer scoring 20 minutes from time. René Hauss, the Standard coach, was full of praise for Revie's side: 'Leeds are the strongest side we have ever met in Europe.' Revie, meanwhile, made a bold prediction that the winner of this tie would win the European Cup.

Celtic were in excellent form in Glasgow and beat Fiorentina 3-0, which left the Italian coach, Bruno Pesaola, crestfallen. 'The Scots have got capital in the bank. And they will be prudent. If the ground is heavy [in the second leg], goodbye our hopes,' he admitted.

Leeds won 1-0 again at Elland Road, with a Johnny Giles penalty, while Celtic were beaten, but Fiorentina could only reduce the deficit by one goal. The possibility of an all-British final was still on – but not for long. Two days after they won through to the last four, Leeds United and Celtic were pulled out of the hat one after the other. Only one of them would play in the final. It was a draw of mild disappointment, but Stein just shrugged his shoulders: 'You can't pick or choose your opponents at this stage of the competition. But we will be having a real go.'

Leeds were in the middle of fixture congestion problems. After their win against Standard on 18 March, they would play five games in ten days, including two FA Cup semi-final meetings with Manchester United. They almost seemed to be punished for their own success, for 24 hours after playing Celtic on 1 April, they faced West Ham in London. By the end of March, though, the league title was as good as won by an exciting Everton team. Celtic had clinched the Scottish League just a few days before they travelled to Yorkshire.

In hindsight, Leeds United's schedule was quite ludicrous, but there was always an element of *schadenfreude* whenever they failed. They never had a squad of great depth, although their starting XI was outstanding in so many ways, but trying to fight battles on multiple fronts was always extremely taxing on their players. Furthermore, they invariably suffered from misfortune, such as the loss of Paul Reaney between the two legs against Celtic with a fractured leg and, two years later, a similar injury to Terry Cooper ahead of the 1972 FA Cup Final. Sometimes, it felt as though Leeds were often undone by simply trying too hard.

The strain was starting to show when Leeds prepared for the first leg with Celtic. The injury list was frightening for Revie: Norman Hunter (knee), Billy Bremner (groin), Giles (calf), Jones (ankles), Reaney (hamstring) and Cooper (stitches) were all battling to be fit. Leeds were tough, so their players often worked off pain and it was rare to see them whingeing about knocks. They played hard and often received the same in return. Billed as 'the premature finale', Leeds United versus Celtic was a titanic struggle on a sticky pitch and was much anticipated on both sides of the border. This was the eighth game in 14 days for Leeds and, over the course of the 90 minutes, it showed. Both sides had barely drawn breath when Celtic struck to change the mood immediately; only 90 seconds had passed when Bertie Auld sent a long pass out to the left flank, where Paul Madeley and Jack Charlton lost control of the ball and it rolled to George Connolly, whose tame shot took a slight deflection off Cooper and sailed past Gary Sprake. The Leeds crowd was stunned, the Leeds team was equally confused. What had happened?

Throughout the first half, Leeds looked jaded and their passing was not to its usual standards. The midfield battle of Auld and Bobby Murdoch versus Giles and Bremner was being won by the Celtic boys. Bremner, who received a blow that gave him mild concussion, had to leave the field and, with that, the hopes of Leeds seemed to fade.

There was no shortage of effort on the part of Leeds, but they looked to have finally run out of juice. Phil Brown, a regular Leeds reporter, came to the conclusion that, after such a campaign, 'the elastic has gone' in the team. Stein was euphoric and asked whether the English press would finally give Scottish football the credit it deserved. The reporters declared that the odds had swung wildly in favour of Celtic, who would host the second leg at Hampden Park rather than Parkhead. This was a game that everyone wanted to see.

Leeds had another three games in a ten-day period before they went to Scotland, and it was a slog. They drew 2-2 at West Ham the day after losing to Celtic, while losing Reaney; they then beat Burnley ahead of the FA Cup Final with Chelsea, where Leeds were dominant at Wembley, but Chelsea's pluck earned them a 2-2 draw. Another game was now on the list, a replay on 29 April at Old Trafford. Celtic, on the same day as the FA Cup Final, were surprisingly beaten 3-1 by Aberdeen in the Scottish Cup Final. Four days after that, on 15 April, Leeds and Celtic met again. A phenomenal crowd of 136,505 packed into Hampden Park to witness an England vs Scotland game in all but name. Actually, there were 14 Scots on the pitch and only six Englishmen, as well as an Irishman and a Welshman.

Celtic started furiously, pressuring Leeds from the kick-off. But it was the visitors who took the lead to level the aggregate score after 15 minutes, Bremner hitting a long-range piledriver into the top corner of Evan Williams's net. The Leeds skipper, who had been living on his nerves as much as anyone for weeks, demonstrated his joy at scoring in front of his countrymen by punching the air in defiance. Two minutes into the second half, John Hughes headed Celtic level, and in the 51st minute, they went ahead when Bobby Murdoch shot home from inside the area. Leeds were now 3-1 down over the two games and looking desperate. Things got worse when Hughes ran into Sprake, who was replaced by the Scot David Harvey, an equally competent goalkeeper. Celtic were now confident and assured, causing Leeds problems, notably with David Hay's overlapping runs and the intricate skill of Jimmy Johnstone that tormented hard men like Hunter and Cooper. It was all over for Leeds, who now had to lift themselves for the FA Cup Final replay in two weeks. Revie was sanguine in defeat: 'A club can never be too ambitious, though I personally never believed we could do the treble of league, FA Cup and European Cup. In fact, months ago, I said that to win the three would be the eighth wonder of the world.'

Revie believed his team had lost the tie at Elland Road and praised Celtic, hoping they would win the European Cup. Leeds lost the FA Cup Final replay, too, despite leading Chelsea for the third time in the final's two-game saga. Celtic, though, set their sights on the final in Milan's San Siro stadium against Feyenoord. Celtic's schedule could not have been more different than the team they beat at Hampden Park and they were now able to rest before the final on 6 May. Feyenoord won the Eredivisie title in 1968/69, finishing three points ahead of Johan Cruyff's Ajax, who reached the European Cup Final at the end of that season. Feyenoord had an easier path to the final than Celtic, beating KR of Iceland, AC Milan, the holders, Vorwärts of East Germany and Legia Warsaw. There was no doubt they were surprise finalists, although the world was starting to wake up to the rise of Dutch football after Ajax had finished runners-up in 1969. Nevertheless, Celtic were overwhelming favourites to lift their second European Cup in four seasons.

England's representatives in the European Cup may have faltered at the penultimate stage, but another less celebrated club did return from the continent with a prize, albeit a modest bauble of wood and silver. Swindon Town won the inaugural Anglo-Italian Cup, the brainchild of Gigi Peronace, a long-time acolyte of English football. Swindon, who won the Football League Cup while in the Third Division, were denied the chance of European football because of their status. The Anglo-Italian Cup gave them the opportunity to take part in a prestigious competition involving English and Italian clubs. There were six clubs from each country: Middlesbrough, Sheffield Wednesday, Sunderland, Swindon Town, West Bromwich Albion and Wolves from England; Fiorentina, Juventus, Lazio, Napoli, Roma and Vicenza from Serie A.

Swindon pulled off some impressive results, beating Juventus 4-0 at home and 1-0 away, and winning 2-1 in Naples. They had the best record of the six English sides and qualified for the final. Napoli topped the Italian clubs. The final, at the end of May 1970, was played in Napoli's San Paolo stadium with 50,000 attending. Swindon silenced the normally vociferous Neapolitan crowd with three goals within an hour, two from Peter Noble and one from Arthur Horsfield. The locals did not like it and invaded the pitch. There was tear gas and Swindon's players were pelted with stones by Napoli fans. The referee, Mr Paul Schiller from Vienna, had no choice but to abandon the game and declare Swindon the winners. However, questions were asked about the validity of the competition as it seemed to attract violence on and off the pitch. Another tie between Vicenza and West Bromwich Albion had to be abandoned and there was trouble at Molineux, home of Wolves, when Lazio's Giorgio Chinaglia was sent off. It was supposed to be a 'friendly' competition of a sort. The Anglo-Italian

Cup in its early 1970s form, ran from 1970 to 1973. After Swindon's win, Blackpool beat Bologna in 1971 and gamely tried to defend their trophy in 1972 against Roma in the final in front of 75,000 spectators, losing 3-1. Finally, Newcastle won the 1973 final, beating Fiorentina.

Italy was the location for the European Cup Final between Celtic and Feyenoord. The San Siro stadium in Milan was accustomed to drama and was one of the most eye-catching arenas in Europe. Celtic seemed a little too casual ahead of the final. Camped out by Lake Como, they were relaxed and ready to go. There were 30,000 Scots in and around Milan waiting to cheer them to victory. The Dutch also arrived en masse, at least equalling the tartan-clad Scottish fans in number. However many there were, they seemed to drown out the noise of the Celtic masses.

Stein seemed a little dismissive of the qualities of Feyenoord: 'They have a basic method and I don't think they can change.' Stein also did not rate them as highly as Celtic's semi-final opponents: 'They have not the calibre, the fitness or the fight of Leeds. A quick goal and we should do it.' Today, such comments would serve as motivation for the opposition, and it was not long before Stein was eating his words. Celtic were at full strength, but it really demonstrated the lack of knowledge British clubs had of most foreign football teams. His summing up of Feyenoord was a little out of character for the great man. Feyenoord were certainly no fools. As well as their smart coach, Happel, they had outstanding midfielders in Wim van Hanegem and the Austrian Franz Hasil, an experienced winger in Coen Moulijn and a prolific striker in the Swede, Ove Kindvall.

Feyenoord dominated the game for long periods and it was against the run of play when Celtic opened the scoring, Tommy Gemmell shooting low into the net after Bobby

Murdoch had back-heeled the ball to him from a free kick. Feyenoord levelled soon after when captain Rinus Israël headed home after a brief game of head tennis, the ball going in off the post. And it stayed that way for a long time, although Feyenoord continued to make Celtic look leaden-footed and lacking in creative ideas. The game went into extra time and was poised for a replay when Feyenoord scored with three minutes to go. A quickly taken long free kick was misjudged by Billy McNeill, who appeared to handle the ball as he fell backwards, and Kindvall nipped around the Celtic skipper and lifted his effort over the head of the advancing Williams. Time was running out and Feyenoord knew they were going to win. As photographers invaded the pitch, Kindvall was carried back to the centre circle by his team-mates.

Celtic were beaten and rather shell-shocked. Stein admitted his team had not been at their best. 'Feyenoord played very well and deserved victory, I must say that, and we played a poor match. We really had too many bad players tonight,' he said. There was, though, mutual respect between the teams. Happel commented: 'We made more chances, but I am pleased the way Mr Jock Stein accepted it. He was one of the first to congratulate me. This is sportsmanship.' Wim van Hanegem added: 'Jimmy Johnstone came up to me at the end of the match, a tough battle it had been, and told me we deserved to win and wished us all the best. You are a big man if you can react like that after losing a European Cup Final.'

Down the years, Celtic historians have revealed that the mood at the club just did not seem right at the end of the 1969/70 season and there may well have been some complacency among a team that had become very used to winning all the time. The Scottish League, for example, had been won very easily in 1969/70 with a

12-point margin. In October 1970, Celtic were beaten in the Scottish League Cup Final, meaning they had lost three cup finals in a six-month period. Stein, meanwhile, decided to rebuild a team that had started to show its age.

Feyenoord's triumph was the start of a four-season period of Dutch dominance. Ajax kept the trophy in the Netherlands for the next three years. The balance of power in Europe had definitely swung to the Low Countries, but British football had enjoyed a spectacular season across the three competitions in 1969/70, two cup winners and a finalist. In fact, starting with Celtic's 1967 European Cup win, Britain had won six trophies, and there was more to come.

Although nobody could deny the glamour of European football, it also came with certain challenges, such as violence on the pitch, xenophobia, nationalism and no small amount of tension. Some critics wondered whether it was really worth it, while others pondered on the idea of a British Isles competition. For decades, football romantics had toyed with the concept of Celtic and Rangers playing in the Football League, but the possible consequences for Scottish domestic football always deterred any reformers from taking any tangible steps to make that a reality. However, in 1970, Texaco, the oil company, sponsored a competition involving English, Scottish, Northern Irish and Irish clubs. It would not include any club who had qualified for Europe, but its compact, 16-team format did have its appeal.

There were six teams from England – Burnley, Nottingham Forest, Stoke City, Tottenham, West Bromwich Albion and Wolves – six from Scotland, including Hearts, Dundee and Dunfermline, and two apiece from the Irelands. The eventual winners of the inaugural competition were Wolves, who beat Hearts in the two-legged final. Both Wolves and Tottenham got a taste for their return to Europe in 1971/72. The Texaco Cup lasted four seasons and the English contingent won the rather impressive trophy every single time: Derby, Ipswich and Newcastle followed Wolves.

The competition pointed the way for the growing commercialisation of football. Sponsorship of this type had been slow to enter football, but the door was now open. The Watney Cup also started in 1970, a pre-season competition of eight teams, the two top scorers who had not qualified for Europe in each of the four divisions. Some saw it as selling out, but in truth it proved to be the salvation of the game. Qualifying for Europe started to become a tangible sign of success for clubs. There were only three major trophies in English football – league, FA Cup and League Cup – so securing a place in Europe was the next best thing. The growing importance of pan-European competition was one of the reasons why the ugly child, the Inter-Cities Fairs Cup was disbanded and UEFA took over with a 64-team UEFA Cup. From 1971, this became a very strong, highly coveted competition that was also a test of endurance.

11

A Recopa Treble

UNTIL MANCHESTER United won the European Cup in 1968, it was largely felt that English clubs fared better in the two lesser competitions. By 1969/70, English clubs had won the Cup Winners' Cup in 1963 and 1965 and the Fairs Cup in 1968 and 1969.

This could have been explained away as a symptom of the strength in depth of the English game or, in the case of the Cup Winners' Cup, indication of the importance of the FA Cup.

It was a popular opinion in Britain that the rest of Europe did not take their cup competitions as seriously as the English and Scottish. The FA Cup Final in the 1960s was a 'must-see' event that left the streets of England's towns and cities empty of activity as even the most uncommitted person sat in front of the television to see the blanket coverage that dominated from breakfast to tea time.

The British perception that the cup did not matter elsewhere was flawed, however, as in Portugal, Spain and West Germany, the cup winners were generally higher-placed teams than in England. Only Italy came near to England's list of middling winners between 1961/62 and 1967/68.

Tottenham had disappointed in 1967/68, going out of the Cup Winners' Cup in the second round to Lyon. West Bromwich Albion, who had surprisingly won the FA Cup in 1968, rose to the challenge well in 1968/69, as did their Scottish counterparts, Dunfermline Athletic. The two sides had worked their way through to the last eight, with Albion beating Dynamo Bucharest – emphatically – and then Brugge on away goals. Dunfermline had thrashed Apoel of Cyprus 12-1 on aggregate and went back to the Mediterranean region to beat Greece's Olympiacos, 4-3. The draw paired the two British clubs together in a mini-England versus Scotland clash.

Most pundits expected West Bromwich Albion to win, although they were enduring a rather patchy and inconsistent season. They eventually reached the last four of the FA Cup, losing to Leicester City, but their league form was poor by the time they met Dunfermline. The first match at East End Park finished goalless, although Dunfermline pounded the Albion defence, who were taken aback by the speed of the home attack. Albion had a good team in 1969, which included talented players such as Jeff Astle, Tony Brown, Asa Hartford and Bobby Hope. They were confident of winning through at The Hawthorns during a period of extremely cold weather. Given that the stadium, at 168 metres above sea level was – and still is – the highest of all the 92 Football League grounds, the weather could be bitter.

Albion's gloved players found it difficult to play well in the second leg; in fact, both teams were having trouble on the bone-hard pitch. The crowd was restless and began chanting 'we want football', so poor was the entertainment. Dunfermline took a second-minute lead when a free kick deflected into the air and Pat Gardner headed past a static John Osborne. Albion had 90 per cent of the play, but resorted to punting high balls into the penalty area towards Astle. It did not work and Dunfermline went through 1-0. Sadly for the Scots, they were unable to get past Slovan Bratislava, who went on to win the cup, beating Barcelona 3-2 in Basel.

Manchester City won the FA Cup in 1968/69 and returned to Europe as England's representatives in the European Cup Winners' Cup. City had tasted UEFA competition in 1968 when, as league champions, they entered the European Cup. They were confident as their team was young, played adventurously and they had a brash coach in Malcolm Allison, who dovetailed nicely with manager Joe Mercer. When City were drawn to meet Turkey's Fenerbahçe in the European Cup, Allison promised that City would 'terrify Europe'. Unfortunately, they went out at the first hurdle, 2-1 on aggregate.

They were determined to put on a better show this time, especially as their cross-town rivals, Manchester United, were not in Europe in 1969/70. Their first opponents were Athletic Bilbao, who were managed by former England forward Ronnie Allen, a prolific goalscorer who netted more than 230 goals for West Bromwich Albion. Allen had moved to Spain in 1969 and led Bilbao to the league runners-up spot in his first season.

City made a protracted journey to Bilbao and drew 3-3 with the home team, who were backed by a fiery crowd. City were the first to admit that they had been lucky and that the draw was rather flukey. Their final equaliser was an own goal by Echeverria but Allen blamed legendary goalkeeper José Ángel Iribar for a series of blunders that allowed City back into the game. 'Sometimes he is the best goalkeeper in the world, but tonight he was the worst,' he said, rather harshly. Today, Iribar's statue stands outside Bilbao's San Mamés stadium.

City were fancied to win the tie and, at Maine Road, they easily disposed of the Basque team. But the game did not pass without a hint of controversy for at half-time there seemed to be a scuffle in the players' tunnel. Allen claimed that several of the Bilbao players saw City's number four, Mike Doyle, strike midfielder Betzuen. Whatever did happen, Betzuen could not finish the game due to a nasty back injury. City won 3-0 with goals from Alan Oakes, Colin Bell and Ian Bowyer.

Lierse SK were next for City, a club that went bankrupt in 2018. Lierse won the Belgian Cup in 1969, beating another club that is no longer around, Racing White. City were simply too strong for Lierse, and Francis Lee and Colin Bell were in exceptional form, making strong claims for a place in the England squad for the 1970 World Cup. They were 3-0 up at half-time in the away leg but there were no more goals in the second half; however, City earned a rousing ovation from the home crowd.

The tie was more or less settled, which explained why only 26,000 attended the second leg at Maine Road on a cold, frosty November night. The pitch was slippery, but once City settled they scored five more goals past an uncertain Lierse defence. Once more, Lee and Bell were on song, scoring two apiece, with another England hopeful, Mike Summerbee, also on the scoresheet. City were through to the quarter-finals, but Rangers did not join them after losing 3-1 on the night and 6-2 on aggregate against a strong Górnik Zabrze side.

City's season was inconsistent to say the least; while their league form was patchy, they were definitely feared in cup competitions. Their Football League Cup campaign saw them beat Liverpool, Everton and Manchester United on the way to a final with West Bromwich Albion. Going into 1970, City seemed to have lost their way with two wins in 11 games. They ended a barren spell with two league wins before they went to Portugal to face Académica de Coimbra, an amateur team of students. They had qualified for the Cup Winners' Cup by losing to Portuguese double-winners Benfica after taking a first-minute lead in the final of the Taça de Portugal.

The first leg in the university town of Coimbra ended goalless but there was a scare for City captain Tony Book, who limped off and faced a battle to be fit for the Football League Cup Final three days later. Book won that fight and City beat West Bromwich Albion 2-1 after extra time on an energy-sapping Wembley pitch. City were expected to overcome Académica at Maine Road in the second leg, but the Portuguese side were tough and could be uncompromising. The match was frustrating for City and they had a succession of players who were injured by the tackles and challenges of the 'tough-guy students' of Coimbra. Doyle was carried off, Bell left the field with a thigh injury and George Heslop had to be heavily bandaged. It was still 0-0 after 90 minutes, so an extra half-hour was required. It was more of the same, with Académica adopting a stifling approach and a strategy aimed at upsetting City's skilful players. The *Manchester Evening News* declared that they were a team of 'Portuguese men o' war' and they very nearly took City to a play-off game in Amsterdam. That was until 17-year-old substitute Tony Towers scored an 119th-minute goal from 20 yards after Neil Young's high cross landed well for him.

City were tipped to win the competition, but the other semi-finalists were all difficult opponents: Schalke 04 of West Germany, Italian side Roma and Górnik Zabrze of Poland. City drew Schalke, a team from the Ruhr region and a well-supported club that had won a place in the competition as runners-up to Bayern Munich in the DFB

Pokal. Bayern had also won the Bundesliga, so as double-winners they went into the European Cup. Schalke were now a mid-table side, but they had Reinhard Libuda and Klaus Fichtel in their line-up. Libuda had made an impact in European competition earlier in his career with Borussia Dortmund. He was a clever wing-man who acquired the nickname 'Stan' as a reference to Stanley Matthews. Fichtel, although less spectacular than Libuda, was a versatile professional who could play in defence or midfield.

Schalke had made hard work of some of their games in the competition, beating Shamrock Rovers, Norrköping of Sweden and Yugoslavia's Dinamo Zagreb. The press of the time made the most of the England versus Germany reference, but mostly they were warning City of the threat posed by Libuda. And it was a threat, because he scored the only goal of a tight game in Gelsenkirchen, running 50 yards before sending the ball past Joe Corrigan, who was left sprawling on a treacherous pitch. Joe Mercer was far from downhearted, however, as City had played well and deserved a draw in a game hampered by snow and ice. 'These fellows are by no means dancing in the Vienna woods yet,' he quipped, referencing the venue for the final.

City's league season was almost over, but they clearly had their minds on other things. After beating West Bromwich Albion at Wembley, they forgot how to score goals and were thrashed at Maine Road by West Ham. Prior to the second leg against Schalke, they had failed to find the back of the net in four of their five games. They had, however, recently beaten Manchester United at Old Trafford, but, essentially, City were destined for a mid-table finish.

Their game with Schalke was one of three big semi-final ties involving British clubs: Arsenal were as good as home and dry in the Fairs Cup after taking a three-goal lead against Ajax, while Celtic and Leeds were meeting at Hampden Park. City had the potential to wipe out the one-goal deficit from the first meeting in Germany. And so it proved, for within nine minutes Doyle had cancelled out Libuda's strike that had given Schalke that fragile advantage. Then Young, who had been suffering from a crisis of confidence, scored twice, in the 14th and 27th minutes. City were in command and had a three-goal first-half lead. Lee added a fourth, and nine minutes from the end of a scintillating game Bell made it five. Libuda, inevitably, scored a consolation for Schalke in the final seconds. City had made it through to the final, their third in two seasons, but they did not know who their opponents would be until 22 April when Górnik and Roma met in a play-off in Strasbourg. After three drawn encounters, the Polish side went through after the flip of a coin!

City's fans were overjoyed. One trophy already in the Maine Road cabinet, United struggling, and another final to look forward to, in Vienna, one of the most charming cities in Europe. This really was a golden period for the club; they had won all the domestic honours in a three-year period, and now they had the chance to show Europe who they really were. After the semi-final second leg, City fans rushed to make their plans for the final. One travel agency in the heart of Manchester, a specialist in overseas football trips, was besieged by 500 supporters as flights were booked. By the end of 17 April, some 1,300 had booked their places for the Austrian capital.

This was the start of the 1970s, so industrial action was not an uncommon threat to smooth-running airports. As City prepared to fly to Vienna, a strike was threatened by ground staff at Manchester airport. The team eventually made it to Austria along with around 4,000 fans from Manchester versus 150 from Poland. The Prater stadium was at the end of the famous Prater Park, which was featured in Carol Reed's award-winning movie, *The Third Man*. It was one of Europe's most iconic arenas at the time, but in 1970 it was completely uncovered and exposed to the elements. Vienna was wet on 29 April 1970 and for all but around 15 minutes of the final it rained heavily. This undoubtedly affected the attendance and restricted it to less than 10,000.

City were without Summerbee, but young Tony Towers was an able replacement. Along with Joe Corrigan and Tommy Booth, they were the only changes from the club's 1968 league title win. City started well in Vienna, going ahead after 12 minutes when Young finished from close range after Lee's 30-yard shot had struck the post and rebounded invitingly. Shortly afterwards, Doyle was replaced after damaging his ankle tendons and Górnik started to threaten, notably through Włodzimierz Lubański. But City strengthened their hold on the cup when they scored a second goal two minutes from the interval. Young was brought down in the area and Lee's powerful penalty went in via the legs of Górnik keeper Hubert Kostka.

Górnik pulled a goal back in the 68th minute when Lubański created a chance for Stanisław Oślizło, but it was not enough to save the game. At the final whistle Malcolm Allison sprinted on to the pitch to congratulate his players. 'It was a great triumph and all-round show. I am delighted most of all because we've done it on the continent. Manchester United and West Ham won their trophies at Wembley.' Joe Mercer, meanwhile, could not praise his players enough: 'Tonight the lads proved they are the greatest. Naturally, the goals won it for us, but the overriding factor was that we had the moral courage to have a go at them.' Mercer felt that if Doyle had stayed on City's victory would have been more comprehensive. There was also praise for George Heslop, who had been brought in as a second centre-half to counter the threat of Lubański, as well as Young, whose season had taken a turn for the better.

Not even reports of crowd trouble in Vienna and the behaviour of some fans could spoil the day for City. Their fourth major prize in three seasons underlined what an exciting team they were. But, with the exception of the Football League Cup in 1976, a golden age was drawing to an end in the Prater.

On the same evening, Chelsea qualified for the 1970/71 Cup Winners' Cup by beating Leeds United in the FA Cup Final replay, so there would be two English clubs in the competition and, little did they know it, they would come face to face for a place in the 1971 final.

Chelsea had one of the stronger squads in the First Division and in the summer of 1970 had paid £100,000 for Millwall's Keith Weller. He had slotted in well at his new club but their star man, Peter Osgood, who had netted 31 goals in 1969/70 and played in the 1970 World Cup in Mexico, was struggling to find his goal touch. Chelsea were drawn against Greece's Aris Salonika in the first round of the Cup Winners' Cup and were expected to win comfortably. They had lost just once in their eight league games, but five of these had been drawn and only two won. They were not quite clicking as they had in 1969/70, but they were notorious slow starters.

The big problem for Chelsea was the heat in Greece. When they prepared for the first leg in Salonika, the temperature was over 90°F. Aris had some good players, notably internationals Nikos Christidis, Angelos Spyridon and Takis Loukanides. They also had a proven goalscorer in Alekos Alexiadis, who was regularly near the top of the goalscorers list in Greece. Aris did not make Chelsea feel very welcome on the pitch and adopted a strategy of upsetting the Londoners with high tackles, gamesmanship and shirt-tugging. The pitch, described as a 'tufted desert' by renowned journalist Geoffrey Green, made life very difficult for the FA Cup holders. They lost centre-half John Dempsey in the 36th minute, a minute after Osgood had missed a penalty, largely because he had been distracted and unnerved by several minutes' protest at the decision. Aris went a goal ahead through Alexiadis, who shot home after Bonetti had turned a cross on to the woodwork. Chelsea had a reputation for coming back from deficits, as they had done in the replayed FA Cup Final earlier in the year. They showed those qualities in Salonika, equalising ten minutes from the end through Ian Hutchinson, who volleyed past Christidis after Charlie Cooke had crossed and Osgood nodded the ball back for his strike partner.

Two weeks later, Aris arrived for the second leg. 'We have come to London to make a good show and we accept, after watching Arsenal play Ipswich, the English game is very powerful. We shall be determined but we hope to play without trouble,' said an Aris official. Chelsea were in excellent form and constantly battered the Greek defence at Stamford Bridge. By half-time, it was 3-0 to Chelsea, with two goals from tireless midfielder John Hollins and a header from Hutchinson. Two more goals followed early in the second half, one from Marvin Hinton and another from Hutchinson. It was not until five minutes from the end that Alexiadis scored for Aris, who were given a good reception by the 40,000 crowd. They departed as friends and promising Chelsea that should they reach the final in Athens they would have the help of 50,000 fans in Greece.

Their next obstacle was CSKA Sofia, a very strong team, rated one of the best in Europe. CSKA was an abbreviation for 'The Central Sports Club of the Army' and they were the most successful club in Bulgaria at the time. Along with Levski, their big rivals, the city of Sofia dominated Bulgarian football. In 1969/70, Levski had won the double, beating CSKA in the Bulgarian cup final and finishing three points ahead of them in the league. Virtually every member of the CSKA squad was an international – the advantage of being the army club – and, by the time the players finished their careers, they had a combined haul of caps in excess of 500. Dimitar Yakimov, Dimitar Penev, Dimitar Marashliev, Boris Gaganelov, Asparuh Nikodimov and Petar Zhekov – the UEFA Golden Boot winner in 1970 – were all part of the Bulgarian squad that went to Mexico for the World Cup. CSKA's coach, Manol Manolov, predicted his team would win the first leg by three goals, but the Bulgarian press were generous in their praise of Chelsea, describing them as the strongest side to visit the country in years.

So enthused were the locals that 500 people turned up to watch Chelsea train. The Vasil Levsky Stadium, where the game was played, had an excellent surface and floodlights far advanced of those seen in England. Chelsea settled well in these conditions and a first-half goal by Tommy Baldwin after Keith Weller had sent a low cross to the far post was enough to win the game 1-0. Osgood stole the show, however, with his elegant play, even if his finishing was still below his high standards. CSKA had a similar problem with their own Zhekov, who had struggled to find the form that made him Europe's top scorer.

CSKA adopted a muscular approach for the second meeting in London. As well as bruising challenges and cynical tackles from behind, they simply tried to upset Chelsea's flow. It did not work, however, for Dave Sexton's team demonstrated restraint and patience. They also played rather cautiously, aware that CSKA were a dangerous team who were experts in counter-attacking. Similar to the first leg, Chelsea scored just before the half-time whistle; Peter Houseman's cross was headed on by Weller, and David Webb, the club's FA Cup hero just a few months earlier, slid the ball past goalkeeper Yordan Filipov.

CSKA had Kiril Stankov sent off for punching substitute John Boyle in the stomach and the game became very untidy, but the Bulgarians never looked as though they would score a goal, even though Bonetti had to pull off a spectacular save from Nikodimov. Their coach, Manolov, was not over-impressed with Chelsea: 'I do not think they will win the cup because they are not a good footballing side.'

Chelsea's players, in recalling the 1970/71 Cup Winners' Cup, regarded CSKA as the hardest opponents they faced in the competition. Chelsea were through to the quarter-finals along with Manchester City, the holders, and Cardiff City. City had made hard work of Linfield in the first round but then put on two excellent performances against Honvéd. Their 1-0 win in the Kispest Stadium, Budapest, was regarded as being a very important moment for English football by Malcolm Allison. 'Now these Hungarians know we can play a bit here, too,' he said, referencing England's humbling at the hands of the Mighty Magyars in 1953. It was a little bit of bravado by Allison but, nevertheless, an impressive result. The second leg was played in incessant Manchester rain and City won 2-0. The Honvéd coach, Kalman Preiner, blamed the weather: 'My players were lost in the heavy going. Manchester City's players were not. They rose above it, but we had it on our minds. We were not able to play our normal game and we got worse and worse.'

Cardiff had thrashed Cypriot side Pezoporikos Larnaca 8-0 at Ninian Park in the first round, with a young John Toshack scoring twice. They drew the second leg 0-0 and went on to meet France's Nantes in round two. The Bluebirds were goal-happy again at home, winning 5-1 after conceding a goal in the first minute. Even more notable was the second leg, which they won 2-1. The draw in Paris had a touch of glamour about it as French singer Mireille Mathieu picked the teams out of the hat. Cardiff were rewarded with a phenomenal tie for Welsh football, Real Madrid, arguably the biggest club in Europe. Cardiff's manager, Jimmy Scoular, was hoping for a big game for his club: 'It's just what we wanted, I really am very pleased about it and, what's more, I think we stand a good chance of beating them.' Chelsea and Manchester City avoided each other and were drawn against Brugge and Górnik, respectively. The other tie was between PSV Eindhoven and East Germans Vorwärts.

By the time the quarter-finals came around in March 1971, Chelsea had lost some of their verve and had suffered injuries and had endured a long-term suspension for Osgood. Chelsea's other main forward, Hutchinson was sidelined with various ailments and became one of football's unluckiest players in the early 1970s. Furthermore, Peter Bonetti had suffered from illness and Sexton had been using young reserve keeper John Phillips. They missed Bonetti, but the form of Phillips meant that the real loss to the team was Osgood. Chelsea still won matches, but they looked more workmanlike without their talisman. The Brugge stadium was not big, but the supporters were close to the pitch and the incessant noise of klaxons made for an intimidating atmosphere. Around 1,500 Chelsea fans crossed the English Channel to attend the game. Brugge dominated and went ahead very early on with a header from an in-swinging corner by Raoul Lambert. Chelsea were outplayed at times and really could not get into the game. Only John Hollins emerged from the game with any credit, but once Brugge scored their second just before half-time through Marmenout, it was clear Chelsea faced a real challenge at Stamford Bridge. A two-goal defeat was not the end of the world and Dave Sexton tried desperately to talk things up: 'We'll win the return [...] I am confident we can wipe out the deficit.'

Meanwhile, Cardiff City sent 47,000 fans into a frenzy by beating Real Madrid in the first leg of their quarter-final. Admittedly, this was not the Real of old, but they were still one of Europe's top clubs. Cardiff won 1-0 when Brian Clark, who had been brought in to replace the ineligible Alan Warboys, met a cross from Nigel Rees and headed home. Their midfielder, Ian Gibson, was outstanding, but picked up an injury that would keep him out of the second leg. Manchester City, like Chelsea, had a two-goal defeat to contend with in Poland. Górnik, who City had beaten in the 1970 final, gained some revenge with a 2-0 win, and not many pundits expected them to overcome the Poles in the return in Manchester.

When the second legs came around, it was largely seen as a night that could see British hopes decimated. Chelsea had decided to bring in Peter Osgood after his two-month suspension and he had clearly decided to avoid the hairdressers during his time out – the fans' favourite returned with a hairstyle that looked remarkably like an Afro. Although he was running on fumes for much of the game due to his enforced absence, Osgood lifted the crowd and the team. The first half saw Brugge play very cautiously to contain the home team, but Houseman, who had an excellent game, put Chelsea ahead. It stayed that way until eight minutes from the end when Osgood scored and embarked on something that resembled a war dance, eventually being engulfed by fans. Into extra time, Hudson created goals for Osgood (114 minutes) and Baldwin (120) to give Chelsea a spectacular 4-0 win that people who were in the 46,000 crowd still talk about more than 50 years after the event.

Manchester City, thanks to goals from Ian Mellor and Mike Doyle, turned around their tie against Górnik and booked a play-off in Copenhagen, which they won 3-1. Cardiff City put on a brave show in Madrid, holding out until the second half, but goals from Velasquez and Fleitas gave the Spaniards a 2-1 aggregate victory. Chelsea and City were drawn to meet each other in the semi-final, which was met with some disappointment. Joe Mercer, the City manager, would have preferred an all-English final, but he was only too aware that Dave Sexton's team would be out to gain some revenge on City after they had ended Chelsea's FA Cup hopes earlier in the year at Stamford Bridge. The other semi-final was between Real Madrid and PSV Eindhoven.

Chelsea and Manchester City had met each other twice already during 1970/71; the league game in London ended 1-1, but City won 3-0 in that FA Cup fourth-round tie, with Colin Bell tearing Chelsea apart. Both teams had lost some momentum in the second half of the season and, by the time they came face to face in the Cup Winners' Cup, both were suffering from injuries, particularly City. For the first leg, Chelsea could only call on six of their FA Cup-winning line-up, while City were without Bell, Summerbee, Doyle, Alan Oakes and Glyn Pardoe. Chelsea's wounded included Osgood, Hutchinson, Hudson and Bonetti. There was an unfamiliar look about both sides, with Chelsea including South African forward Derek Smethurst, a young centre-half in Micky Droy and using regular defender Webb as centre-forward.

Chelsea laid siege to the City defence for most of the game, but they lacked the guile to take advantage of a team that had arrived at Stamford Bridge to simply contain the home team. The crowd was restless but Chelsea were limited to a 1-0 win thanks to Smethurst's goal just after half-time. It was a very narrow margin for Chelsea and the smart money was on City winning through to the final. Three days after the first leg, the two teams drew 1-1 in a league game at Maine Road.

The second leg was, once more, a case of two teams deprived of regulars – 'the lame, the sick and the inexperienced' – although Chelsea's squad had more depth, so they could bring in players such as John Boyle and Paddy Mulligan, although they were now without the ever-reliable Hollins. City blooded young players such as Ron Healey, Jeff Johnson and Derek Jeffries, and their rawness showed through on 28 April. Chelsea relied on counter-attacks and grit to settle the semi-final. With three minutes remaining of the first half, Keith Weller sent an in-swinging free kick towards goal, which deceived Healey, who could only help the ball into the net. The young keeper was distraught, but Chelsea knew that they had done enough to win the tie. They deserved to go through and players such as Boyle and Cooke had been outstanding in a very industrious performance. Dave Sexton must have been relieved that Bell had not been fit enough to play, for he was always a difficult opponent for Chelsea. Malcolm Allison, City's assistant manager, was not able to take part in the game as he was on a two-month ban, but he was as outspoken as ever after the match. 'City's players were afraid before they started, they didn't really try to win,' he said.

Just a year after winning the FA Cup in Manchester, Chelsea had pulled off a major victory in the same city to secure a place in the European Cup Winners' Cup Final.

Their opponents were Real Madrid, who had beaten PSV Eindhoven in the other semi-final. Real were in unfamiliar territory; they were not in the European Cup for the first time since 1955. There were stories that the club was rather embarrassed to be in the Cup Winners' Cup, but they had won the Spanish Cup in 1970, beating Valencia, and they would not be returning to the premier competition in 1971/72.

Real did have some outstanding players, even if they were not quite the equals of the team that won five consecutive European Cups. Almost all of their team were internationals and there were notables like Paco Gento, Amancio, Pirri and Ignacio Zoco. Gento, arguably the last link with the glory days, was 37; Amancio, who had appeared in the 1966 World Cup and 1964 European Championships, and Zoco, the captain, were both 31; Pirri, who could play in defence or midfield, was 26 and still had plenty of mileage in his career. Real's manager was their former captain, Miguel Muñoz, who was part of the history of the European Cup. He claimed that he did not know much about Chelsea, but he had heard about Sexton and Osgood. Muñoz had little chance to see them in action, but he did get to Ipswich for their final league game, an uninspiring 0-0 draw at Portman Road. There were 18 days between that game and the final in Athens. Hollins faced an uphill struggle to get fit and Osgood was wrapped in cotton wool to ensure he was available. The England forward was crucial for Chelsea, not just for his sublime skills, but also from a team morale perspective. He was over his injury, but clearly lacking match fitness. He had, prior to the final, played just three times in four months.

In the Karaiskakis Stadium in Athens, the locals were behind Chelsea, but that would soon change. It was a tetchy opening but, ten minutes into the second half, Cooke and

Boyle combined to set up Osgood, who sent a low shot wide of Borja. The deadlock had been broken, but it seemed to inspire Real to start displaying their talent. Chelsea held out until the 92nd minute when Zoco, who had been pushed into attack, finally beat Bonetti. Psychologically, Real had the upper hand as the game went into extra time. Bonetti, who had been sidelined for long periods in the season, was in superb form and pulled off a series of saves to underline why he was, until the ill-fated 1970 World Cup, England's second-choice goalkeeper behind Gordon Banks. So the final went to a replay, to be held two days later in the same stadium.

Chelsea lost half of their support and there was a slight feeling of deflation among players and fans. Hollins, who had been substituted in the first game, was not fit, but Sexton brought in Baldwin to partner Osgood. They started well, despite the general consensus that Real were now favourites, and went into a 2-0 lead inside 38 minutes. Firstly, John Dempsey, who felt some responsibility for Real's late equaliser, volleyed home on 31 minutes after Borja had punched out a Houseman corner. Then Osgood was on target again, shooting low into the net after receiving a pass from Baldwin. For a while, Chelsea looked comfortable, but Real pressed for much of the second half and, with 15 minutes to go, Fleitas pulled a goal back. Again Bonetti was on song, with support from Webb, described as a 'Trojan' by the Greek press, and Cooke continued to keep Real focused. Bonetti's very late save from Fleitas effectively won the day and allowed Chelsea to beat the mighty Real Madrid 2-1. The Spaniards were crestfallen and refused to enter their dressing room for almost an hour after the final whistle. 'This gives me more pleasure than winning the FA Cup last season,' admitted Sexton. Who would have known, at that moment, that Chelsea would not win another prize for 26 years?

Chelsea were among the favourites for the Cup Winners' Cup in 1971/72, and being drawn against Luxembourg's Jeunesse Hautcharage in the first round was a good way to find their shooting boots after a poor start to the season. They won 21-0 over two legs, including a 13-0 victory at home in which Osgood scored five goals, bringing his total to eight in the tie. However, Chelsea made a mess of the next round against unfancied Åtvidaberg of Sweden, going out on away goals. Liverpool, who had qualified as runners-up to double-winning Arsenal in the FA Cup, also exited in the second round, losing to Bayern Munich. British hopes were left in the hands of Rangers, who eased past Rennes 2-1 on aggregate and then won on away goals against Sporting Lisbon. The Gers almost self-destructed against the Portuguese after going 3-0 ahead in the first half of the first leg at Ibrox, conceding two goals after the interval to take a narrow advantage to Lisbon. They lost 4-3 in the second leg but went through on away goals.

Rangers did not have an easy path in the competition and had to work hard for their quarter-final victory against Torino. In Italy they stunned the 35,000 crowd into silence when they took the lead through Willie Johnston then held out until the hour mark when Guido Toschi equalised. Rangers played an unfamiliar defensive game, but it worked wonders against a technically gifted Torino team. The return was tight, with very little flair on show, but Rangers scored the only goal in the 47th minute when Alex MacDonald bundled the ball over the goal line after Tommy McLean had run from his own half down the wing and crossed to the far post.

Now it was the semi-finals for Rangers and a tough tie with Bayern Munich, who had beaten them in 1970/71.

Rangers demonstrated their character by carving out a 1-1 draw in Munich, thanks to an own goal by Rainer Zobel that equalised Paul Breitner's opener for Bayern. There were great expectations for the second leg and 80,000 filled Ibrox. Within a minute, Sandy Jardine opened the scoring and, 20 minutes later, 18-year-old Derek Parlane added a second. The tie was as good as won by half-time and Bayern were very frustrated, so much so that Franz Beckenbauer was seen taunting the crowd, who had ironically cheered a bad ball by the legendary West German skipper. Rangers were through to their third European final, to face Dynamo Moscow, who had beaten Dynamo Berlin in the last four.

The Rangers team that lined up in Barcelona's Camp Nou was a mix of home-grown talent and some costly signings. Colin Stein was signed from Hibernian for a Scottish record of £100,000, while McLean and MacDonald both cost £65,000, from Kilmarnock and St Johnstone, respectively. The team also included Jardine and John Greig in defence and Johnston on the wing.

Dynamo Moscow had made an impact in Britain in 1945 when they toured the country and played Chelsea, Arsenal, Cardiff and Rangers. They remained unbeaten, drawing 2-2 with Rangers in Glasgow and 3-3 with Chelsea, while beating Cardiff 10-1 and Arsenal 4-3. The crowd for the final was a paltry 25,000 but, for obvious reasons given the international climate of the time, there was very little presence from Moscow. The Scots made the most of it, however, arriving in Barcelona and nearby resorts such as Lloret de Mar, where trouble had broken out ahead of the final. The Rangers fans had Barcelona to themselves, packing the bars and restaurants and treating the occasion as a holiday. They travelled by over 100 chartered flights from Glasgow as well as by car and train.

They were convinced that Rangers would win what was their third European final.

The game itself was exciting and full of drama. Stein opened the scoring after 23 minutes, flicking home a cross from Johnston. Then Johnston himself netted the first of his two goals in the 40th minute, heading a Dave Smith centre into the net. Five minutes into the second period, Johnston, looking suspiciously offside, raced towards goal and shot past goalkeeper Vladimir Pilguy. Three goals ahead, the trophy looked won, but Dynamo scored twice midway through the half and added some tension to the remainder of the game.

The final whistle heralded a pitch invasion, which got rather nasty at times. A Dynamo Moscow player was hit over the head with a bottle, and seating was ripped up and thrown around the pitch. Some Rangers fans fought with police, who had been reinforced with a special riot squad. Gustav Wiederkehr, the Swiss president of UEFA, was incensed: 'The Scottish fans behaved like savages. We must find ways to keep such people away from the stadiums.' It was so frenetic that Rangers had to be presented with the cup in the dressing room, with a very muted reaction from UEFA, who simply handed it over with the words 'winners, Glasgow Rangers'.

There were over 100 arrests at the game and many fans missed their flights back to Scotland. The Dynamo Moscow officials – including legendary goalkeeper Lev Yashin, who was team manager – were angry and confused. They called for the game to be replayed due to the abnormal conditions – there had been no less than five pitch invasions – and the Russian Football Federation sent a telegram to UEFA supporting their club. The Soviet press agency, TASS, hoped that UEFA would take notice: 'We pin our hopes on the objectivity of UEFA, who must order a replay.' It did not happen and Rangers eventually got home to be greeted by 25,000 fans jockeying for a glimpse of the Cup Winners' Cup. The finale had not been what people had wanted, but Rangers had, at last, carved their name on European football, even if it did come with a two-year ban, which was later reduced to 12 months.

12

An All-English Affair

THE INTER-CITIES Fairs Cup, which was effectively administered by FIFA officials, had an uncertain future from the mid-1960s. There were proposals for the competition to come under the auspices of UEFA, but there was a certain reluctance from figures such as Sir Stanley Rous to pass the baton on. The Fairs Cup was self-regulated and there was often a lack of consistency in the way it was scheduled and how it sat within the international calendar.

In the spirit of bringing the Fairs Cup concept in line with the European Cup and European Cup Winners' Cup, UEFA was supposed to take the competition over in 1969, but it took two years to come to fruition. Initially, it was expected to be called 'The European Union Cup', but they settled on the UEFA Cup and, for a while, the media and clubs were not sure if it was EUFA or UEFA. Although it was, essentially, a case of same bottle, different label, the competition was no longer an ugly duckling and had moved from representative teams in its early days to include some of the continent's top clubs. UEFA commissioned a new trophy, engaging Italian sculptor Silvio Gazzaniga to come up with something that was modern and clearly of its time. The Milan-based Gazzaniga also designed the

FIFA World Cup. The UEFA Cup weighed 15 kilograms, was made of silver and sat on two onyx discs. Although the Fairs Cup was a beautiful piece of *objet d'art* in itself, it was more representative of another age. The first winners, Barcelona, beat the 1971 winners, Leeds United, in a play-off to decide who kept the redundant trophy.

The Fairs Cup had a ruling that only one club from each city could enter but UEFA decided to discard that rather inane rule. But the Football League decided to impose its own restriction, which was not well received by clubs from London, Manchester and Liverpool. There were 63 clubs from 31 associations in the first competition in 1971/72, with four from England, three from Scotland and one apiece from the two Irelands. There were also four clubs from each of West Germany, Italy and Spain. There were some very notable teams involved, including previous European Cup winners AC Milan and Real Madrid, and other huge names such as Juventus, Napoli, Hamburg, Porto, Atlético Madrid, Athletic Bilbao and, of course, Leeds United, Tottenham Hotspur, Wolverhampton Wanderers and Southampton were also in the mix. And then there were the big names from Eastern Europe: Spartak Moscow, Ferencváros, Rapid Bucharest, Dinamo Zagreb and Legia Warsaw, among others.

There was considerable enthusiasm for the competition, but it could never compete with the European Cup; in 1971/72, games in the UEFA Cup had an average crowd of 17,000 compared to the 33,000 that attended European Cup ties. However, in those leagues that had a certain strength in depth, the competition's 64 teams and the possibility of some big fish being involved meant the UEFA Cup gained a reputation for being a tough competition to win. In the early stages, though, it was not unusual to be confronted with some weak opposition. Tottenham, for example, were drawn against Keflavík, a little-known club that had finished third in the 1970 Icelandic league. Iceland was a footballing backwater in 1971 and the national team did not enter the World Cup in 1970. They were also absent from the European Championship. Everton had played Keflavík in the 1970/71 European Cup and had beaten them 9-2 on aggregate. Bill Nicholson admitted that he expected his team to win through comfortably: 'We've never been here before and I have no first-hand knowledge about the team we must beat.' Nicholson did call on Everton manager Harry Catterick to get some idea of how Keflavík would play and this only confirmed what he expected – Spurs would have to be at their very worst not to win handsomely.

Fewer than 2,000 people saw the first leg, which ended with Spurs winning 6-1 in Iceland. Alan Gilzean scored a hat-trick, Alan Mullery netted twice and Ralph Coates, Spurs' close-season signing from Burnley, grabbed his first goal for the club. The Keflavík goalkeeper, 20-year-old Thorsteinn Ólafsson, who had just won his first cap for Iceland, had a very busy evening as Spurs bombarded his goal. In the second half, Nicholson decided to send on 18-year-old Graeme Souness as a substitute for Mullery. Souness was a player who would make his mark with Liverpool and Scotland in the years ahead; however, his brief run-out in Iceland was his only appearance for Spurs.

The second leg offered no respite for Keflavík as Spurs tore them apart at White Hart Lane. The game ended 9-0, with Martin Chivers, revelling in the loose marking, now helping himself to a hat-trick and Gilzean adding two to his three from the first leg. Steve Perryman, Coates and Cyril Knowles also got on the scoresheet as well as another Spurs youngster, Phil Holder. The Keflavík coach, Einar

Helgason, was brimming with compliments for the hosts, claiming his team had been beaten by 'the best team in European football'.

Praise indeed, but that title was often used to describe Leeds United, who were still smarting from losing the league title race in 1970/71. Leeds were getting to grips with playing their first four home games away from Elland Road due to crowd trouble in the latter part of the season. They also had a spate of injuries to deal with, one of the problems of having a rather minimalist squad.

Leeds, who appeared to have perfected the art of two-legged ties, were drawn against Lierse SK of Belgium, a team described as 'fit and well organised' by Don Revie. Leeds fielded a weak side by their own standards, bringing in Terry Yorath, John Faulkner, Chris Galvin, Rod Belfitt and Mick Bates. They won 2-0, but Lierse were impressive and very eager into the tackle. In the second leg, Revie gambled by leaving his first-choice goalkeeper, Gary Sprake, on the bench along with Norman Hunter and also resting Jack Charlton. It was another below-strength line-up, but a two-goal margin looked to be enough. It was a gamble that completely backfired as the Belgians went into a three-goal lead by the interval. It was a shock result for readers of the national newspapers the next morning, but the sceptics might have seen it as a way for Leeds to reduce their load – the 1969/70 and 1970/71 seasons had demonstrated that fighting campaigns on several fronts was a near-impossible task. Had they sacrificed the UEFA Cup to concentrate on the league and FA Cup?

Southampton went out of the competition at the first hurdle, losing to Athletic Bilbao, but Wolverhampton Wanderers comfortably accounted for the students of Académica Coimbra of Portugal by 7-1 on aggregate. Derek Dougan, their 33-year-old Northern Ireland international, scored four goals across the two legs, including a hat-trick in the 4-1 away win.

St Johnstone, in their first foray into European competition, captured the headlines in Scotland after beating Hamburg 4-2 on aggregate. They had lost the first game in Germany by 2-1 and many considered they were unlucky not to have returned home with a draw. In the second game at Muirton Park, the Saints performed a miracle by winning 3-0 in front of 15,000 passionate fans. The *Daily Record* proclaimed that it was one of the greatest performances ever by a Scottish team in Europe. The home crowd were ecstatic and invaded the pitch at the end of the game to congratulate their heroes. The Saints went through another round, beating Hungarians Vasas, before losing to Željezničar of Sarajevo 5-2, but the Perth side had certainly got a taste for European football. Unfortunately, they had to wait 18 years for their next adventure.

Aberdeen went through one round before coming up against what could be described as 'European royalty' in Juventus, while Dundee reached the last 16 to meet AC Milan. In a near-empty San Siro, Milan, who had Gianni Rivera in midfield and Karl-Heinz Schnellinger in defence, won 3-0, a result that seemed to make the second game at Dens Park a mere formality for the Italians. The Milan goalkeeper, Fabio Cudicini, had a tremendous night keeping Dundee at bay, but the incessant pressure from the Scots clearly rattled Milan. Goals from Gordon Wallace and John Duncan, who would try his luck in England with Tottenham in the mid-1970s, gave Dundee a 2-0 lead with a quarter of an hour to go. Cudicini was still a barrier to success and Dundee just could not manage it. Nevertheless, their brave effort won them many friends. 'The Scots chased every ball, ran marathons and fought like champions,' said *The Scotsman* newspaper. This became something of a quality of Scottish sides in Europe as well as the national team in the coming years. Scotland and their clubs fought like tigers, but were often gallant losers.

Tottenham's second-round opponents, Nantes, were significantly more difficult than the Icelandic side that so easily capitulated in round one. Like Spurs, Nantes finished third in their domestic league in 1970/71 and they had some very useful players. Erich Maas, a tricky winger, was a West German international, while Ángel Marcos, from Buenos Aires, had played half a dozen games for the Argentinian national team. Spurs had the advantage of playing away in the first leg. Even a trip to France was seen as an excursion into the unknown and the Spurs players were suspicious of foreign food. Hunter Davies's excellent book, *The Glory Game*, recalls how the squad scraped any remnants of garlic from their steaks at their modest hotel in Nantes.

The game ended goalless but Spurs found it difficult to break down a robust Nantes defence who gave Chivers and Gilzean very little room. Chivers, to quote a contemporary report, was a 'severe disappointment' and there is evidence of some tension with manager Bill Nicholson in the Davies book. Tottenham had kept a clean sheet and were well-placed for the second leg, even if they felt rather deflated at the post-match reception hosted by the mayor of Nantes.

Wolverhampton Wanderers, who had won 3-1 in The Hague against ADO, were enjoying their European journey. Wolves had been outplayed for long periods of the game, but ADO, who had in their line-up a future globetrotting manager in Dick Advocaat, could not score. Dougan, Jim McCalliog and Kenny Hibbitt did score, however, giving Wolves a commanding lead for the return.

Tottenham laboured against Nantes in the second leg, although they completely outplayed their visitors. They had to be satisfied with a Martin Peters goal early in the game at White Hart Lane. Meanwhile, Wolves completed their task against ADO at home, winning 4-1 in a quite bizarre 90 minutes in which the Dutch side scored three own goals. For both English representatives, the next round brought with it a little mystery. Spurs were paired with Rapid Bucharest of Romania, while Wolves were destined to travel behind the Iron Curtain to East Germany. Their opponents were Carl Zeiss Jena.

Jena, in 1971, was a city of some 88,000 people. It was renowned for its glassware and optical manufacturers, Zeiss and Schott, both of which were moved to the Soviet Union. It seemed a bleak place in the winter, and when Wolves travelled to East Germany there was snow on the ground at the Ernst-Abbe-Sportfeld, accompanied by a cold wind from the east. Carl Zeiss Jena were unbeaten and topped the East German league. They had beaten Bulgaria's Lokomotiv Plovdiv and OFK Belgrade of Yugoslavia in the previous rounds. While some East German sides could be very difficult to play against, others were found wanting in European games. Carl Zeiss Jena had talent and they provided a cluster of players for the East Germany squad in the 1974 World Cup. On paper, it was a tough task for Wolves, but they scored early through the promising John Richards and came away from Jena with a 1-0 victory. It was relatively easy for Wolves in the return, a 3-0 win against opponents who seemed out of sorts from the start.

Tottenham, meanwhile, welcomed a Rapid Bucharest team that was languishing in mid-table in Romania. Bill Nicholson had watched them win 5-1 against Jiul Petroşani but felt their first-choice side had been only partially on show. Their squad for London included four players from Romania's 1970 World Cup squad, including the eccentric black-clad goalkeeper Ricâ Raducanu, plus

Nicolae Lupescu, Ion Dumitru and Alexandru Neagu. Rapid manager Marian Bazil refused to announce his team for the game at White Hart Lane before Nicholson had revealed his selection. It was widely believed they considered Chivers to be the danger man and that they would assign Alexandru Boc to mark the England centre-forward. Rapid had been vulnerable away, but they were strong at home. Against Napoli, for example, they had recovered from a 1-0 deficit to win the first-round tie 2-1 on aggregate. They had also won their home leg against Legia Warsaw but lost in Poland. Spurs set the tone of the game at White Hart Lane within just 20 seconds, as Chivers took one of his trademark long throws and Peters scored. Chivers himself scored two to give Spurs a 3-0 win, a handsome margin to take to Romania. Raducanu, for all his flamboyance, was at fault for at least one of the goals. One report described the goalkeeper as 'part Groucho Marx, part Harlem Globetrotter, part performing seal'.

Tottenham's management seemed nervous about a trip to Bucharest and sent their staff out to buy copious amounts of English food to take on board their BEA flight to Romania. In deep-freeze units, Tottenham's players could look forward to lamb, chicken and steaks. Nicholson and his colleagues had received reports that Romanian food might be unsuitable. They were met by British Embassy representatives at Bucharest airport, no doubt carefully watched by members of the secret police that were rumoured to be in attendance. Rapid were confident of turning around a three-goal deficit, but the locals clearly did not feel the same way as only 10,000 in an 80,000-capacity stadium saw the game. The weather was fiercely cold but Rapid did their best to warm things up. It was an ugly encounter and became known as 'the battle of Bucharest'. Tottenham won 2-0, with goals from substitute

Jimmy Pearce, who was later sent off after being on the pitch for only 12 minutes, and the bruised and bedraggled Chivers. When the second goal went in, Raducanu ran towards the referee and threw the ball at him. He should have been sent off and would certainly have been shown the way to the dressing room in England.

Spurs limped off after a gruelling 90 minutes and Nicholson was incensed by the approach of the Romanians: 'We have never played against a dirtier side. This was the worst experience of dirty football I've had in 30 years at Tottenham. If this is European football, you start to feel that you would be better off out of it. Look at the injuries we've got. The Romanians were not interested in playing the ball. They just wanted to kick people.' The English press supported Nicholson's view. Norman Giller in the *Daily Express* said Spurs had been 'hacked and kicked about like rag dolls', while Jeff Powell of the *Daily Mail* described it as one of the most 'savage matches in the riot-torn history of European football.' Nicholson had to deal with a shell-shocked squad carrying lots of injuries but was pleased that his team had emerged from the battle with dignity. That spirit would be tested again in the quarter-finals as Spurs were drawn to meet another Romanian team – UT Arad. Wolves, however, had a very different challenge in the form of Italian giants Juventus.

UT Arad promised the tie would not be a repeat of the brutal matches with Rapid, but Spurs were only concerned with winning, and nothing else. Arad, in Transylvania, had a population of around 130,000 in 1972 and had a thriving textiles industry. In fact, UT Arad's full name was Uzine Textila Arad. They were Romanian champions in 1970 and were known as a team that liked to play fairly and honestly. In Arad, a huge banner tried to nurture good relations with their English visitors: 'Welcome to the dear England footballers'. Nicholson admitted that 'we have never gone into a European match knowing less', such was the lack of information available. Half a dozen of the team that won the Romanian title in 1970 were included in UT Arad's starting line-up. Spurs were still carrying some injuries, but they were simply too strong for the home side. Roger Morgan, a player who had been very unlucky since joining from Queens Park Rangers in 1969 for a fee of £110,000, scored one of the goals, and Chivers added another as they won 2-0. This time, the Romanians made Tottenham feel more welcome and, in the streets around the stadium, residents took off roof tiles in order to watch the team from England from neighbouring houses. They were as curious about Spurs as the Londoners had been about them.

Wolves pulled off an outstanding 1-1 draw with Italy's top side of the moment, Juventus, who would go on to win Serie A in 1971/72. Juve had star names in the form of experienced Helmut Haller, the West German striker who had played and scored in the 1966 World Cup Final, and expensive acquisition Pietro Anastasi. Wolves won the second leg 2-1 with Danny Hegan and Dougan scoring, while Haller converted a penalty for Juve, who paid the price for fielding a weakened team. They seemed to be more concerned with keeping everyone fit for the Turin derby a few days later. Wolves had also benefitted from the experience of Welsh footballing great John Charles, who had played for Juventus and was acting in an advisory role for the club. Mike Bailey, the club's captain, told the media that 'our lads played exceedingly well and were never in danger of losing'. There were some nervous moments in the closing stages, however, as a second Juventus goal would have eliminated Wolves on away goals.

Twenty-four hours earlier, Spurs had drawn their second leg in a strange, cautious atmosphere at White

Hart Lane, but they had already completed the hard work in Romania. Two teams from England in the semi-finals, but they were not drawn together. Spurs had a daunting clash with AC Milan to look forward to, while Wolves had another communist adventure with Ferencváros. Nicholson considered Milan to be the best side left in the competition but there was now a very realistic possibility of an all-English final. Spurs had played for some time without Alan Mullery, their captain and a member of the England squad. Mullery had a pelvic injury that had proved troublesome. He needed total rest and, when he started his rehabilitation, he was sent on loan to Fulham, his former club. At Craven Cottage, Mullery was Fulham's best player and he earned a surprise recall to Spurs, just in time for the semi-final first leg against Milan.

The two-times champions of Europe were not happy about the return of Mullery. Their coach, Nereo Rocco, felt that as he was arriving from another club, it was the equivalent of a transfer, but Spurs had always retained Mullery's registration. Rocco was accustomed to a different practice in Italy. As for Mullery, he was delighted as it had looked, from the outside, as though Spurs had abandoned him. Needless to say, he received a rapturous welcome back to White Hart Lane when he led the team out against Milan before over 40,000 people. Milan had won the European Cup three years earlier and would eventually finish runners-up to Juventus in Serie A in 1971/72. They brought with them all the less pleasant aspects of *catenaccio*, time-wasting, shirt-tugging, amateur dramatics and plenty of 'what me?' when they fouled a Spurs player. It did not need Milan to score first, but they did in the 25th minute, through hard man Romeo Benetti, which triggered off all their tricks. Perryman, now firmly established in the Spurs line-up, scored twice with well-struck shots to win the game, but the crowd had to endure a scruffy contest. Nicholson called them 'spoilers': 'From a spectators' point of view they ruined the game with their petty fouls and acting.' The referee did take notice and sent off Riccardo Sogliano for excessive time-wasting. Spurs had a frustrating evening and a one-goal margin was rather flimsy to take to Italy.

On the same night in Budapest, Wolves faced a decent Ferencváros team of nine internationals that had some skilful ball-playing individuals, such as Flórián Albert and Gyula Rákosi. They had enjoyed a relatively comfortable path to the semi-finals, having beaten Fenerbahçe, Eintracht Braunschweig, Panionios and Željezničar. Wolves did well to leave Budapest's Népstadion with a 2-2 draw, but it could have been a defeat had goalkeeper Phil Parkes not saved a penalty. With the second leg to come at Molineux, Wolves were favourites to reach their first European final.

Certainly, of the two English clubs, Tottenham had the more daunting task ahead of them. Mullery completed his romantic comeback story by putting Spurs in front at the San Siro with a curling effort that gave goalkeeper Fabio Cudicini no chance. Milan were now 3-1 down and their fans were getting irate. They finally equalised with 20 minutes to go with a penalty from Rivera, but Spurs held on to secure a notable victory on aggregate. Some bonfires were lit on the terraces, a sure sign the locals were unhappy, and Spurs needed some escorts to get back to their base at Lake Como. Milan's coach, Rocco, was sporting in defeat and wished Spurs good luck in the final.

Their opponents would be Wolves, which was disappointing for some of the Spurs players, who were hopeful of another European trip. They had beaten Ferencváros 2-1 in the second leg to take the tie 4-3 on aggregate. Steve Daley, who would become one of the first £1m players in Britain, scored in the first minute in his first full game in Europe. Centre-half Frank Munro, who had found the back of the net in Budapest, notched up another goal, and Parkes, rather spectacularly, saved another penalty to ensure his side went through. So the first UEFA Cup Final would be between Tottenham and Wolves, who would finish sixth and ninth in the league in 1971/72, respectively. It was the first all-English final and underlined the strength in depth of the Football League's First Division. In fact, up to 1972, there had been just one European final involving two teams from the same nation – the 1962 Inter-Cities Fairs Cup between Valencia and Barcelona. For English football it was a boost, for the national team had just been knocked out of the European Championship in mid-May 1972 by West Germany, which many consider was the start of a long and slow decline. The other home nations – Scotland, Northern Ireland and Wales – had all been eliminated before the knockout stage of the competition.

At club level, though, England and Scotland had certainly made their mark in recent years. The Inter-Cities Fairs Cup had ended with four consecutive English winners – Leeds United (twice), Newcastle United and Arsenal – the Cup Winners' Cup had three successive British winners – Manchester City, Chelsea and Rangers – and Britain's European Cup duck had been broken with Celtic and Manchester United lifting the European Cup in 1967 and 1968, respectively. After the early years of struggling to deal with the more rugged and ultra-professional approach of the Italians, the Spanish and Portuguese, England had found a way to compete. The complaining had been replaced by mastering the art of the two-legged tie.

Tottenham had finished their home programme in the league, rounding off with a 4-3 victory against Leicester

City that saw defenders Cyril Knowles and Mike England score three of the four goals. Their season had been patchy at times and they had not been quite as exciting as in 1970/71. However, they had reached the semi-final of the Football League Cup, the last eight of the FA Cup and here they were, in their second final in two seasons. Wolves had been even more inconsistent, but their form in Europe had been excellent. While Spurs had one away game to go, at Arsenal of all places, Wolves had to host Leeds in what would prove to be a vital match for the visitors. Ironically, the two teams kicked off their seasons playing each other and they would also end their campaigns meeting in very different circumstances.

Spurs were considered favourites to win the final, partly because Wolves had some injuries that were worrying them. Bailey, their skipper, had been out for some time and McCalliog was struggling with an eye infection. Spurs were only too aware of the danger man from Wolves, Dougan, who had scored eight goals in the competition. He was well known to them, and their young striker Richards was seen as one of English football's most promising players.

Although the prospect of an all-English final was a reflection of the relative strength of the nation's club football, the two games struggled to capture the attention of many people. In hindsight, it has become something of a 'forgotten final'. As Geoffrey Green said in *The Times*, 'the concrete truth was that the game lacked magnetism'. At Molineux, the game was officiated by Tofiq Bahramov, the so-called 'Russian linesman' from the 1966 World Cup Final who was actually from Azerbaijan. It was not until the 57th minute that the game came alive, when a free kick by England was headed home by Chivers as the Wolves defence lacked conviction. Wolves equalised through McCalliog and it looked like a 1-1 draw until Chivers sent a 30-yard shot past Parkes. The difference between the two teams was Chivers, who shrugged aside early lethargy to remind people of his worth to Spurs and England.

Spurs went home to North London as firm favourites to lift their second European trophy. Ahead of the clash at White Hart Lane, Spurs' veteran forward Gilzean was being linked to other clubs. The 33-year-old's contract as coming to an end and speculation was rife that Nicholson would dispose of the Scot. Spurs had players with plenty of mileage in their careers, but Mullery, England and Gilzean were all over 30. Only Dougan was over 30 in the Wolves starting line-up. Mullery headed Spurs in front with a brave diving header on 30 minutes. The Spurs captain was hurt in the process but he recovered to keep the romantic story of the comeback hero going. Wolves equalised through David Wagstaffe, who sent a long-range effort in off the post. Tension grew and Wolves enjoyed the upper hand for the last half-hour of the game. However, Pat Jennings kept them at bay and there was no small amount of relief when the final whistle blew. The fans streamed on to the pitch and Mullery was dragged around the stadium with the huge modernist UEFA Cup in his hands. The game may not have been one of the greatest seen at White Hart Lane, but Spurs had won the inaugural UEFA Cup and, pretty soon, Mullery, the hero of the hour, was off to Fulham.

For the next two seasons, Spurs had very productive UEFA Cup campaigns, reaching the semi-finals in 1972/73 but losing to Liverpool, and then in 1974 running out of steam against Feyenoord in the final. Crowd trouble and an ageing squad underlined that Spurs were approaching a transition period, one that would see the end of the Nicholson era and the departure of some well-loved figures at the club.

13

Trans-Europe Distress

AFTER THE efforts of Manchester United and Leeds United, not to mention Celtic's triumph of 1967, the English champions struggled to adapt to the new order that was gradually sweeping across Europe. Everton, Arsenal and Derby County, the champions of 1970, 1971 and 1972, respectively, all failed to make their mark, although they had the consolation of knowing that they had been eliminated by eventual finalists. Everton were surprisingly knocked out by Panathinaikos in 1971, but it was clear from their league results that they were a team beyond its peak.

A year later, Arsenal, the double winners of 1970/71, were beaten by Ajax, a team they had comfortably disposed of in the Fairs Cup in 1970. While Arsenal were a tough, determined outfit, they were made to look rather lumbering by an Ajax team that was approaching its zenith in 1971/72. Arsenal lost 2-1 in Amsterdam, although it could have been worse for Bertie Mee's team. The second leg at Highbury offered little comfort and, within a minute of the kick-off, a George Graham own goal made Arsenal's uphill task even steeper. It proved too much for them, and the way Ajax managed the tie over the two games suggested that English football was losing ground to teams from across the English Channel. And the technical expertise of Cruyff and his team-mates was far more advanced than the best that England had to offer.

In 1972/73, Derby County, who had struggled to repeat the form of their title campaign, were finding European football more to their liking. They had beaten Yugoslavia's Željezničar, Benfica, including Eusébio, and Spartak Trnava of Czechoslovakia to find themselves up against Juventus, arguably the most uncompromising team in Europe. In the first game in Turin, Derby lost 3-1 in an intense contest in front of a passionate crowd. Brian Clough refused to concede, however, and told the press ahead of the second leg: 'We are well aware that this is going to be one hell of a game, but we are optimistic enough to think we can do it.'

Derby were weakened by suspensions, both Roy McFarland and Archie Gemmill having picked up two bookings in the competition, their places taken by Peter Daniel and Alan Hinton, the latter still not 100 per cent fit after injury. The game ended 0-0, and within a few months Clough had left Derby in controversial circumstances.

Derby's successors as English champions were Liverpool, who had a new star in their ranks in the form of Kevin Keegan. In their title-winning season, Bill Shankly's side also won the UEFA Cup. Bizarrely, they played German opposition, East or West, in four of their six ties. Eintracht Frankfurt, Dynamo Berlin, Dynamo Dresden and Borussia Mönchengladbach were all beaten by the Reds. In the semi-final, Liverpool knocked out the holders, Tottenham, on the away goals rule. Liverpool, who had been crowned league champions already, faced Mönchengladbach in the final. This was a team that had some outstanding players, including Rainer Bonhof, Berti Vogts and Herbert Wimmer. They also had the great

Günter Netzer in their midfield, a brilliant player who was West Germany's difficult-to-handle maverick.

The first meeting at Anfield was abandoned after 30 minutes due to torrential rain. A few days earlier, Shankly had told his ground staff to keep the pitch wet in order to make the going soft. It was his belief the Germans did not like spongy turf, but it almost backfired on the canny Scot. The weather was appalling, the pitch became unplayable and this delayed the game by 24 hours. John Toshack, Liverpool's former Cardiff City forward, was left out of the aborted first leg, but Shankly had noted that Gladbach looked vulnerable in the air and brought the Welshman in for the rerun. 'Tosh' proved to be too strong for the Gladbach defence at Anfield. He assisted Kevin Keegan to score twice to give Liverpool a 3-0 lead, which was seen as a formidable advantage to take across to Germany. However, the media felt that even a three-goal margin might not be enough against such skilful opponents. Shankly knew the final was far from won, describing Gladbach as 'a great attacking side'. Liverpool were backed by locally based British army troops in the second leg, which was played against a backdrop of lightning and very crude, cold rain. Two goals from Jupp Heynckes, who had missed a penalty at Anfield, and would later make his reputation as a manager, gave Mönchengladbach a 2-0 win, leaving Liverpool hanging on by that important third goal from Larry Lloyd in the first leg.

Liverpool went into the 1973/74 European Cup believing they could win the competition, but after an easy first-round game against Jeunesse Esch of Luxembourg, they faced Red Star Belgrade. The Yugoslavs beat Liverpool twice by 2-1 and left the club's management rather shell-shocked. But this defeat was the catalyst for changes at Liverpool and in the way they approached and played games.

The result laid the foundations for the club's domination of football at home and abroad that really only ended in 1990.

In 1973/74, English success in Europe was confined to Tottenham Hotspur's second UEFA Cup Final in three years. The Spurs team was little changed from their last final, but players such as Martin Chivers, Martin Peters, Ralph Coates and Philip Beal were all nudging or beyond 30. Their opponents, Feyenoord, were Dutch champions in 1974 and had taken advantage of the departure of Johan Cruyff from Ajax to Spain. Spurs had finished in mid-table in the league and there were signs of discontent at White Hart Lane. Little did anyone know at the time but the UEFA Cup Final would be Bill Nicholson's last European tie with the club. The first game in London ended 2-2, with Spurs leading twice before Theo de Jong scored an 85th-minute equaliser to deny them victory. Eight days later, Spurs were beaten 2-0, but the match is remembered for the violence that broke out in the De Kuip stadium. Van Hanegem, Wim Rijsbergen and Wim Jansen went off to West Germany for the World Cup, while Spurs were left to reflect on what was the beginning of the end of an era.

British clubs, who had enjoyed a successful run, especially in the Fairs Cup, UEFA Cup and Cup Winners' Cup, had drawn a blank in 1974 for the first time since 1966. Ironically, the England team had also gradually slipped into a period of mediocrity and had seen their shortcomings exposed in both the 1972 European Championship and the 1974 World Cup qualifying campaign. In 1974, Don Revie, who had led Leeds United to their second league title, became England manager and ended the Yorkshire club's golden age. Although the most successful club manager in a job at the time, Revie was not the right choice and, for Leeds United, the appointment of Brian Clough also proved to be a rash move. Leeds, however, recovered from a bad start to the season and reached the European Cup Final.

It was always Revie's ambition to win the European Cup and his failure to do so was highlighted by his successor when he arrived at Elland Road. Clough himself felt that his Derby team had been robbed by Juventus in 1973, and one of the attractions of the Leeds job was the chance to have a stab at the European Cup. However, he had been sacked by the time the competition got underway in mid-September 1974. Leeds had won just one of six games in the league and it was clear the players and the manager were not singing from the same song sheet. Clough never lost the Leeds dressing room, because he never seemed to have it in the first place. Leeds started their European campaign against FC Zürich. They were still without the suspended Billy Bremner, but won 4-1, a reminder that the ageing Leeds side could still turn it on when needed. Although they lost 2-1 in Switzerland in the second leg, they were comfortably through to the second round.

Jimmy Armfield of Blackpool was the surprise choice as Leeds' new manager and he had already settled in ahead of the next European Cup games, against Újpest of Hungary. In Budapest, Leeds pulled off an outstanding 2-1 victory with a side weakened by injuries. They could have won more convincingly but Peter Lorimer, along with Gordon McQueen a first-half scorer, struck the woodwork with a penalty kick. Leeds had to play with ten men for 75 minutes after Duncan McKenzie was sent off after he reacted to a string of fouls by András Tóth. Nevertheless, Armfield felt the win was the best display his team had produced so far: 'We won on guts and also because we kept the ball away from them.'

The return at Elland Road was less combative than the game in Hungary and Leeds had a little more fire in midfield due to the return of Bremner, who had not played since 17 August. Leeds won 3-0, with Bremner getting on the scoresheet along with McQueen and Terry Yorath. Leeds were through to the last eight, joining the likes of Barcelona – Cruyff included – and Franz Beckenbauer's Bayern Munich. That had to wait until 1975, so Armfield had time to concentrate on improving Leeds' poor league position. They were drawn to meet Belgian champions Anderlecht, who like Leeds had almost given up on retaining their league title. They had shown some vulnerability away from home in the European Cup and had lost to both Slovan Bratislava and Olympiacos in the first two rounds. Each time they had done enough in the home legs, which suggested that Leeds' best chance to win the tie would be at Elland Road.

Anderlecht were no fools and had established internationals in their line-up. Paul Van Himst was one of several Anderlecht players who were over the age of 30, including Jean Dockx and Erwin Vandendaele. They also had the silky skills of Robbie Rensenbrink, one of the stars of the Netherlands side that finished runners-up in the World Cup in 1974. Leeds had problems with injuries and suspensions, but established a very valuable 3-0 lead at Elland Road, with goals from Joe Jordan, McQueen and Lorimer. Anderlecht had arrived in Yorkshire with the sole intention of stifling Leeds but it did not work. Ahead of the second leg, Leeds' ex-manager, now in charge of England, had promised his old club a celebratory banquet in Paris should they win the European Cup. They won 1-0 in Brussels, with Bremner nonchalantly chipping the only goal on a very heavy surface littered with huge puddles of water. Armfield had gambled, to a certain degree, by dropping both Eddie Gray and Johnny Giles, whom he felt would struggle on a sodden surface at the Émile Versé stadium. It paid off and Leeds found themselves in the last four. 'We have as good a chance of winning the European Cup as any side left in. This was a team performance and I would not single out any player,' said Armfield. A couple of days later, he got the semi-final draw he did not particularly want – Barcelona. He had hoped for the rising French club, Saint-Étienne, who had been drawn to meet Bayern Munich.

Barcelona, coached by Rinus Michels, now had Johan Cruyff's old Ajax foil, Johan Neeskens, playing alongside him, but Barça had an awful away record in La Liga and in 1974/75 lost 12 of their 17 games. They finished third in the league, well behind Real Madrid. Cruyff's impact in his first season in Spain had been considerable, scoring 24 goals in 38 games, but in his second year his goal tally went down by ten. He had not scored in the European Cup before the Leeds games. Barcelona, for all their forward power, had demonstrated their defensive solidity by keeping clean sheets all the way through as they disposed of Linz, Feyenoord and Åtvidaberg.

While Leeds United feared Cruyff and Neeskens, the former Ajax duo were a little underwhelming over the two legs. The Dutch press noted that Cruyff appeared to lack the speed and reflexes that had differentiated him so much from his rivals. Neeskens, meanwhile, was not fully fit. Barcelona seemed surprised by Leeds United's raw intensity at Elland Road, but they had enough skill and technique to make the game a tight, keenly fought 90 minutes. There was an underlying feeling that for most of the home side's players it may be their last stab at the European Cup. Certainly the backbone of the Revie era was now approaching the end – Bremner was 32, Giles 34, Hunter 31, Reaney and Madeley 30. Younger players such as McQueen and Jordan had claimed their place, but

Clough's mercurial big-money signing, McKenzie, had not slotted in particularly well.

Leeds played as if they knew it was a swansong campaign for some of their older hands and won 2-1 at Elland Road before 50,000 people. Bremner, as was his habit, scored in a big game, putting Leeds in front in the ninth minute. Cruyff set up his team-mate, Juan Manuel Asensi, for the equaliser with 20 minutes to go but Leeds continued to push for a winner, knowing only too well the second leg would be very tough in the Camp Nou. They got the vital goal with 12 minutes to go, Allan Clarke volleying home after Jordan had nodded the ball into space for the Leeds striker. The game was fractious at times, with Barça's defenders snapping at the heels of the home team's forwards. Tempers also frayed and there were numerous minor skirmishes, in which Cruyff was also involved.

The general consensus was that Leeds had failed to give themselves a secure buffer for the return leg in Spain. The locals in Barcelona were concerned about the arrival of 800 English fans, who now had a reputation for unruly behaviour. It was another tense occasion but Leeds managed the game superbly, taking an early lead through Peter Lorimer, who hit a trademark shot into the net after Jordan's flick-on. It would not have been a surprise had Leeds run out of steam as they had played 13 games in five weeks, compared to Barça's fourth game in a month. Leeds received no help from the FA or Football League in dealing with fixture congestion. In Barcelona, said *The Times*, Armfield's team was 'direct, functional and economical' in their approach, but it took Barcelona a long time to get on level terms after Lorimer's goal, a header from Manolo Clares with 20 minutes to go. Just after the equaliser, McQueen was sent off, so Leeds were really up against it for the final stages. They hung on to win 3-2 on aggregate and silence the Catalan crowd. Their opponents in the final would be the holders, Bayern Munich. The European Cup Final had been on Leeds' agenda for almost a decade – as the players ran to the end of the ground to celebrate with the travelling fans, it felt like the cycle was almost complete.

There was one lap to go and it could not have been more formidable. Bayern Munich may have had a dire domestic season, but they had the core of the West German World Cup-winning team of 1974: Sepp Maier, Beckenbauer, Uli Hoeneß, Gerd Müller and Hans-Georg Schwarzenbeck. They had lost 11 of their first 21 Bundesliga games, which some observers felt was down to fatigue and mental stress. In January 1975, they sacked coach Udo Lattek and brought in the cerebral Dettmar Cramer, a football intellectual. Some felt that the diminutive Cramer was not the ideal choice and it certainly took time for results to turn. They were in better shape by the time they travelled to Paris for the European Cup Final, although they still had two league games remaining. They eventually finished tenth, 16 points behind champions and rivals Borussia Mönchengladbach.

Bayern Munich were well prepared: they played two training games before the final and had given themselves ample time to get ready. They had also incentivised their players handsomely to win – a bonus of the equivalent of £7,000 per man to retain the trophy. By contrast, their opponents arrived in Paris the day before the final, which raised some eyebrows among the Germans. Bayern Munich's route to the final had been somewhat easier than the path taken by Leeds: they had a bye in round one, they came out on top against Magdeburg of East Germany and overcame Soviet side Ararat Yerevan. The Magdeburg clash was a curious one, with Beckenbauer and his colleagues coming face to face with some of the players – Jürgen Sparwasser, Martin Hoffmann and Wolfgang Seguin – who had beaten West Germany 1-0 in the World Cup just a few months earlier. However, Bayern's toughest tie, on paper, was against Saint-Étienne in the semi-finals.

After beating Barcelona, many experts felt Leeds were marginal favourites, but Bayern had the experience of a tough final in 1974 when they beat Atlético Madrid 4-0 after a 1-1 draw. Leeds were no strangers, of course, to European finals – the game against Bayern would be their fifth, having taken part in three Fairs Cup finals and finishing runners-up in the 1973 European Cup Winners' Cup to AC Milan. In all competitions, Leeds were playing their tenth final since 1965, and six of their players – Reaney, Bremner, Hunter, Lorimer, Giles and Paul Madeley – had been involved in every campaign. Hunter was the only one to play in all ten. The team was, however, nearing its end, and there had been talk of Bremner and Giles both moving on in the summer. McQueen was suspended for the final so the ever-reliable and versatile Madeley would line up in the centre of defence alongside Hunter. Once again, McKenzie was on the bench, while Welsh hard man Terry Yorath, who had been an understudy in Leeds' peak years, was preferred in midfield to Eddie Gray. Leeds would be followed by 10,000 fans, but in the end it was their presence that captured the wrong type of headlines.

The 20th European Cup Final was preceded by a parade of some of the competition's big names over the years – Alfredo Di Stéfano, Ferenc Puskás, Paco Gento and Raymond Kopa, among others. The first-ever final had been played in the Parc des Princes, but this was the third incarnation of the stadium, a modern, brutalist version that was very reflective of the early 1970s. Leeds dominated the first half for long periods, and in the 38th minute they were convinced they should have had a penalty when Beckenbauer brought down Clarke. Bayern had lost their Swedish defender Björn Andersson in the fourth minute, but they did not let this upset them. They quietly absorbed Leeds' energy and enthusiasm but they also had to contend with an injury to Hoeneß three minutes from the interval.

Leeds felt further injustice in the 62nd minute when Lorimer volleyed home after the ball had been headed out from a free kick. The referee adjudged Bremner, who had gone close to scoring seconds earlier, was offside, so Bayern breathed again. Leeds were still smarting over that incident, and their fans had started to cause a commotion, when Bayern opened the scoring in the 71st minute. Conny Torstensson fed Franz Roth, who ran wide and sent a left-footed shot low past David Stewart. Leeds were stunned as they had been on top for so long and had literally been kept at bay by Maier. The Leeds fans started to throw seats and missiles on to the pitch. As the mayhem continued there were scuffles between the supporters and police, who by now had donned riot gear. With the game rapidly becoming a sideshow to the hooliganism, Bayern scored another goal in the 81st minute, Jupp Kapellmann sending a low cross to the near post and Müller, in typical fashion, shooting on the turn into the net. It was the killer blow, there was no coming back for Leeds, although they tried desperately. Bayern had scored from their only efforts on goal.

Leeds, however, were left bemoaning the penalty that never was and the disallowed goal. These incidents seemed to be the epitome of Leeds United's decade of near-misses at home and abroad. They won six trophies between 1968 and 1974, but they were runners-up on eight occasions. Armfield was proud of his boys, despite the 2-0 defeat. Most pundits felt Leeds had been desperately unlucky, but they had also been undone by the indomitable spirit of German football. 'If anything we had too much of the ball. We did all the running and tired ourselves out. The lads played well, they played their hearts out and I think that makes it worse,' Armfield said. The trouble continued until well after the match in Paris. There were 120 arrests and there were casualties. A TV camera operator lost an eye and a photographer left the stadium with a broken arm. As far as the media were concerned, British football had been dragged through the mud of un-sportsmanship and violence. The headlines said it all: 'Fans shame Leeds'. In the aftermath, Leeds received a ban from Europe, but it did not really matter – the team that Revie built was in decline and the golden days were over.

Leeds United's successors as English champions in 1975 were Derby County, an experienced team that had successfully transitioned the period following the departure of Brian Clough. Under Dave Mackay, they won a very competitive league championship race and in the summer of 1975 signed Charlie George, a player who was in dire need of fresh impetus after losing his way at Arsenal. The North Londoner found his new surroundings a source of inspiration and he scored 24 goals in 1975/76. His finest moment in a Derby shirt came in the European Cup against, of all clubs, Real Madrid. Derby won through the first round against Slovan Bratislava before welcoming Real to the Baseball Ground. George scored a memorable hat-trick as Derby won the first leg 4-1. Sadly, they collapsed in the second game in Madrid, losing 5-1. George's campaign was enough to earn him his solitary England cap, but his time at Derby was never again as productive as in 1975/76.

West Ham United returned to European football in 1975 after a gap of almost ten years. They had finally said goodbye to their England World Cup-winning heroes, with Bobby Moore the last to leave in 1974. They had also moved the much-respected Ron Greenwood upstairs and appointed club stalwart John Lyall as manager. West Ham had long been regarded as a good footballing side under Greenwood, but there was always a soft touch about them. But in 1975 they won the FA Cup, beating Second Division Fulham 2-0, a team that included Moore and his England colleague Alan Mullery. West Ham started 1975/76 running on the fumes of their FA Cup success. They had a new shirt design that was still claret and blue but there was something quite 'European' about it. They went unbeaten in their first nine games, playing some very progressive football, but they could not sustain their form and dramatically slipped down the league table, eventually finishing 18th, six points off relegation. They saved their best moments for the European Cup Winners' Cup, creating some great memories under the Upton Park floodlights. They warmed up for their first-round tie with Finland's Reipas Lahti with the first of two meetings with Fiorentina in the totally unnecessary Anglo-Italian League Cup, a game the Hammers lost 1-0. They also lost the second leg in London by the same scoreline in December.

The Finnish side switched the game to Helsinki's iconic Olympic stadium, but the crowd was little more than 4,500 in a vast arena. West Ham predictably dominated but had to work hard for a 2-2 draw. The second leg was easy, a 3-0 victory with all the goals arriving in the second half. The second round was also relatively simple as West Ham became the first English club to travel to Armenia, which was then in the Soviet Union. The trip to Ararat Yerevan was an astonishing 3,000 miles, which drew some criticism from European football sceptics who questioned the value of such a journey. Lyall, along with Greenwood and the recently hired Bill Nicholson, gave a quick response: 'Those who disapprove of European football have never managed a club. It is a status symbol.' West Ham played well in Armenia and led through Alan Taylor, only for a controversial goal, resulting from an old-fashioned shoulder charge on goalkeeper Mervyn Day, to deny them a win. Once more, the Hammers secured the victory in the home leg, a 3-1 scoreline sending them into the last eight.

When European football returned in March, West Ham's season was falling apart on the domestic front. They travelled to The Hague to meet Den Haag and the first half was a complete nightmare. There was crowd trouble that threatened to halt the game, the renowned East German referee, Rudi Glöckner, made some bizarre decisions that affected the scoreline and by half-time West Ham were 4-0 down, with Den Haag's Aad Mansveld netting a hat-trick that included two debatable penalties. Fortunately, the Hammers staged something of a recovery in the second half after Lyall had ordered them to simply go out and attack. Billy Jennings scored after 52 and 59 minutes, thanks to assists from Graham Paddon, to give the scoreline a little respectability.

West Ham's fans had not given up on their team and almost 30,000 packed into the Boleyn Ground to see the second leg. Lyall's men put on a scintillating display of attacking football and, by half-time, goals from Alan Taylor, Frank Lampard and Billy Bonds had put them 3-0 up and 5-4 ahead on aggregate. Den Haag pulled a goal back on the hour, which created some nerves on and off the pitch, but West Ham won through on the back of their two away goals. Eintracht Frankfurt were next for West Ham in the semi-final. They were an attacking team that included Bernd Hölzenbein and Jürgen Grabowski, both heroes of West Germany's 1974 World Cup triumph. They also had useful players who could score goals, such as Rüdiger Wenzel and Bernd Nickel. The first leg in the picturesque Wald Stadion was an entertaining affair with West Ham taking an early lead with an excellent strike from Paddon. Frankfurt responded and equalised on the half-hour through Willi Neuberger, and three minutes into the second half Wolfgang Kraus netted the winner. Although West Ham were beaten, they had played well, and the away goal, as they had found out against Den Haag, proved very helpful.

West Ham, after all, only needed to win 1-0 to reach their second European final. What unfolded was a match that has been talked about for decades, 90 minutes of raw passion and virtuoso performances from some of the club's outstanding players. The crowd had to wait until the second half, however, for the dam to be breached. Trevor Brooking, with a rare header, put them ahead four minutes into the restart, and midway through the half Keith Robson made it 2-0, and 3-2 on aggregate. With ten minutes to go, Robson created a third for Brooking, who gleefully rounded the goalkeeper to score. Frankfurt netted very late on, but it was not enough. While Ron Greenwood, now the club's general manager, claimed Frankfurt were the best team they had played in Europe, Lyall was ecstatic, claiming he had watched the best display in the club's history: 'Tonight we have showed English football can produce skill equal to anyone. The whole side produced everything that we needed. We proved just how much we have learned in Europe.' Indeed they had, for West Ham were set to meet Anderlecht in the final.

The Belgians had finished third in the league in 1974/75 and had won the cup by beating Antwerp. In 1975/76, they were runners-up to Club Brugge. On paper, their team was stronger than West Ham's, as only two of the Hammers' line-up – Lampard and Brooking – had represented England, whereas only one member of the Anderlecht starting XI –

Michael Lomme – was not a current or future international. The men to watch were Rensenbrink and Arie Haan from the Dutch national team, and the young François Van der Elst, who would later join West Ham.

There had been no denying West Ham had really been motivated by European football, their displays against Den Haag and Eintracht Frankfurt showing what they were capable of, as opposed to their very forlorn league performances in the second half of the season. At the same time, they had failed to win any of their away games in the Cup Winners' Cup and they had lost 12 of their last 14 league fixtures on the road. The final was in Brussels, the home of Anderlecht, so the Hammers had to shake off their form away from the Boleyn Ground. Anderlecht, by contrast, had lost just once in the league at home and had won all four of their Cup Winners' Cup ties on their own turf, without conceding a goal. They had beaten Rapid Bucharest, Borac Banja Luka, Wrexham and Sachsenring Zwickau.

West Ham were certainly not overawed and they started the final with confidence. They went ahead through the underrated Pat Holland on 29 minutes, but just before the break Lampard's poor back-pass was seized upon by Peter Ressel, who squared the ball to Rensenbrink to score with a left-foot drive. Lampard, usually so reliable, later revealed that his slip-up was down to a groin injury that could have been career-threatening. Rensenbrink was in excellent form and created a second Anderlecht goal for Van der Elst early in the second half. West Ham refused to give up and Robson scored with a crouching header from Brooking's cross. Anderlecht then took control and in the 73rd minute they were awarded a penalty after Holland brought down Rensenbrink. He got up to score the kick to put the Belgians ahead for the first time. The

Dutchman was not finished, however, and his 88th-minute through ball to Van der Elst ended with the 21-year-old striker rounding goalkeeper and defender to score number four. West Ham were finished, but they had been gallant losers. Lyall was quick to hand the plaudits to Anderlecht's Rensenbrink: 'He was unplayable today, nobody could hold him. I am terribly disappointed but I must congratulate Anderlecht for their fine showing.' The better side had won, but it had been a richly enjoyable European journey for the Hammers that has never been forgotten.

West Ham's campaign provided further proof that their customary style was well suited for European football. Certainly their record in the 1960s and in the 1975/76 season indicated that they felt at home in that environment. Similarly, in 1976/77, two other teams that had entertained the crowds, Queens Park Rangers and Manchester United, were expected to enjoy lengthy runs in the UEFA Cup. QPR were managed by former Chelsea boss Dave Sexton, and United were now being coached by Tommy Docherty, Sexton's predecessor at Stamford Bridge. QPR played a progressive style of football that was influenced by Continental methods, while United's approach was attack at all costs. QPR looked very much at home as they disposed of Brann of Norway (two Stan Bowles hat-tricks), Slovan Bratislava and Köln, but they came unstuck in the last eight against AEK Athens. After winning 3-0 in the first leg, they capitulated in the second leg in Athens and were beaten on penalties. United beat Ajax in the first round but found the strong-arm tactics of Juventus too much, despite beating them 1-0 at Old Trafford, where the home crowd chanted 'animals' at the visitors. They lost 3-0 in the second leg, but the experience had been quite chastening for Docherty's young team. Success was just around the corner for English football, however.

14

The Paisley Pattern

WHEN BILL Shankly departed Liverpool in 1974, the club looked from within for his replacement. Shankly was immensely popular and was a builder of dreams, taking his beloved Liverpool to the top once more. It was an impossible task to succeed him, but they pushed the avuncular and understated Bob Paisley into the job. He did not look like anyone's idea of a modern football coach, but Paisley became the most successful English manager of all time and did so with the minimum of fuss. He lacked the wise-cracking, Cagneyesque wit of Shankly, but Paisley not only continued the work of his mentor, he bettered it.

Like Shankly, he was not a 'Scouser', he was from the North East, but he was as much part of the scene at Anfield as the Spion Kop. Paisley had to get to work as Liverpool got used to the idea of his predecessor's departure. The last player signed by Shankly was Ray Kennedy, a muscular young forward who moved from Arsenal, where he had been part of the club's double-winning side of 1971, ironically clinched at Wembley in the FA Cup Final against Liverpool. Kennedy struggled to establish himself at first, but it was Paisley that saw something in him that would transform his career. He had an inkling Kennedy would be more effective in midfield rather than as a striker.

Liverpool had a big-man, little-man pairing up front in John Toshack and Kevin Keegan, so opportunities might prove to be limited. In midfield, Kennedy's left foot and vision, not to mention his powerful shooting, made him into a valuable player for both club and country. In 1974/75, though, Liverpool were acclimatising to the post-Shankly era and just fell short of winning the league. They might have achieved it if they had not played without Kevin Keegan for a few weeks at the start of the season due to suspension. Keegan and Billy Bremner had been involved in a punch-up in the Charity Shield and were punished accordingly. Derby County were league champions, but Liverpool finished just two points behind.

Liverpool were, nevertheless, favourites for the title in 1975/76, but they had new rivals at the top of the table in the form of Queens Park Rangers, who led the way for long periods with a team playing imaginative football that had undoubtedly been influenced by the total footballers of the Netherlands. Liverpool eventually came out on top, but they coupled this success with their second UEFA Cup triumph in four seasons. However, the other British clubs did not fare well. Aston Villa and Ipswich Town both lost to Belgian sides, Villa being knocked out in round one by Antwerp and Ipswich winning 3-0 at home and then losing 4-0 to Club Brugge. Liverpool's Mersey rivals Everton were beaten at the first hurdle by AC Milan. There were two sides from Scotland, but Liverpool beat one of them, Hibernian, in the first round. Dundee United had an easy task in Iceland before they went out in round two to Porto.

As well as beating Hibernian in the first round, Liverpool slalomed their way past Real Sociedad, Śląsk Wrocław and Dynamo Dresden before meeting Barcelona in the semi-finals. Barcelona had an expensive side, but there was considerable unrest in the dressing room. Cruyff and Neeskens were still at the heart of the team, but Rinus Michels had gone, replaced by Hennes Weisweiler. Cruyff and the German coach did not see eye to eye and Weisweiler was convinced that Barça's poor away form – six wins in two seasons – was partly down to Cruyff not trying too hard when they were on the road. Other critics felt that Cruyff and Neeskens reserved their best for European games rather than the domestic programme.

Liverpool, by contrast, were going well and were a tight-knit group. They won 1-0 in the Camp Nou thanks to a Toshack goal, prompting Paisley to decare that it had been 'a perfect night's work'. In fact, Liverpool's margin could have been better, and players such as Emlyn Hughes felt disappointed that they had not won by two or three goals. In the return game, Tommy Smith made a nuisance of himself with Cruyff and the Catalans in a 1-1 draw. Liverpool were through to the final and the Barcelona crowd chanted 'Weisweiler out'. Cruyff, who had threatened to leave the club at the end of the season, was blamed for the departure of the coach, but Barça could not risk losing their most prized asset.

Liverpool's second UEFA Cup Final was against Club Brugge, who were managed by Ernst Happel. The Belgian side were highly respected and not unfamiliar with English clubs, having beaten Ipswich in round two. Brugge had a pair of Danes in their side, goalkeeper Birger Jensen and Ulrik le Fevre, as well as an Austrian and several well-known Belgians in Raoul Lambert, Roger Van Gool and René Vandereycken.

Most of the drama was confined to the first leg at Anfield on 28 April. Brugge took a two-goal lead through Lambert and Julien Cools inside 12 minutes. The home crowd was stunned, but at half-time Paisley replaced Toshack with young Jimmy Case and the game changed dramatically. Liverpool scored three goals in the space of six minutes, from Kennedy, Case and a penalty from Keegan. It gave Liverpool a narrow advantage, but they were equally impressive away from home, so they went to Belgium with a confidence boosted by clinching the league title at Wolverhampton Wanderers. Brugge had also been pronounced league champions by the time the two sides met at the Olympiastadion, Bruges. The home side took an early lead once more, a penalty from Lambert, but Keegan levelled almost immediately afterwards from a free kick. The Reds won 4-3 on aggregate to trigger the start of a golden era for Liverpool, but there were even greater prizes to be won over the next few years.

The 1976/77 season was the end of another era for Liverpool. Keegan, who would become England captain and also be named Ballon d'Or winner in 1978 and 1979, announced in mid-season that he would be leaving the club at the end of the campaign. While Keegan was a much-loved figure, the next few months became a counting-down period as he repeatedly reminded the public that 'it is time for me to go'. At the same time, Liverpool were on the brink of unprecedented success – they were chasing the league, the FA Cup and the European Cup. This had proved to be a near-impossible task, although Celtic in 1967 and Ajax in 1972 had achieved the hallowed treble. Keegan eventually joined Hamburg, a somewhat left-field choice, which suggested that his name did not have as much cachet as British audiences believed. Nevertheless, Keegan, as always, gave 100 per cent and exploited his skills to good effect, but the rumours persistently hinted that he was bound for Spain (Real Madrid) or Italy.

The European Cup was a priority for Liverpool and memories have rightly lingered on for the 40-plus years that have passed since the competition was won for the first time. It was the quarter-final against Saint-Étienne that really made people believe that Liverpool could win the trophy. The first two rounds had been relatively stress-free for Paisley's side, Crusaders of Northern Ireland and Turkish side Trabzonspor both beaten, although the Reds had lost the first leg in Trabzon. Saint-Étienne had fallen prey to Bayern Munich in the 1976 final, who more or less replicated their display against Leeds in 1975, soaking up pressure before striking. The French team lost 1-0 to Bayern, but spent decades bemoaning the fact that the shape of the Hampden Park goalposts – square rather than rounded – cost them the cup. They were a beautiful team to watch and had some outstanding individuals in the Bohemian Dominique Rocheteau, the Argentine defender Osvaldo Piazza and the busy Gérard Janvion at full-back. Saint-Étienne lost their French crown in 1977, but looked a good bet to return to the final. In the first leg at the Stade Geoffroy-Guichard, they looked a shadow of the team that had scared Bayern to death in Glasgow.

Regardless, they beat a Liverpool team that was lacking Keegan, who had a troublesome thigh injury, with a Dominique Bathenay goal ten minutes from the end. Liverpool were confident of victory at Anfield and, within two minutes, they had wiped out the one-goal deficit, Keegan sending a dipping effort over confused goalkeeper Ivan Ćurković to send the home crowd into a frenzy. But that same body of people was silenced in the 50th minute when Bathenay shot home from 30 yards to level the scores and put Saint-Étienne ahead on aggregate. It was an excellent game, with both sides creating numerous chances, but Liverpool finally got control of the tie in the 59th minute when Kennedy made it 2-1. They were still in trouble at this point, however, because Saint-Étienne had the away goal advantage. Elimination seemed likely until Kennedy sent a long ball through the middle, which found the marauding run of substitute David Fairclough, who had made his name as an impact substitute over the past year or so. Fairclough brushed aside two defenders and fired a low shot past Ćurković. This triggered a crescendo of sound that could be heard for miles. The French team had entertained and had played some lovely football, but, at 3-1, Liverpool were through to the semi-final.

The draw for the last four could be have been far worse for Liverpool; Borussia Mönchengladbach were well known, but Dynamo Kyiv were something of a mystery. They had an outstanding winger in Oleg Blokhin, who was capturing a lot of attention, and in 1975 he was named European Footballer of the Year. FC Zürich were undoubtedly the weakest of the four semi-finalists and represented the best chance for Liverpool to reach the final. Zürich had shown some quality, however, in reaching the last four. They surprisingly beat Rangers in round one, Dynamo Dresden in round two and the Finnish side Turun Palloseura in the quarter-final. They had some fast-paced strikers in Italian-born Franco Cucinotta, who would top the Swiss scoring charts in 1976/77, and the 1975/76 top marksman Peter Risi. Their coach was Friedhelm Konietzka, a West German international who had embarked on his first job in management with Zürich.

Liverpool had to overcome a sixth-minute setback in the Letzigrund stadium in Zürich when Smith brought down René Botteron and conceded a penalty despite protestations that the forward had dived. Ray Clemence almost saved the kick, but Liverpool were nothing if not resilient and quickly clicked into gear. A cross by Ray Kennedy to the far post was controlled by Phil Neal, who shot home to equalise after 14 minutes. Three minutes after the interval, Steve Heighway, who seemed to find an extra yard in European games, put Liverpool ahead. He was also involved in the third goal as he was brought down for an 83rd-minute penalty that Neal converted with ease. A 3-1 win was considered to be a case of having one foot in the final. The second leg at Anfield was, in the eyes of the media, a formality.

And so it proved. Liverpool won 3-0 with two goals from Case and one from Keegan, who admitted afterwards that the prospect of reaching the European Cup Final had been the reason he had stayed at the club. A 6-1 aggregate victory was comfortable, leaving most people to wonder how Zürich had managed to get so far in the competition. They had arrived in Liverpool expecting to be beaten by five or six goals, but the game itself was low-key and a disappointment because Liverpool had more or less killed the tie in Zürich. Chairman John Smith underlined just how important reaching the final was: 'This is a very proud moment for the club and a great boost for the city.' Meanwhile, Borussia Mönchengladbach had also won through to the Rome final, having overcome Valeriy Lobanovsky's Dynamo Kyiv side.

Udo Lattek, Mönchengladbach's coach, claimed his team was currently the best in Europe, but Liverpool had every reason to consider they were the top side; they had won the league championship for the second consecutive season, they had been narrowly beaten by Manchester United in the FA Cup Final and now they had the chance to win the European Cup. They went to Rome having just been beaten by United at Wembley, a game they expected to win. But United's young players had a point to prove, because 12 months earlier they had surprisingly lost 1-0 in the final to Second Division Southampton's team of veterans. Liverpool lost 2-1 to United but that made them doubly determined to win the big prize, even though they were still bitterly disappointed to be denied the historic treble. Their coach, Joe Fagan, told Brian James in his book, *Tividale to Wembley*, that Liverpool's attitude for the FA Cup Final had been wrong and that seven games in three weeks had finally caught up with them.

Around 20,000 fans from Liverpool travelled to Rome and created a carnival atmosphere in the Italian capital. The Stadio Olimpico was not full, but there were still over 50,000 people in the arena. Gladbach included some familiar names for Liverpool fans, including Berti Vogts, Rainer Bonhof, Allan Simonsen, Herbert Wimmer and Jupp Heynckes, who were all in the starting line-up. Liverpool included two old hands in Smith and Ian Callaghan, but younger players like Joey Jones and Case were also selected. There was no place for John Toshack, a player that had tormented Mönchengladbach in the past. The experts predicted that the game would not be like previous encounters between English directness and the Continental possession-based approach. Liverpool, to a certain extent, had already started to develop a similar way of playing that would become most effective in the years ahead.

Terry McDermott opened the scoring after 28 minutes, finishing off a Steve Heighway through ball after running some 50 yards to reach the area. Liverpool were shocked by Simonsen's spectacular equaliser, an angled drive high into Ray Clemence's net but, 12 minutes later, Smith – supposedly playing his last game for the club – headed home Liverpool's second goal. It looked like the old man would be the matchwinner until Keegan, also bidding farewell after the game, went on a typical run and was upended in the penalty area. Neal scored from the spot to seal a 3-1 victory. Not everyone felt Liverpool could do it – even Emlyn Hughes, their captain, admitted he had his doubts: 'I felt we had left it all behind at Wembley. But once we started to play, I knew nothing could stop us. Now ... I didn't know it was possible for any man to feel this happy.'

Some reporters felt Liverpool's triumph was the most impressive by an English team abroad. They had won on foreign soil, whereas Manchester United, nine years earlier, had lifted the European Cup at Wembley. The Liverpool team was the epitome of a modern football machine and this victory was not a one-off, it was the start of a period of unprecedented success. Liverpool's fans celebrated long and hard, bathing in Rome's Trevi fountain among other notable features of the city. The sound of 'You'll Never Walk Alone' echoed in the Roman city for hours. And, unlike in today's partisan environment, most of England joined in – Liverpool were not winning just for themselves, they were also winning for their country. That is how it was in 1977, the year of Queen Elizabeth II's Silver Jubilee and the coronation of new European champions.

Liverpool had to deal with the departure of Kevin Keegan in the summer of 1977, but they acted quickly and signed a player who would assume legendary status at Anfield. Kenny Dalglish was bought from Celtic for £440,000, a player with a strong track record in Scotland, but relatively unknown to most football fans in England. Dalglish was 26, had scored 173 goals in 338 appearances for Celtic and was a fixture in the Scotland national team. In terms of ability, he was arguably a more naturally skilful player than Keegan, whose biggest asset was his energy and ability to make defenders feel uncomfortable. Dalglish scored 30 goals in 1977/78, but Liverpool lost their league title as Brian Clough's Nottingham Forest won the league and Football League Cup, beating Liverpool in the final of the latter. Liverpool were building a new team, however, and in mid-season signed Graeme Souness from Middlesbrough for £350,000. Liverpool could not match Forest's consistency in the league and they also suffered some clumsy defeats against teams at the opposite end of the league table, such as Chelsea, Birmingham, Norwich and Derby. But in Europe, Liverpool were eager to retain the trophy they had won in Rome.

After receiving a bye in the first round, Dynamo Dresden were their first opponents, but they made light work of the East German champions at home, winning 5-1 in the first leg. Toshack, who looked to be on his way out of the club at the end of 1976/77, caused countless problems for Dresden, but he was rather harshly excluded from the second leg. Liverpool lost the game 2-1 in the Rudolf-Harbig-Stadion, but they had earned their passage in the first meeting. Now in the quarter-final, Liverpool had to face a big name from the past in Benfica. The Portuguese champions, managed by former Chelsea centre-half John Mortimore, were still a useful side, but they were no match for the early 1960s version that won two consecutive European Cups. Liverpool had more or less conceded the league title by March 1978 and were languishing in fifth place in the league. But they were good enough to win 2-1 away from home in the first leg, with goals from Case and Hughes, after Benfica had taken an early lead in a game played in torrential rain. When Benfica ran out at Liverpool in the second leg, they looked nervous and not really up for the challenge. They were easily beaten 4-1, giving the home side the easiest of paths to the semi-final.

This meant another clash with Borussia Mönchengladbach. Udo Lattek was still in charge, but his team would be deposed as West German champions by Köln in 1977/78. Graeme Souness was introduced to European football for the first time and immediately made his mark, adding a fresh dynamism to the Liverpool team. Gladbach were without their talisman, Simonsen, but they gained the initiative when Jupp Heynckes scored after 28 minutes. Liverpool played well and patiently and thought their considered approach had earned a draw when substitute David Johnson equalised with two minutes to go. Any celebrations were quickly extinguished, however, when Rainer Bonhof netted a free kick just before the end.

Despite the defeat, the performance of Bob Paisley's side had impressed most people, but the one-goal deficit meant they had to attack from the start at Anfield. Paisley deliberated about his tactical approach, admitting that 'it's going to be one hell of a battle'. On their own patch, Liverpool were inspired by the Anfield crowd. Kennedy scored after just six minutes, levelling the aggregate scoreline. Souness was a revelation, breaking up Gladbach's prodding attacks and driving the midfield. It was very clear he had been a masterstroke of a signing by Paisley. By half-time, a Dalglish goal had made it 2-0, and nine minutes into the second half Case added a third. The battle had been easier than Paisley had envisaged and now Liverpool were firm favourites to retain their crown; Juventus, who were expected to reach the final, were beaten 2-0 by Club Brugge and went out 2-1 on aggregate. Like Gladbach, the Belgians were old foes from the UEFA Cup.

Liverpool would have the distinct advantage of playing on English soil as the European Cup Final was to be staged at Wembley. Brugge were still managed by Ernst Happel and had two Danes, one Austrian, a Hungarian and a Dutchman in their squad. Their road to Wembley had been longer and a shade harder than Liverpool's – Atlético Madrid, Juventus, Panathinaikos and Finland's Kuopian Palloseura (KuPS) had all been successfully dealt with. Liverpool ended the league season with a 12-

game unbeaten run that propelled them to second place, seven points behind champions Nottingham Forest. The team was changing, thanks to the arrival of Souness and a growing understanding with Dalglish. Souness, in particular, was receiving a lot of attention, not just as a key Liverpool player, but also in anticipation of Scotland's 1978 World Cup campaign. His career had started with Tottenham, but he left London as he was homesick. He joined Middlesbrough and was soon identified as a tough, influential midfielder. His early appearances for Liverpool had marked him as 'a furnace of endeavour as a vehicle for skill', according to the *Daily Express*. His performances in the semi-final against Borussia Mönchengladbach had impressed everyone and he was seen as a potential matchwinner in the final.

The Brugge side was older than Liverpool's line-up and they were without Raoul Lambert, a striker who had traces of both Gerd Müller and Dalglish about him. But he was now 33 years old and unfit. Happel kept his team selection secret for as long as possible, but insisted that Brugge were travelling to London with little fear. 'Liverpool's strength is their collectivity and spirit. But we have nothing to lose and are certainly not afraid of Liverpool or anyone else,' he said. The final was built up as a bigger occasion than the 1977 game against Gladbach, and politicians wasted no time in commenting in the media. While Prime Minister James Callaghan wished Liverpool well, leader of the opposition, Margaret Thatcher, sent her own message of support: 'I have always admired the way in which Liverpool play their football and I am delighted that they have reached the final for the second consecutive year.' Meanwhile, highly rated Yugoslav coach Miljan Miljanić sang Liverpool's praises: 'Britain doesn't really deserve a club like Liverpool because they are not appreciated by your press and your public.'

Paisley, an unsung hero for so long in his career with Liverpool, was asked about the club's success, and his response was typically self-effacing: 'I'm a lorry driver with a load of talent in my van.' Everyone within and outside the club knew that it was not that simple. Brugge were without Lambert, but Paisley was denied the services of Steve Heighway, who sat on the bench while Fairclough started the game. Paisley predicted a great attacking spectacle, but he was wrong, largely because the Belgians arrived at Wembley with the sole intention of preventing Liverpool from playing. Paisley felt they merely aimed to keep the score down. Liverpool dominated, but the match failed to live up to expectations. The winning goal after 65 minutes came from a link-up between the club's two major signings of the season – Souness playing a delicate ball through to Dalglish, who chipped the ball beyond Brugge's Danish lager-loving goalkeeper Birger Jensen. Brugge did have a chance to score when Alan Hansen played a poor back-pass but Jan Sorensen was thwarted by Clemence. It was a close call, but Liverpool were worthy winners and Paisley immediately targeted a third European Cup in 1978/79, but highlighted Nottingham Forest as the biggest threat to a hat-trick.

Happel, a European Cup winner himself, tried to defend his team's lacklustre display. 'It was a weak final. It's no excuse, but we were handicapped by injuries. I was disappointed with Liverpool because we played them two years ago and tonight they were just a shadow of that team,' he said.

Liverpool were the only British club to get beyond the last eight in the three European competitions in 1977/78. Aston Villa reached the quarter-finals of the UEFA Cup but lost to Barcelona, who had earlier knocked out Ipswich Town. Manchester United, in the European Cup Winners'

Cup, beat Saint-Étienne, despite playing the second leg at Plymouth, a neutral ground appointed because of crowd trouble at the first game in France.

There was no hat-trick for Paisley in 1978/79, because the very team he feared, Nottingham Forest, eliminated them in the first round. Two English teams – West Bromwich Albion and Manchester City – made it to the quarter-finals of the UEFA Cup, and Ipswich were again beaten by Barcelona in the last eight of the Cup Winners' Cup. A year later, Liverpool surprisingly went out to Dynamo Tbilisi, losing 4-2 on aggregate. Arsenal carried the English flag into the Cup Winners' Cup Final in 1980 after a run that saw a memorable win in Turin against Juventus in the semi-final, a game that was the finest moment of young Paul Vaessen's career. He scored the only goal of the game after the two teams had drawn 1-1 at Highbury. Sadly for Arsenal, they were beaten in the final on penalties by Valencia after the game had ended goalless in the Heysel Stadium.

After winning the league championship in 1980, Liverpool embarked on another run that would end with Paisley winning his third European Cup. Just as in 1977/78, Liverpool lost their league title in 1980/81, with Aston Villa and Ipswich Town emerging as the main title contenders and Liverpool finally finishing in fifth place, their lowest position since 1971, but they won the Football League Cup for the first time, beating West Ham United in the final. They also introduced a young striker to their squad in Ian Rush, who had been signed from Chester for £300,000. His time would soon come. The 1980/81 European Cup included some huge names – Ajax, Bayern Munich, Inter Milan, Real Madrid and Sporting Lisbon were all among the participants. Nottingham Forest were also in the mix after two successive triumphs in the competition. Liverpool began with an easy tie against Oulun Palloseura of Finland. They drew 1-1 away from home and then hit the hapless Finns for ten at Anfield. Both Souness and Terry McDermott scored hat-tricks in a 10-1 win in front of just 21,000 people.

Aberdeen were beaten 5-0 on aggregate in the second round and then CSKA Sofia trounced at Anfield by 5-1, with Souness getting another treble. Across three rounds, Liverpool had scored 26 goals in six games and had conceded three. The road to the semi-final had been relatively stress-free, but the draw paired them with Bayern Munich. The other semi-final was between Real Madrid and Inter Milan – rarely had the competition had such a star-packed last four. The Bayern team was not as accomplished as the side that won three consecutive European Cups between 1974 and 1976 but they had one of Europe's top forwards in Karl-Heinz Rummenigge, who scored 26 goals in the Bundesliga in 1980, and would go on to be top scorer in 1980/81 with a further 29 goals. Bayern also had 1974 World Cup winner Paul Breitner, who was now playing in midfield. Breitner was less than complimentary about Liverpool, claiming they were an 'unintelligent and generally poor team'. Such an unfair assessment was obviously designed to undermine Liverpool, but it merely served to motivate them; in fact, the story was pinned on the dressing-room wall at Anfield.

Liverpool were suffering from an injury crisis and Souness was missing from the first leg. It was expected that the Scot and Breitner would battle away in midfield, with Souness spurred on by the Bayern man's verbal dismissal of Paisley's men. The game ended goalless, which seemed to swing the pendulum Bayern's way, but by 1981 Liverpool had perfected the art of two-legged European ties.

Souness was back for the second game in the vast Olympic stadium in Munich where 75,000 people had assembled to see whether Bayern could dispose of the English champions. Liverpool began nervously and lost Dalglish to an ankle injury in the sixth minute. He was replaced by Howard Gayle, a fast and enthusiastic youngster, and Liverpool's first black player. Liverpool took the lead with seven minutes remaining, a goal from Kennedy that stunned the Bayern crowd. They had a valuable cushion at this point as they were not only 1-0 ahead on aggregate, but they had an away goal to fall back on. Bayern responded and equalised through Rummenigge, but it was too late. Liverpool, after a brave and patient display, were through to their third European Cup Final.

Real Madrid had lost the Spanish title they won in 1980 to Real Sociedad so their only hope of silverware was the European Cup. They had in their ranks Laurie Cunningham, an England international who had joined Real in 1979 from West Bromwich Albion for £950,000. Cunningham was an exceptionally skilful forward who became one of England's first black internationals. Real also had outstanding individuals such as Santillana and Juanito, as well as future coach Vicente del Bosque. Their current coach, Vujadin Boskov, talked of Liverpool's 'veterans', which was a little misleading as they had only three players over 30 in Ray Clemence, Phil Neal and Dalglish. There was no denying that the team that had won the competition in 1977 and 1978 was getting older, though, as Kennedy, Johnson, McDermott and Souness were all approaching 30. Only one player, Sammy Lee, was under 25 years of age.

The final was to be played in the Parc des Princes in Paris, the venue for the first final 25 years earlier. Liverpool fans, who had been given just 12,000 tickets, swarmed to the French capital, but some were not well behaved. There were 100 arrests ahead of the game and some hotels were damaged in the centre of the city. Liverpool's secretary, Peter Robinson, had to apologise for the incidents, but also gave a hint of what the future looked like: 'It is something we very much regret. But neither ourselves nor the British government can accept responsibility. It is something we have no control over.'

Liverpool won their third final 1-0, but the game was underwhelming in many ways. They had some injury concerns regarding Dalglish, who had not trained for weeks, Phil Thompson, and Alan Kennedy, who had been recovering from a broken wrist. Ironically, it was full-back Kennedy who scored the only goal, receiving the ball on his chest from a Ray Kennedy throw-in, dashing past a defender and shooting past goalkeeper Agustin. Kennedy later described it as the best moment of his football career, but he admitted that he thought he had miskicked the ball when he tried his luck.

Paisley had made history as the first coach to win the competition three times: 'We have won the European Cup with better performances but there was a lot of close marking out there and it was difficult to get things going. It was a very hard game to win. It may not have been a classic but we showed tremendous character.' It was England's fifth European Cup win in a row, a sequence that began with Liverpool's victory against Mönchengladbach. The run of success continued in 1982, but it was a different club that got its hands on the 'cup with the big ears'.

15

Something Stirs
in the Midlands

LIVERPOOL'S INITIAL European Cup wins came to an end in the early weeks of the 1978/79 season, a campaign that saw one of the club's best teams play some exhilarating football. Brian Clough's Nottingham Forest had surprisingly won the Football League in their first season back in the top flight after a few years in the Second Division. Forest was an unlikely place for Clough to resurface after he had left Leeds United, but he created the kind of momentum he enjoyed at Derby County and went one better. In that title-winning season, his Forest team combined skill, organisation, determination and good football to shock the league. Liverpool found them something of a thorn in their side and Forest wore down Bob Paisley's team to win the Football League Cup. Paisley had feared Forest in the European Cup, and when the draw was made for the first round, the two clubs were drawn together. While Clough probably relished the chance to unseat the holders, Liverpool would surely have preferred anyone else but Forest.

Clough always wanted to win the European Cup and recalled Derby County's unfortunate and controversial exit at the hands of Juventus. He also pointed out when he arrived at Leeds United that Don Revie had won 'almost everything' but not the European Cup. Forest were not regular European participants, but then they had never won the league championship. Clough joined the club in January 1975 at a time when he was being linked with the England job. But his forthright views were never going to curry favour with the FA. He took the club to promotion in 1977 but nobody really expected Forest to be title contenders. Clough and his partner, Peter Taylor, were good at identifying players who they considered to have the skill and qualities to be successful but had perhaps fallen short of expectations. John Robertson at Forest was a prime example, a winger whose lifestyle stymied his early progress. He became a pivotal figure in Clough's team. Peter Withe, an unspectacular but functional journeyman forward, enjoyed a career-best campaign in 1977/78, while other signings such as Larry Lloyd, Archie Gemmill and Kenny Burns, revitalised their careers at Forest. Others, including Martin O'Neill and Tony Woodcock, suddenly became very different players. Clough also spent big on England goalkeeper Peter Shilton, a signing that was something of a coup. And then there was a young full-back, Viv Anderson, who went on to become the first black England international. Forest stunned the First Division in 1977/78, losing just three games. Clough was back and he had his eyes on the big European prize once more.

The critics were slow to give Forest credit for their success in 1977/78, but the way the team had been constructed was a classic case of leveraging untapped potential. They were also very strategic in the way they played certain games, and they also knew how to get under Liverpool's skin, in much the same way that Jürgen Klopp's Liverpool seemed to know exactly how to play Pep

Guardiola's Manchester City some 45 years later. When the draw was made for the first round of the 1978/79 European Cup, most experts felt Liverpool, with their vast experience and track record, would be too strong for Forest. The league season had not started terribly well for Clough's side. They lacked punch up front and clearly needed a new forward or two. Withe, their top scorer in the title-winning season, was deemed to be surplus to requirements and was sold for £200,000 to Newcastle United. Forest replaced Withe in their team with Garry Birtles, a relatively unknown 22-year-old who had been signed from non-league Long Eaton United in 1976 for just £2,000. He had not seen first-team action since March 1977 but, after Withe had gone and Steve Elliott had failed to impress, Birtles was thrown into the deep end. A left-footed player, who looked a little clumsy at times, his big moment came in the first leg of the Liverpool tie.

The City Ground was packed and the atmosphere vibrant for the latest chapter of the Forest versus Liverpool saga. Forest played their most enterprising football of the campaign so far, relying on swift counter-attacks to keep Liverpool on their toes. For the 1978 European champions, this was a far tougher game than they were used to meeting in the competition at this stage. In the 26th minute, Birtles' moment of glory came as he finished off a move that started in defence. Tony Woodcock ran towards goal and, in doing so, confused Emlyn Hughes as the ball went through the Liverpool defender's legs. Woodcock drew Clemence towards him and then squared his ball to Birtles, who simply stroked it into the net with his favoured left foot.

Liverpool laid siege on the Forest goal for long periods, but they had built a strong wall of defiance that frustrated their opponents. With three minutes to go, Birtles was involved in the second goal, getting past Jimmy Case and Phil Thompson before crossing for Woodcock to head down to full-back Colin Barrett, who volleyed past Clemence. A 2-0 win looked impressive, but Clough was only too aware of Liverpool's credentials. 'Obviously I am pleased to beat Liverpool, it is always an achievement for any club, English or European. But Liverpool are well capable of scoring three goals at home. It would be insulting 14 years of European competition if I were to say we had a great chance at Anfield.'

The second leg ended 0-0 and Forest staged another splendid rearguard action in front of the Liverpool crowd. It was a one-sided game, described by Clough as 'a damned sight harder than I expected'. After two years of triumph in Europe, Liverpool's bid for a third successive trophy had been thwarted in the first round by their new 'bogey' team. Bob Paisley insisted that 'we are still the best team in Europe ... yet we are out of it. That is not sour grapes. It is just being realistic. Good luck to Forest in Europe. I think they will need it.' The sentiment did sound a little bitter on Paisley's part and that was echoed by some Liverpool players. Clough, always quite respectful of the Liverpool dynasty, used them as a benchmark to a certain degree. 'We want to do more than win the European Cup. We want to set Liverpool's kind of standard,' he said. Forest had beaten one of the favourites for the cup in a season in which the competition looked weaker than in previous years. Juventus, another of the highly fancied teams, had been knocked out by Rangers. Real Madrid, although incomparable to their great teams of the past, were still involved, though.

Forest's next challenge came from Greece's AEK Athens, a side renowned for their power and passion at home. They were a free-scoring side that would go on to net 90 goals in 34 league games in 1978/79. They had some prolific forwards in their line-up, including Thomas Mavros, Dušan Bajević and Takis Nikoloudis. Forest were coming into form as they flew to Athens. They had drawn six of their ten league games, but were still unbeaten. Clough had remarked in the press that his priority was not to win the European Cup but to retain the Football League title. Forest were confident in Greece and won 2-1, with John McGovern and Birtles scoring the goals. AEK, who had hosted Forest in pre-season, were disappointing and played with ten men in the second half. The second leg was one-sided and relatively easy for Forest, who were also dealing with an injury crisis. Clough never used injuries as an excuse, as he believed they should be overcome without complaint. But he did like his players looking smart and one of his squad, Larry Lloyd, had been fined £200 for not wearing the club blazer. The friction between manager and player seemed to be forgotten by the time the second leg came around as the big central defender was made captain and led Forest to a 5-1 win.

The quarter-finals looked remarkably average after Real Madrid were eliminated by Grasshopper Zürich. Rangers were still involved, while Eastern Europe was represented by Dynamo Dresden and Wisła Kraków, and the West German champions, Köln, were arguably the biggest threat to Forest. Sweden's Malmö and Austria Vienna completed the last eight. Forest struck lucky in being paired with Grasshopper, but the mere fact the Swiss side had overturned a 3-1 first-leg defeat to knock out Real Madrid meant they had to be treated with respect.

Forest were still having problems scoring goals when 1979 arrived. They had only lost twice, but too many draws were costing them dear. They were sixth in the league table and the lack of firepower led Clough to claim that 'we have a crisis on our hands'. Increasingly, Forest were being named as possible winners of the cup, but Clough, always keen to downplay his team's chances, pointed to the 'goals for' column, which revealed just 28 goals in 24 games. 'With our poor scoring record at home, I don't see how we can be favourites for this competition. I honestly don't know where the next goal is coming from.' But Clough had a plan and it revolved around signing one of the most sought-after players in the country.

Trevor Francis was approaching his peak and had spent all his career with a Birmingham City side destined for relegation. Francis had won his first England caps but there was an underlying feeling the best of him was still to come. Birmingham were also keen to cash in on their prize asset while they could, but if anyone wanted to sign Francis, they would have to pay good money. The record transfer fee in England was £500,000, which had been paid for two players, Kevin Keegan when he moved from Liverpool to Hamburg and David Mills of Middlesbrough, who was signed by West Bromwich Albion in December 1978. Eventually, Clough persuaded the Forest board to break the record with a fee that exceeded £1m. If any player was going to be the first million-pound man in Britain, it was arguably always going to be Francis, but Clough, in his own inimitable style, attempted to defuse the hullabaloo by naming Francis in a reserve game and also by turning up at the signing in his squash kit. However, Forest could not play their new asset in either the Football League Cup or European Cup just yet. If they reached the final of the latter, Francis would be eligible to play, if selected, of course.

Grasshopper had their own star man in Claudio Sulser, a 23-year-old striker who had scored five goals in a 34-minute period in the first round against Valletta as the Swiss side won 8-0 in Zürich. They netted another five in the away leg to run up an emphatic 13-3 aggregate win. Sulser went on to become top scorer in the competition with 11 goals in 1978/79. He was a law student and was fast and powerful. So impressed was Clough when he saw the young forward that he contemplated signing him. Sulser silenced the City Ground as he opened the scoring in the 11th minute of the first leg. It took Forest 20 minutes to draw level through Birtles, and just after half-time, Robertson netted a penalty. The crowd anticipated a second-half onslaught, but Forest struggled to overcome tight man-to-man marking and Grasshopper's ability to quickly break out of defence. The game dragged on and even Clough had given up hope of further goals when Gemmill added a third on 87 minutes and then Lloyd headed a fourth. In three minutes, the complexion of the tie had changed completely. 'Goals in the bank,' screamed the headlines and they were absolutely right; unless Forest imploded, the quarter-final was as good as won.

In between the two legs, Forest won the Football League Cup for the second successive season, beating Southampton 3-2. They were scoring goals again and Woodcock and Birtles seemed to be blending. They scored Forest's three goals at Wembley.

The Zürich football community obviously felt Grasshopper had little chance of overturning a three-goal deficit. Only 8,000 people turned up at the Hardturm stadium but they did, at least, see a spirited performance by their team. Forest were a little rattled by Grasshopper's approach, and a 33rd-minute penalty from none other than Sulser put them ahead. But five minutes later O'Neill levelled to extinguish any thoughts of heroic comebacks. Nevertheless, Forest were relieved to get the game finished. In the other ties, Rangers had been narrowly beaten by West Germany's Köln, depriving the Scottish champions of an all-British semi-final with Forest. Köln were possibly the hardest opponent remaining and Forest were now up against them. Malmö and Austria Vienna were both unlikely semi-finalists, but one of them would make it to the final. Forest just had to get past a team that had won the double in West Germany in 1977/78 and included Toni Schumacher, Bernd Cullmann, Roger Van Gool and the free-scoring Dieter Müller in their line-up.

After disposing of AEK Athens and Grasshopper, Forest were facing their toughest task since the first round when they met Liverpool. Gemmill, arguably their most seasoned European campaigner, hinted that Köln might be a trip into the unknown: 'We know what English football is all about, yet we stand on the threshold of a European triumph with not too much knowledge of the opposition.' Clough, however, remained confident: 'Köln cannot throw anything at us that we have not already experienced and dealt with.' There was no lack of respect on Clough's part, though, he emphasised that German football was very strong, as evidenced by five of the 12 semi-finalists in the three UEFA competitions coming from the Bundesliga.

A packed City Ground was convinced Forest were on their way to the final, but the home crowd was stunned by their team's performance in the first 20 minutes. After six minutes, Van Gool sent a low shot in off Shilton's right-hand post. It got worse in the 19th minute when Köln counter-attacked and Van Gool teased out Shilton and squared the ball to allow Müller an easy tap-in. Forest were being torn apart by Köln's pace and ability to break out of defence, despite the muddy pitch. But in the 27th minute, Forest gained some relief when John Robertson's cross was nodded goalwards by David Needham and Birtles sent his free header past Toni Schumacher. Forest were in recovery mode now but they lost Gemmill just before half-time.

They remained patient and eventually equalised in the 58th minute when Ian Bowyer sent a low drive into the net after another Robertson cross was knocked down by Birtles and fell invitingly for Forest's underrated utility man. No sooner had the equaliser found the net, than Forest went in search of a third goal, and within five minutes they went ahead for the first and only time. Birtles, showing very intricate skill, sent over a dangerous cross from the byline and Robertson dived to head past Schumacher.

Forest thought they now had the advantage they needed to take to Germany, albeit a very slender margin, but their hopes were dashed five minutes from the end. Köln brought on Yasuhiko Okudera in the 80th minute as substitute and his first notable touch was to shoot beneath Shilton's body to make the final score 3-3. It had been a very engaging 90 minutes, but it was not the scoreline Forest were looking for. However, after their disastrous start, a draw was not a bad evening's work. The media, naturally, were already starting to write off Forest, although Clough was defiant in his post-match interview, finishing with a little snipe at the press. 'I hope anybody's not stupid enough to write us off,' he said to BBC TV's John Motson. His cheeky last words were made in the knowledge that the Clough-Taylor partnership had made a living out of surprising people, going back to their days at Derby County.

Forest were on a good run in the league and were destined for a top-three final placing. They warmed up for the second leg in the Müngersdorfer stadium with a couple of draws against Leeds United and Manchester United and a 2-0 win at Birmingham City. Clough declared that his team was well prepared for Köln: 'They [the Forest players] have been bitten once, it won't happen twice. I believe we have a good chance.' Still the media felt Forest were as good as out of the competition, claiming they had lost the tie in those calamitous first 20 minutes in Nottingham. Viv Anderson, who had missed the first game through suspension, was back, adding more pace to the back line, but Gemmill was out through injury. Kenny Burns also returned to the side. The hero of the hour was none other than Bowyer, who ducked to head the only goal in the 65th minute from a Robertson cross. 'Everything fell into place for us. It was a lovely night,' beamed Clough, also insisting that Bowyer was 'worth a million'. Köln's coach, Hennes Weiswieler, felt that the loss of Müller in the first half through injury had influenced the outcome.

So, the remarkable Forest story continued and Clough was eagerly anticipating the final, to be held on 30 May in Munich's iconic Olympic stadium. 'Everything about Germany is right for us. We like the people, we like the towns and we like the football they play.' Their opponents were Malmö, Sweden's champions, who were managed by a 32-year-old Englishman named Bobby Houghton. Forest were red-hot favourites, especially as they could field their £1m signing, Francis. 'He will be in the squad,' joked Clough. Malmö's squad were nearly all Swedish internationals, and players such as Roland Andersson, Ingemar Erlandsson and Staffan Tapper had been part of their country's squad for the 1978 World Cup. Houghton, a friend of future England coach Roy Hodgson, was relatively unknown in his native country and, on first appearance, he could be mistaken for being a Swede. Houghton was quite imaginative in his coaching style and introduced zonal marking to Sweden. He joined Malmö in 1974 and won three Allsvenskan titles in 1974, 1975 and 1977. Houghton enjoyed a very colourful and eclectic career, managing in ten different countries, including spells as national team coach with India, China and Uzbekistan. In 1979, his Malmö team beat Monaco, Dynamo Kyiv, Wisła Kraków and Austria Vienna. They had useful players, including midfielders Anders Ljungberg and Jan-Olov Kindvall. Clearly, they were no fools as their path to the final showed but, as far as the pundits were concerned, the European Cup was Forest's to lose.

Forest had finally clinched the runners-up spot in the Football League to Liverpool with a 1-0 win against fellow Midlanders West Bromwich Albion, who had also had their eye on second place. Forest only lost three league games in 1978/79, but they had drawn 18. Clough took a brief holiday before linking up with his squad ahead of the final. Most writers predicted a comfortable Forest win, perhaps by three goals, but it was clear that Malmö were keen to prevent a drubbing on the big stage. Interestingly, while some warned Forest not to be complacent, headlines like 'Forest to waltz it' suggested that perhaps the media were being a little presumptuous about the outcome. Meanwhile, Houghton told the press that 'our duty is not to football as a spectacle, but to our club', which suggested they would try to prevent Forest playing. Houghton was clear that Malmö could not match Forest for skill, but they would have to combat the English side with 'tactical togetherness'. Others anticipated Malmö would put on a display of 'dogged efficiency'.

Forest were without Gemmill and O'Neill, who both failed fitness tests before the final, although they were assigned to the bench as possible substitutes. As for Francis, he was about to make his European debut on the right side of midfield. Bowyer started on the left. Francis had a sublime first half and one minute before the interval ducked to head home a Robertson cross at the far post. Francis showed his full array of skills and seemed to be out to show the world why he cost Forest a million pounds. But Malmö did offer stubborn resistance, and although Forest were in control, they were frustrated. The big win did not materialise, although Robertson could have added another goal when he struck the post after being set up by Francis. There were 20,000 Forest fans in the Olympic stadium, a third of the 60,000 attendance, but they made plenty of noise as the final whistle blew. Two years earlier, they had claimed the third promotion place from the Second Division, so it was a truly remarkable achievement by a unique team built by Clough and Taylor. 'This is a milestone in my career. We are worthy successors to Liverpool,' insisted Clough. It was actually a milestone for every one of the Forest players, especially Francis, who was dubbed 'Euro man in a million' by the tabloids.

Forest's prized asset had a delayed start to the 1979/80 season due to a groin injury sustained in the US while playing for Detroit Express. There were rumours that Francis was unhappy at Forest, but he dismissed these claims as nonsense, but in truth he never seemed like a good fit. The same could be applied to Asa Hartford, who was signed as a replacement for Gemmill, who had moved to Birmingham. Forest paid £385,000 for the Manchester City midfielder, but he played just three games before being sold to Everton. Frank Clark had retired, so Forest brought in Leeds United's Frankie Gray, a transaction that cost the club £500,000. Clough also took minor gambles on some individuals who could never be described as his type of player – Charlie George, a mercurial forward who made his name with Arsenal, arrived on loan from Southampton, and Stan Bowles was signed from Queens Park Rangers later in the season. In mid-season, Woodcock was also sold to Köln for £875,000. In hindsight, did Forest need to sell in order to accommodate their expensive acquisition of Francis?

England had two representatives again in the European Cup, Forest and Liverpool, but this time they were kept apart in the first-round draw. Liverpool had to face Soviet side Dinamo Tbilisi from the Georgian capital. They were a very talented group of players and Liverpool struggled to beat them 2-1 in the first leg at Anfield. The second meeting was always going to be tough, but the Liverpool team were hampered by crowds of Tbilisi fans singing and chanting outside their hotel at 4am on the day of the match. Tired and under pressure in a partisan atmosphere, Liverpool lost 3-0 in torrential rain and tumbled out at the first hurdle. Celtic fared better, overcoming a one-goal deficit to beat Albania's Partizani 4-2 on aggregate. The Scottish champions had a decent run that saw them beat Dundalk before losing 3-2 on aggregate to Real Madrid. Celtic had won the first leg 2-0 and were only eliminated in the latter stages of the return in the Bernabéu stadium.

Forest's first opponents, ironically, were one of Malmö's rivals, Öster from the city of Växjö, who adopted a similar defensive approach to the 1979 finalists. Forest were patient, however, and two goals in the second half from Ian Bowyer gave them a satisfactory if unspectacular 2-0 victory. The game in Sweden ended 1-1, enough to see off tough-tackling but well-drilled opponents. If Öster were an unknown quantity, Forest's next task was a trip into the unknown to meet the Romanian champions, Argeş Piteşti. Clough and Taylor wanted to watch this team, based some 60 miles north-west of Bucharest, but they were unable to obtain the necessary visas in time. They had to be guided by hearsay and any intelligence they could gain from their contacts. Arges arrived for the first leg in Nottingham shorn of their two best players, a young midfielder called Ilie Barbulescu and a 23-year-old front man, Marin Radu, who was top scorer in the Romanian league in 1978/79. They were not optimistic about their chances against the holders. Their coach, Florin Halagian, was expecting a heavy defeat. However, a certain amount of respect was due as they had won the title in a league dominated by teams from the capital, Bucharest. Everyone knew about Steaua, Rapid and Dinamo, but Pitești were not on anyone's radar.

Forest were without Francis, who was ineligible owing to a delay in returning from his loan spell in the US. It is still a mystery why Forest, who had paid so much money for Francis, allowed him to play in the US in the first place. One can only assume that it had something to do with economics. Forest possibly found it too easy against Argeș, scoring twice in the first 17 minutes through Woodcock and Birtles. After this whirlwind start, they appeared to lose their way and there were no further goals. While it was obvious that Argeș were not particularly strong, they would surely be motivated on their own turf. Clough insisted Forest would not alter their style in Romania, but they might try to hold on to the ball longer. The locals turned out in force in a stadium where the snow-capped Carpathian mountains could be seen in the background. Forest killed the tie with two goals – Bowyer and Birtles – in the opening 22 minutes and, although Argeș managed to get a goal on the hour, a penalty from Barbulescu, Forest had put on a professional 'away performance' that guaranteed their place in the last eight. And just as in 1978/79, the quarter-finals did not look too daunting. Britain had two representatives, Celtic, who had beaten Dundalk, and Forest. Celtic were drawn to meet Real Madrid, while Clough had to take his troops on another trip east to meet Dynamo Berlin.

Dynamo were the club that the East German state expected to win the DDR-Oberliga, and from the late

1970s through to the end of German division they were perpetual champions. They were a well-organised, hard-working team, used to winning every week, but were not in the same class as Forest. They had an impressive goalscorer in 24-year-old Hans-Jürgen Riediger and another useful forward in Wolf-Rüdiger Netz. The team was prolific in front of goal, as evidenced by their 9-1 victory against Stahl Riesa. Clough's team had just lost to one of the First Division's worst sides in Bolton Wanderers, but he was not worried about Dynamo's credentials. He did, however, admit that he felt the tie had to be won at the City Ground. 'I don't fancy going to Berlin with the tie still in the balance,' he said. But his wish did not come true, for Forest made it hard for themselves by losing 1-0, with Riediger scoring midway through the second half. 'We will win it in East Germany,' declared Clough, sounding as though he was trying hard to convince himself.

Forest went behind the Iron Curtain after losing the Football League Cup Final – another surprise – to Wolverhampton Wanderers. They were also without the suspended Kenny Burns and Clough decided the maverick Bowles should make way for Bowyer, who had developed a knack of scoring vital goals in Europe. He also called for Trevor Francis to find his goalscoring form after a barren period. 'I would not say he was under pressure, but he has to listen to the criticism.' Francis had been listening, for he was in excellent form in the Friedrick-Ludwig-Jahn stadium where 30,000 of the quarter of a million ticket applicants were watching. He scored twice in the opening 35 minutes and by half-time Forest were 3-0 up and had taken control of the tie. Dynamo scored a penalty in the second half, but it was not enough. Neither was Celtic's two-goal first-leg win against Real Madrid, who finally disposed of the Scots with a late goal that clinched a 3-0 win.

Ajax were next for Forest, but they were not the Dutch masters of old. Of their big names from the early 1970s, only Ruud Krol was in their line-up; in fact, he was arguably the driving force of their team. Ajax had, unsurprisingly, suffered a decline when the likes of Cruyff and Neeskens departed for Barcelona, but in 1979 and indeed 1980, they were Dutch champions once more. Now coached by Leo Beenhakker, a much-travelled individual who would later manage Real Madrid for two spells, they had an emerging team that played in the spirit of their predecessors. They had a trio of Danes in Søren Lerby, Henning Jensen and Frank Arnesen who had become the backbone of the team. Forest expected Ajax to be as good as Köln but, while they were a respected club around Europe, their popularity at home had diminished since their 'total football' highs.

For all their technique, Ajax could be very miserly away from home and it was expected they would arrive at the City Ground to stifle the home team. Certainly, their close marking was difficult to handle, but the speed of Francis caused them problems and he opened the scoring on 37 minutes from close range. Forest scored a second when John Robertson netted his 14th penalty of the season, proving he was more than just a good provider of crosses, so they had a two-goal margin to take to Amsterdam.

Clough and Taylor were ready for a different type of Ajax in the second leg, as they would need to attack to retrieve the two-goal deficit. They had not been beaten at home in European competition for a decade. Lerby scored the only goal in the 66th minute, which meant Forest were under pressure until the end. Ajax at least kept their home record going, but for Forest a second successive European

Cup Final was on the horizon, the chance to retain the trophy and cast Clough into the history books.

Forest's second final, interestingly, was against Hamburg, whose star player was none other than Kevin Keegan, who had announced he was leaving Germany at the end of the season. His last game for HSV, before he would eventually settle back in England with Southampton, would be against Forest on 28 May 1980 in the final. Hamburg had turned around a two-goal defeat in Spain to beat Real Madrid 5-1 in the second leg. Keegan did not score, but he was the inspiration for Hamburg. The final was, ironically, in Real's Bernabéu stadium.

Keegan's time in Germany had been a success; Hamburg won the Bundesliga in 1978/79 and Keegan had been named European Footballer of the Year in 1978 and 1979. He had now received the broad recognition that had eluded him while he was in England. Never a prolific scorer, he did, at the end of his Hamburg career, have a record of 40 goals in 113 games. He was also England captain in an era that was short on heroes.

Forest finished fifth in the First Division in 1980 and their only hope of being in Europe in 1980/81 was through winning the European Cup. They needed the financial rewards of European football as they had a new grandstand to pay for. Hamburg also had their motivation for winning, aside from the glory of being champions of the continent – they had agreed to sign 35-year-old Franz Beckenbauer after his contract with the New York Cosmos ended.

Forest were without Francis for the final as he had an Achilles tendon injury. They had to rely on 18-year-old Gary Mills alongside Birtles as their main attacking threat. Hamburg were denied the chance of starting with Horst Hrubesch, a battering ram of a forward who linked up well with Keegan. This meant the former Liverpool man would have to face Forest's take-no-prisoners defenders on his own. With Hrubesch in the team, Clough's team would have had other distractions. Hamburg were the more positive team, but Forest defended resolutely and gave Keegan an uneasy 90 minutes. The game was not a spectacle; it was a little attritional but was settled in the 20th minute by Robertson, the player who epitomised the Clough-Taylor era at Forest. He received the ball from Mills, went past Manny Kaltz, traded passes with Birtles and then sent a low shot in off the post. Some critics felt Forest had lacked imagination and that Hamburg should have won, but Clough pointed out the merits of the rearguard action. 'They may have had the edge on us in technique, but we beat them for application, determination and pride – all the things that portray our football. We weren't lucky. We were good and any good team would have no option but to defend, but if you have to defend, you have to do it well. It is as important as attacking.' Clough's reward for a second successive European Cup was a new contract that would yield him £100,000 over three years. At the time, that was a considerable salary.

In 1980/81, Forest's run was brought to an end by CSKA Sofia, who beat the twice-winners 1-0 at home and away. Coincidentally, it was the Bulgarians who had ended Ajax's three-year reign in 1973. It had been an extraordinary period for Nottingham Forest, for the people of Nottingham and for the partnership of Brian Clough and Peter Taylor. If Nottingham Forest's success in Europe was a surprise to many people, Aston Villa's triumph in 1982 was even more remarkable. A big club with a rich heritage, Villa had, a decade earlier, been in the Third Division of the Football League. Their last league title win was in 1910 and the club had fallen from its historical highs in a dramatic and somewhat sad manner. They won promotion back to the Second Division in 1972 and, three years later, under the ultra-disciplinarian Ron Saunders, they were promoted to the top flight and won the Football League Cup for the second time.

Saunders built a strong team that had the solid foundations that he always demanded of his sides, but they also benefitted from considerable flair. Villa, after finishing seventh in 1979/80, became title contenders in 1980/81. Saunders had added Peter Withe to his squad, a journeyman striker who had won the league with Nottingham Forest in 1978. He paired this tall target man with a promising and spritely youngster, Gary Shaw, to form a partnership that immediately paid dividends. Consistency was the key for Villa – they used just 14 players in 1981, with seven of their squad playing all 42 league games. This continuity was vital as Saunders' team went head to head with Bobby Robson's popular Ipswich Town for the title. While Ipswich struggled to fight on three fronts, including the UEFA Cup, Villa only had the league title to focus on. In the end, Ipswich ran out of steam, but Villa remained focused and eventually finished four points ahead of their challengers.

Villa had experienced Europe twice before and had reached the quarter-finals of the UEFA Cup in 1977/78, but the prospect of European Cup football excited the Birmingham public. Nobody in their wildest dreams anticipated the club becoming European champions. Likewise, Villa's fans would not have expected their team to climb to the summit without Ron Saunders, the man who led them to the title in 1981. Villa were to relinquish their league title, but their European campaign gathered momentum with a comfortable first-round victory over Valur Reykjavík of Iceland and then a narrow win on away goals against Dynamo Berlin. Saunders had fallen out with the Villa board and had resigned before the quarter-final came around, and his assistant, the unsung and underrated Tony Barton, had taken over.

Villa had been drawn against Dynamo Kyiv, the team that provided the hub of the Soviet Union's national team. Among them was Oleg Blokhin, one of Europe's top players, who had won the European Footballer of the Year award in 1975 by a considerable margin. Kyiv were managed by the innovative and highly rated Valeriy Lobanovsky and a year earlier the British media had eulogised about Dinamo Tbilisi, who had torn West Ham apart in the European Cup Winners' Cup, but the word was that Kyiv were considerably stronger.

Villa discovered very late on that their first-leg tie with Kyiv would not be played in the frozen Ukrainian capital but 350 miles south in Simferopol. They also had to alter their accommodation in Yalta. There was another change when it was revealed that the kick-off time would be 5pm local time, which meant a midweek afternoon kick-off to satisfy television coverage. Such disruptions were not uncommon for teams playing in the old Soviet Union. Nevertheless, Villa carved out a valuable 0-0 draw, prompting Barton to comment that 'take away Blokhin and Kyiv are an ordinary side'. At Villa Park, on a pitch covered with sand, Barton's team clinched their semi-final place with a two-goal victory. Gary Shaw and Ken McNaught scored the goals but Villa lost their captain, Dennis Mortimer, with a dislocated shoulder.

The competition had now become realistically winnable for Villa as Liverpool, the holders, had been knocked out by CSKA Sofia. Villa now had to face Belgium's Anderlecht, while the Bulgarians had to contend with Bayern Munich, arguably the best side remaining. Anderlecht were an experienced club when it came to European competition; they had mastered the art of two-legged ties and had appeared in three European Cup Winners' Cup finals between 1975/76 and 1977/78, winning two. Villa had now appointed Barton on a full-time basis and were confident about negotiating the semi-final. They expected Anderlecht to adopt a defensive stance in the first leg at Villa Park and so it proved. They were so focused on stopping Villa that they could afford to leave their leading scorer, Willy Geurts, on the bench for 'not trying hard enough'. Geurts had scored five goals in the competition, including goals against Juventus and Red Star Belgrade. Villa fielded Mortimer despite him being far from fully fit. Villa won 1-0 on a frustrating evening, Tony Morley scoring after 27 minutes. After that, it was a case of battering against a formidable defensive line while also preventing Anderlecht from launching damaging counter-attacks. Villa were close to their finest hour, but it could easily have gone wrong in Brussels.

The Belgian capital expected an invasion of English fans, and leading up to kick-off there were numerous skirmishes in the city, and arrests. Even inside the stadium there were problems and, during the first 20 minutes of the game, there were disruptions and on one occasion a fan was laying prostrate on the turf. The police brought in reinforcements and the game was delayed for seven minutes while they moved into place. The game ended goalless, but the headlines were mostly about English fans letting the side down again.

Once the dust had settled, Villa could reflect on one of the most momentous occasions of their history. It was now their turn to take the European Cup back to Britain for the sixth consecutive year. They had ended the season well, and if they had achieved that sort of consistency of the previous three months, they would have almost certainly have qualified for Europe. However, the European Cup was their chance to secure another year in the competition. Bayern Munich, their opponents, had turned round a first-leg defeat against CSKA Sofia in the semi-final. They had far more experience than Villa, notably in the presence of Paul Breitner, Klaus Augenthaler, Dieter Hoeneß and Karl-Heinz Rummenigge, among others.

The behaviour of Villa's fans in Brussels had alerted UEFA to a growing problem, and Bayern's secretary, Hans Bergerter, went public in calling for English clubs to be banned. Rotterdam, the venue for the final, expected a repeat of the scenes witnessed in Brussels, but there was a sense of relief that there was very little trouble, although Dutch police did baton-charge a group of bottle-throwing Villa fans. Another group did not even get as far as Rotterdam as they were prevented from getting off a ferry docking at Hook van Holland due to their inebriated state. There were signs that the rest of Europe was becoming a little intolerant of drunken louts on football excursions from England. In just a few years, the situation would come to a nasty climax.

Villa's night of glory got off to a strange start. Just ten minutes into the game with Bayern, Villa's goalkeeper, Jimmy Rimmer, who had been on the bench for Manchester United's 1968 European Cup triumph, had to be replaced by 23-year-old Nigel Spink. Rimmer had been struggling with a shoulder injury in the lead-up to the final and seemed perfectly fit to play, even during the warm-up before the match. But he tweaked his neck and could not continue. Spink was an untried goalkeeper who had joined Villa in 1977 from non-league Chelmsford City. He had played a single league game for the club, but Barton and his team had total faith in the youngster and while his defenders, notably Allan Evans and Kenny Swain, provided cover for

Spink, he performed well for the 80 minutes he was on the pitch. It was a nice bit of football romance to add to the occasion. Spink went on to have a good career and was capped once by England on a tour to Australia, playing 45 minutes as a substitute for Shilton, but he will forever be remembered for his cameo in Villa's European campaign.

Bayern may have been favourites, but it was Villa that won the silverware, thanks to a goal from Withe on 66 minutes, a simple tap-in from Morley's cross. Bayern were a little shocked and proceeded to unleash all their firepower in a rather frenetic fashion. Spink and his protectors stopped everything that came their way and Bayern trudged off defeated and disappointed. Tony Barton was a relative unknown and would have remained so if Saunders had remained Villa manager. However, he was now coach of the European champions after beating one of the continent's top clubs. It was all rather surreal, especially given the introduction of another 'unknown' in the first ten minutes.

Villa, along with Liverpool, carried the flag of England into the 1982/83 European Cup, but both fell at the quarter-final stage. Villa beat Beşiktaş of Turkey and the Romanians of Dinamo Bucharest before losing to a strong Juventus side. Liverpool had a relatively easy route, overcoming Dundalk and Finland's HJK Helsinki and looked a fair bet to reach the semi-finals when they were drawn to meet Poland's Widzew Łódź. They lost the first leg 2-0 in Łódź and found themselves 2-1 down at Anfield before recovering to win 3-2, but it was not enough. The great run of success that began with Liverpool's 1976/77 victory in Rome and ended in Rotterdam in 1982 with Aston Villa was over.

16

The Summit and the Sadness

IN THE mid-1970s, there was a certain fascination for all things Dutch among the football fraternity. Some managers, such as Dave Sexton, Ron Greenwood and Bobby Robson, were students of the European game and attempted to bring elements of the continent to England. It did not always work, for English players were not schooled in the same way as their European counterparts, but these managers at least demonstrated a willingness to learn from Germany, the Netherlands and other countries.

In February 1978, the European Community decreed that the football associations of member states had to allow players from abroad access to England. In the summer of 1978, the Football League lifted a ban that dated back to 1931. Some clubs moved quickly, notably Tottenham Hotspur, who signed two members of Argentina's victorious World Cup squad: Osvaldo Ardiles and Ricardo Villa. It was more a trickle than a torrent of new talent, but by the end of 1978/79 clubs like Ipswich Town, Southampton, Chelsea, Manchester City and Birmingham City had all signed foreign players.

Ipswich Town acquired two Dutch players, Arnold Mühren and Frans Thijssen, arguably the best overseas duo to enter the Football League in the 1970s. They were certainly more consistent than the Spurs pair and helped create an excellent and entertaining team. Under Robson, Ipswich had a reputation for purist football and represented a solid challenge to Liverpool, but were often undone by their lack of strength in depth. They were a small club, playing in front of just 23,000 people at their homely Portman Road ground. They were also popular outside their own environs. Between 1972/73 and 1976/77, Ipswich finished in the top four on four occasions. In 1977/78, a season that saw them flirt with relegation, they won the FA Cup, their second major honour after their shock 1961/62 title win when Alf Ramsey was in charge.

Robson was looking for something different to make his team into championship contenders. His first venture into the overseas market came in the summer of 1978 when he signed Mühren from Twente for £150,000. Mühren had mixed in good circles, growing up among Ajax's golden generation, including Johan Cruyff. He had won the European Cup in 1973 and was still only 27 when he arrived in Suffolk. His cultured left foot was a joy to watch, although his debut against Liverpool was a setback, a three-goal home defeat. Mühren was anonymous as the game bypassed him, prompting a post-match discussion with Robson. The message was clear: 'I need the ball.' It was not long before Robson started to adapt Ipswich's style and also to take notice of some of the methods adopted by Dutch football clubs. Mühren noticed the lack of pre-match preparation, something that was important to clubs like Ajax and Feyenoord.

Ipswich were still inconsistent and after the Boxing Day draw with Norwich were 16th in the First Division, having won just seven of their 21 games. Robson signed Thijssen from Twente for £200,000, providing Mühren with a like-minded partner in midfield. Ipswich's form in the second half of the season was impressive. They lost just twice in 20 games, winning seven of their last eight. They also reached the quarter-final of the FA Cup and were narrowly beaten by Barcelona in the European Cup Winners' Cup. The following season, Ipswich were seen as possible champions, but their start to the campaign was disastrous, with eight defeats in their first 12 games. But after being beaten by Coventry at the start of December, they went 22 games without defeat and finished third, just seven points behind champions Liverpool.

By now, Mühren and Thijssen were the driving force of Ipswich's free-flowing style. Robson said of Mühren: 'I cannot think of anyone I would rate higher as a professional. No one worked harder.' Thijssen, speaking some years later, recalled that when he arrived from Twente, Ipswich played like most other teams: 'The English style was to kick it forward as much as possible, so when you played midfielder you had to run forward and if you didn't get the ball, you would have to run back. Bobby [Robson] changed the style, telling the defenders to play it to the Dutch guys in the midfield. That style suited our team very well.'

The 1980/81 season was supposed to be Ipswich's finest hour. They had an excellent starting XI and played a compelling brand of football. They were unbeaten in their first 14 games and were chasing the title all season as well as fighting on the European front and in the FA Cup. Ipswich lost in the FA Cup semi-final and eventually finished second in the league, four points behind an Aston Villa team they had beaten three times during the season. Thijssen, who was named Football Writers' Association Footballer of the Year, missed the last five league fixtures with hamstring problems and Ipswich lost four of them.

The UEFA Cup provided Ipswich with some consolation for a season that promised so much. They came up against some strong teams, two of which would end 1980/81 as champions of their respective leagues. In the first round they beat Aris Salonika of Greece, with John Wark scoring a hat-trick of penalties in the first leg at Portman Road. Wark, whom Aris had tried to sign a few months earlier, had an outstanding season and scored so many goals in the UEFA Cup that he was nicknamed 'Mr Europe'. He netted four in that first leg, a rugged game in which the Greek side had a man sent off. Ipswich lost the second leg 3-1, but were through with goals to spare. Bohemians of Prague were beaten 3-0 in Suffolk in the next round but, once more, Ipswich made it hard for themselves by losing 2-0 in the Czech capital. The third round saw them put on a tremendous performance at home, beating Widzew Łodź 5-0, with Wark netting a hat-trick. 'In the first half, we had spells when I have never seen us play better,' said manager Bobby Robson. Once more, they were beaten in the away leg.

Ipswich had tough opponents in the quarter-finals, France's Saint-Étienne, who were known as the 'laughing cavaliers of French football'. Michel Platini was approaching his peak and a year away from moving to Italy, but he was the biggest threat to Ipswich. Saint-Étienne also had Dutch striker Johnny Rep in their line-up. But Les Verts were swept aside in the Stade Geoffroy-Guichard, with Ipswich winning 4-1 and leaving the field to loud applause from the French fans. They sealed the tie with a 3-1 win at home, a game that was not screened on British screens as Ipswich had, rather controversially, sold the TV rights to French television. Ipswich now had to deal with Köln, who had Englishman Tony Woodcock, a twice-winner of the European Cup, in their team. They won both legs 1-0 to seal a place in the final against Dutch side AZ Alkmaar, who won the Eredivisie by a margin of 12 points. They would also go on to win the KNVB Cup, beating Ajax in the final. In other words, AZ were strong and included notables such as Kees Kist, Johnny Metgod, Jan Peters, who scored twice at Wembley against England in 1977, and Austrian winger Kurt Welzl. They had a smoother path to the final than Ipswich and had beaten Sochaux of France in the semi-final.

Just before the first leg of the final at Portman Road, Ipswich had lost any chance of the league title and Aston Villa were confirmed as champions. Ipswich had, in April, surprisingly lost their FA Cup semi-final against Manchester City, so the UEFA Cup was their only chance of a trophy. There were very few football followers who would have denied Ipswich some reward for a truly outstanding season. The first meeting was a 3-0 win for Ipswich, with Wark as 'dour and intense as ever' scoring the first goal from the penalty spot, Thijssen adding a second just after half-time and Paul Mariner rounding off the scoring in the 55th minute.

Ipswich's reputation for throwing away a commanding lead in Europe was well known, and their away record in the UEFA Cup was a little unconvincing, so there was hope for AZ. The second game was staged in Amsterdam's Olympic stadium but only 22,000 turned up to see it. Ipswich were, arguably, burnt-out after their gruelling campaign but they came back twice to level the scores before finally losing 4-2. The overall score was 5-4 to Ipswich. It had been a painfully narrow victory, but it would have been a cruel finale for Bobby Robson's team if they had gone into the summer empty-handed.

While Bobby Robson was an established figure in English football and would become England manager and graduate to the status of 'national treasure' in his latter years, Alex Ferguson was an up-and-coming manager in the early 1980s. As a player, he turned out for Queens Park, St Johnstone, Dunfermline, Rangers, Falkirk and Ayr and he won four caps for Scotland. His managerial career started quietly at East Stirlingshire and St Mirren, but in 1978 he succeeded Billy McNeill at Aberdeen. Ferguson built his team to become credible rivals to the 'Old Firm' of Celtic and Rangers. Together with Dundee United, Aberdeen formed part of the 'New Firm' in Scottish football that brought greater competitiveness to the top division. In 1980, Aberdeen were Scottish champions, the first time since 1965 that a team other than the Glasgow giants had won the league title. They went close to completing the double, losing to Dundee United in the Scottish Cup Final. However, they won the cup in 1982 and entered the European Cup Winners' Cup in 1982/83 as one of the outsiders for the competition. There were a plethora of big names for Ferguson to worry about, including Inter Milan, Real Madrid, Barcelona and Tottenham Hotspur.

Aberdeen began their campaign by thrashing Sion of Switzerland 11-1 on aggregate in the preliminary round. They scrambled through two difficult games with Dinamo Tirana, winning 1-0 and had to deal with intense heat in the second leg in the Albanian capital. Lech Poznań were also stubborn opponents in the second round but, after securing a two-goal win at Pittodrie, Aberdeen came away from Poland with a single-goal victory, largely due to a disciplined defensive performance. Aberdeen silenced a raucous home crowd when Doug Bell netted the winner and watched as the locals headed for the exit, convinced that their side could not retrieve a three-goal deficit.

It was the quarter-final that convinced everyone that Aberdeen were credible contenders for the Cup Winners'

Cup. Bayern Munich were among Europe's top clubs, with a pedigree that few could match. The Olympic stadium in Munich, a magnificent arena, staged the first leg but only 28,000 attended the game. The home team was frustrated by an Aberdeen defence that was well marshalled by Willie Miller. A goalless draw was an exceptional result for Aberdeen, but Bayern were just as dangerous away from home, so there could be no room for complacency. The return at Pittodrie proved that point, with Bayern leading twice before being beaten 3-2 by a 77th-minute volleyed goal from substitute John Hewitt. Aberdeen could easily have folded against sustained pressure from Bayern, but Ferguson summed it up perfectly: 'Grit and determination were the decisive factors in taking us through.'

The semi-final draw was kind to Ferguson's team in pairing them with Belgium's Waterschei, meaning that Real Madrid had been avoided. The Spaniards had to meet Austria Vienna in the other semi-final. Aberdeen won 5-1 in the first leg, all but killing the tie. 'It's a great night not only for Scotland but for British football,' said Ferguson. The Waterschei coach, Ernst Kunnecke, realised the game was up. 'I want to praise Aberdeen by saying the score was a fair reflection of their ability … we are out of Europe.' The second leg saw Aberdeen outplay their hosts, but they lost 1-0. Miller declared that 'we should have murdered them' and there was a feeling of anticlimax at the final whistle but, all said and done, the Dons were in the final. They had to wait to discover who their opponents in Gothenburg would be. Ferguson was not worried about the prospect of facing Real Madrid, one of the world's most famous football names. 'We have come too far to entertain thoughts of being frightened by any big-name club.'

Ferguson had a lifelong respect for Real, however, as he had been in the crowd at Hampden Park in 1960 when the team of Ferenc Puskás and Alfredo Di Stéfano had torn Eintracht Frankfurt apart in a dazzling 7-3 win to lift their fifth successive European Cup. Real had never lost to a Scottish outfit, but this particular version of the most celebrated club in the world was incomparable to their great line-ups. However, they were still Real Madrid and full of talent. Their path to the final saw them beat Baia Mare of Romania, Hungary's Újpest Dózsa, old rivals Inter Milan and, finally, the Austrians of Vienna. Real's coach was none other than Alfredo Di Stéfano, who took over in 1982 from Luis Molowny. 'Our biggest threat is losing concentration. In recent European finals, one goal has been enough. One lapse and you're toiling. It's imperative our players concentrate and keep their discipline,' said Ferguson.

The game in the Ullevi Stadium in Gothenburg was played in torrential rain. Aberdeen, backed by the majority of the 17,000 crowd, took an early lead through Eric Black, who seconds earlier had hit the crossbar, but Real responded in the 14th minute with a penalty from Juanito. The game swung Real's way for a while, but the second half was a very even affair and it eventually ended 1-1. Ferguson did not want penalty kicks, but in the 12th minute of extra time, John Hewitt, coming on as a substitute, headed the winner. Di Stéfano was a sad figure at the end, but wished Aberdeen the best of luck. 'The terrible conditions and the state of the pitch affected us and we were not prepared for the way the ground cut up and caused our players to tire.' Aberdeen's triumph was a remarkable one in a season in which the competition was extremely strong. 'I am absolutely delighted that my team have justified everything we've worked for by winning the Cup Winners' Cup,' Ferguson said.

There would be more prizes for Aberdeen under Ferguson, including the Scottish Cup in 1983, 1984 and

1986 and further league titles in 1984 and 1985. Midway through 1986/87, he would move on to eventually become Manchester United's most successful manager. But it all really started at a club in the far north of Scotland when Aberdeen were cup kings of Europe. They even went close to retaining their trophy in 1984, losing in the semi-final to Porto.

Manchester United also enjoyed a run to the penultimate stage, beating, on the way, a Barcelona side managed by César Luis Menotti and including Diego Maradona. United were beaten by Juventus in the semi-final, with Italy's 1982 World Cup hero, Paolo Rossi, scoring the winner in the final minute of the second leg in Turin. Tottenham Hotspur and Nottingham Forest reached the last four of the UEFA Cup, with Forest going out to an Anderlecht side described by Brian Clough as the best European side he had seen in years. Watford, playing in Europe for the first time, also enjoyed their time on the continent, beating Kaiserslautern and Levski Sofia before going out to Sparta Prague. Aston Villa were eliminated rather clumsily by Spartak Moscow at Villa Park after drawing 2-2 away from home.

Spurs had an incident-packed journey to the UEFA Cup Final. They notched a 14-0 aggregate scoreline against Ireland's Drogheda before meeting Feyenoord, who ten years earlier had beaten them in the final of the same competition. There was added spice to this occasion as Feyenoord had signed Johan Cruyff, the man who had often been their bête noire when he was captain of Ajax. Cruyff's move was controversial, but very much reflected the nature of the man. His quality shone through at White Hart Lane, but the star of the night was Glenn Hoddle, who inspired his team to a 4-2 win, with all four Spurs goals scored in the first half. Hoddle was very much one of English football's hottest talents, but he had expressed an interest in moving on from the club that had nurtured him. This made him, albeit temporarily, unpopular with fans, who talked of betrayal, but he was the player that made Spurs tick.

They won again in Rotterdam to secure a third-round tie with Bayern Munich. Spurs were slightly needled by comments made about Hoddle by Bayern's former stars, but over the two games they were made to eat their words. Spurs lost 1-0 in Munich but won 2-0 at home, with Steve Archibald and Mark Falco scoring the goals. It looked as though the club was paving the way for their first European trophy since 1972. Their next tie was against FK Austria Vienna, then sporting a sponsor-led club name Austria Memphis. As expected, Spurs won through, with Osvaldo Ardiles on the scoresheet, a player whose career had been interrupted by the Falklands War between Britain and Argentina. Ardiles had also been sidelined with injury, so while his technique was never questioned, his stamina was now an issue.

Spurs were next drawn to meet Hajduk Split of Yugoslavia, a club they had met before, in the Cup Winners' Cup of 1967/68. In the first game in Croatia a fan ran on to the field and slaughtered a chicken. Against this rather macabre background, Spurs lost 2-1, but a goal from Micky Hazard in the second leg took Spurs through to the final to face Anderlecht, the holders.

Spurs appeared to be a club at the crossroads in 1984. Their underrated but highly respected manager, Keith Burkinshaw, had told them he was leaving at the end of the season. His parting words about the way the club was changing and that the 'money men' were taking over the game suggested that he was a disillusioned football person walking away from the game he loved. He made it clear that his next job would be on his terms. 'The manager's job in football is being eroded. I will accept nothing less than complete control at my next job,' he said. Although he was rarely out of work in the years following Tottenham, Burkinshaw's peak was certainly at White Hart Lane. The Spurs squad wanted to send him off with a trophy. They had won the FA Cup in 1981 and 1982 and often promised more than they delivered. Burkinshaw's Spurs always tried to live up to the club's long-time reputation of playing entertaining football.

Anderlecht, their opponents were European experts in many ways. As well as beating Nottingham Forest, they had slalomed their way past Spartak Moscow, Lens, Baník Ostrava and Bryne of Norway. Most of their team were internationals and they were managed by former Belgium international Paul Van Himst. The first leg of the UEFA Cup Final was in Brussels, an easy journey for Spurs fans to make. Unfortunately, there was trouble in the Belgian capital and one Spurs fan was shot dead in the red light area of the city. There were 100 arrests and a policeman was stabbed. Spurs' European sojourn had seen trouble earlier in Rotterdam, which led the club to be fined. Sadly, this was a sign of the times. The game ended 1-1, with Paul Miller the unlikely scorer as Spurs went ahead, while Anderlecht's Danish captain, Morten Olsen, equalised for the home team. For Spurs, a draw against very accomplished opponents was a good result. Burkinshaw could still have his big send-off.

Spurs were without goalkeeper Ray Clemence for both games with Anderlecht, so Tony Parks, a 21-year-old understudy from Hackney, took his place. It was not an easy night in the second leg, and when Alexandre Czerniatynski ran on to Olsen's pass and put the visitors ahead on the hour, it did not look good for Spurs. But six minutes from time a high ball into the Anderlecht penalty area fell to Graham Roberts, who slipped his effort wide of Jacky Munaron from close range. Extra time did not separate the two teams, so it was down to a penalty shoot-out. Step forward Parks, who dived to his right to push away Arnór Gudjohnsen's kick to give Spurs a 4-3 win on penalties. This memorable moment gave Parks a special place in the club's history, but he played just two games over the next three seasons. But nobody could take away from him the two games in May 1984 when he won Spurs their third European trophy. Burkinshaw said farewell to Spurs on the night of 23 May with his third trophy, making him one of the club's most successful and yet intensely modest managers.

Liverpool also had an unsung hero in charge in the form of Joe Fagan, a boot room graduate who had taken over from Bob Paisley in the summer of 1983. Fagan led Liverpool to a truly glorious campaign of success – three pieces of silverware in his first season as manager. Paisley had, of course, won three European Cups among his 13 major trophies, so he had set a benchmark that few could ever hope to match. Liverpool won the Football League for the seventh time in nine years, finishing three points ahead of Southampton. They also lifted the Football League Cup for the fourth consecutive year, beating an emerging Everton side 1-0 in a replay at Maine Road. In Europe, they won through four rounds, winning seven and drawing one of their eight games. Although they met Benfica and Bilbao, they avoided the heavyweights, and their semi-final opponents were Dinamo Bucharest, whom they beat 3-1 on aggregate.

The final, in Rome, was against none other than Roma, who were playing on their home ground, a rather peculiar characteristic of UEFA's planning for final venues. One of Italian football's underachievers in many ways, Roma had won Serie A in 1983 with a four-point advantage over

Juventus. They had a strong home record but away from home they drew ten of their 15 games. The Roma side went close to retaining their league title in 1983/84, but their lack of goalscoring power often let them down. In the European Cup they had got past CSKA Sofia, Gothenburg, Dynamo Berlin and in the semi-final had turned around a two-goal defeat at Dundee United by winning 3-0 in Rome. They had Roberto Pruzzo, one of the best Italian forwards of his generation, in their team, along with Bruno Conti and Francesco Graziani. They also had Brazilians Falcão and Toninho Cerezo, both of whom had starred in the 1982 World Cup in Spain. This was a strong side who had the advantage of playing on familiar turf.

Graeme Souness, Liverpool's tough midfielder, was not intimidated by the prospect of a fiery Roman audience: 'It puts you on your toes when practically every fan in the ground seems to be against you. It gives you something to react to.' Souness had an excellent game and was one of the outstanding performers as Liverpool refused to bow to the 'home' side. Phil Neal opened the scoring but Pruzzo equalised in the first half; however, there were no more goals as the contest moved into extra time and penalties. The pressure seemed to be on Roma rather than Liverpool and, after Steve Nicol missed the first penalty kick, Fagan's men scored their next four, of which Alan Kennedy's was the winner. After scoring the only goal in 1981, the former Newcastle man had been the matchwinner in another European Cup Final. Little did he know it, but it would be the last European Cup-winning moment by an English club until 1999. Drama and tragedy was just around the corner, but 1983/84 was one of British football's most impressive seasons in Europe.

Everton had never really made a mark on European club competitions until 1985. After winning the Football

League title in 1970, the team built by Harry Catterick went into decline and they had certainly been cast into the shadows by neighbours Liverpool, who had dominated the period from the mid-1970s to mid-1980s. When, in 1984, Everton won the FA Cup against Watford, nobody really anticipated that in 1984/85 they would enjoy one of the most momentous seasons in the history of any club. Former midfielder Howard Kendall – 'the best uncapped player in England' – who might have lost his job before he stumbled upon a group of players and a style that suited them, built a side that was exciting and a great example of the team ethic. Between 1984 and 1987, Everton went face to face with Liverpool as Merseyside stood astride English football.

Lifting the FA Cup in 1984, their first since 1966, meant Everton were in Europe once more. Across the 1984/85 season, Kendall's team got stronger as the campaign progressed and they fought battles on three fronts – league, FA Cup and European Cup Winners' Cup. They won at Anfield, the home of Liverpool, thrashed Manchester United by five goals and went on a 28-game unbeaten run. There seemed to be no stopping them as they focused on winning three trophies. Everton's team was so settled that it almost picked itself – outstanding Welsh goalkeeper Neville Southall, Gary Stevens and Kevin Ratcliffe, not to mention Pat Van den Hauwe and Derek Mountfield in defence, Kevin Sheedy of the silky left foot, Peter Reid, Paul Bracewell and Trevor Steven in a dynamic and hard-working midfield, and Scots Andy Gray and Graeme Sharp up front. Everton hit the top of the table well before the end of 1984 and nobody had the consistency to remove them from the leadership position. They ended the season as champions with a 13-point margin over second-placed Liverpool. They also reached the FA Cup Final and were favourites to retain the trophy they had won a year earlier. However, they lost 1-0 to Manchester United, who had been reduced to ten men when Kevin Moran became the first player to be sent off in an FA Cup Final.

Everton made an impact on European football by winning the European Cup Winners' Cup. The first two rounds did not prove too difficult for them, a narrow win against UCD of Ireland and a comfortable 4-0 aggregate success against Inter Bratislava. Even the quarter-final was favourable for Kendall and his emerging team. Fortuna Sittard of the Netherlands were only taking part in the Cup Winners' Cup because they had finished runners-up to Eredivisie winners Feyenoord in the KNVB Cup. Gray scored a hat-trick in the first leg at Goodison as Everton won 3-0, and they finished the job with a 2-0 success in the Dutch province of Limburg.

The semi-final, particularly the second leg, against Bayern Munich became one of the defining matches of Kendall's Everton. There was a growing feeling that the critics and the football public had not given the players the credit they deserved for a great season reaching its climax. One school of thought was that Everton may be stop-gap champions while Liverpool regrouped and reasserted their authority in 1985/86. Pitting their wits against Bayern Munich was Everton's opportunity to show everyone just how far they had come in a relatively short timeframe. In Munich, they successfully 'drew the sting' of Bayern and came away with a 0-0 draw that seemed to upset the home fans in the Olympic stadium. Not even Bayern's young fleet-footed winger, Ludwig Kögl, who had been tipped to be a big star, could faze the resolute Everton defence.

Bayern Munich and Everton were both champions-elect in their respective leagues and both were now in their cup finals, so they had the chance of winning a treble. Kendall remained confident, despite the daunting task ahead of him and his team: 'Each different challenge provides its inspiration. The players do not want to lose another game this season.' By the end of the game at a packed and passionate Goodison, Bayern's hopes had been dashed. Everton won 3-1 after falling behind to a Dieter Hoeneß goal, Sharp, Gray and Steven scoring the goals that were greeted by a crescendo of noise.

Everton clinched their title at the beginning of May 1985 and, 21 days after beating Bayern, they faced Rapid Vienna in Feyenoord's iconic De Kuip stadium in the Cup Winners' Cup Final. Rapid, one of the grand old names of Central European football, had some notable names in their squad, including the Viennese-born Hans Krankl, a silver-haired figure who could still score goals, and Antonín Panenka, the Czechoslovakia international whose penalty in the 1976 European Championship Final became part of football folklore. Nevertheless, Everton were firm favourites to win the final and they did not disappoint. It was an emphatic victory, especially after they took the lead on 57 minutes through Gray. Steven increased their lead after 72 minutes but Krankl reduced the deficit with six minutes to go, only for Sheedy to round off a 3-1 victory.

The media were quick to proclaim that Everton's win had put a smile back on English football's face after a tragic fire at Bradford City and crowd violence at Birmingham. 'It was something special tonight, a truly tremendous performance. We showed what a good team we are. In terms of possession football, you will see nothing better. I think the treble is certainly on,' said Howard Kendall afterwards. A few days later the FA Cup Final was lost, and by the end of May, Everton's hopes of rubbing shoulders with Europe's elite in the European Cup were in tatters.

Nobody could take away their achievements of 1985, but Everton will never know what their vibrant team might have achieved in the years ahead.

Liverpool, by contrast, were accustomed to success at home and abroad. In 1984/85, they had suffered from the loss of midfielder Graeme Souness to Sampdoria in Italy. Liverpool were weakened by his departure but they still had enough to win through to the European Cup Final once more. They had few problems, beating Lech Poznań, Benfica, Austria Vienna and, in the semi-finals, Panathinaikos of Greece. They thrashed the Greeks 4-0 at home, but Panathinaikos and their players were unhappy about the referee and left the field angry and very animated. The second leg had an extra edge to it as the media had attempted to stir things up: 'People want victory here and now. These fanatical people will be difficult to control,' said one Greek daily newspaper. Meanwhile, Panathinaikos coach Jacek Gmoch whipped his players up: 'As you were leaving Liverpool, you asked for revenge. I am asking you if you are ready, because I am.' Liverpool won 1-0 and got out of Athens in one piece, with the crowd applauding politely. They were through to meet Juventus in the final in Brussels.

Juventus had never won the European Cup but had lost finals by a single goal in 1973 and 1983. They had an excellent team, coached by Giovanni Trapattoni, with star players of the highest quality. Michel Platini, Zbigniew Boniek, Marco Tardelli, Gaetano Scirea and Paolo Rossi were among Europe's top players. After winning Serie A in 1984, they finished sixth in 1985, so they needed to win the trophy to return to Europe. Brussels was expecting some 14,000 Liverpool fans for the final at the Heysel Stadium. About an hour before the game started, a group of Liverpool fans gained entry to a neutral area mostly occupied by Juventus supporters. As they ran from the threat of trouble, the Juventus fans were crushed in a section of terracing that had a concrete retaining wall, which collapsed. Thirty-nine people were killed, 32 of whom were Italian. The scenes were horrific, the chaos very visible, but the game went ahead. Juventus won 1-0 thanks to a Platini penalty, but nobody seemed to care too much. There was, of course, a major inquest, accusations, denials and recriminations, but this terrible incident came at the end of a period in which the English game had been tarnished by the behaviour of football fans up and down the country, as well as in European games. Liverpool fans were blamed and 14 of them were found guilty of manslaughter. This story is not about Heysel or who was responsible, but it could so easily have happened to any other large group of fans. The more people in a crowd, the more wrongdoers there will be. Sadly, football played into the hands of a government that was not too fond of the game and also had little interest in solving some of the social problems that influenced crowd behaviour.

English clubs were banned from Europe from 1985/86 until 1990, with Liverpool receiving an additional year of exile. Teams such as Everton, Norwich City, Southampton, Sheffield Wednesday, Luton Town, Oxford United, Wimbledon and Coventry City, as well as Arsenal, Tottenham and Nottingham Forest, among others, were all denied European football during that period. Some have never gone close to qualifying again. The absence of English clubs brought to an end a run in which they had featured in eight of the last nine European Cup finals, seven of which had been won. In the period 1955 to 1985, 16 British clubs won a total of 25 major European prizes; no other country can boast such depth. In the end, they must have been doing something right.

Bibliography

Barclay, Patrick: *Sir Matt Busby: The Definitive Biography*. Ebury (2017)

Burns, Jimmy: *Barça, a People's Passion*. Bloomsbury Paperbacks (2011)

Caremani, Francesco: *Heysel. The Truth*. Bradipolibri Editore (2015)

Davies, Hunter: *The Glory Game*. Mainstream (1972)

Dietschy, Paul: *Origins and Birth of 'The Europe of Football'*. Routledge (2020)

Ferris, Ken: *The Double: The Inside Story of Spurs' Triumphant 1960–61 Season*. Two Heads (1996)

Fieldsend, Daniel: *Local, a Club and its City: Liverpool's Social History*. Fieldsend (2019)

Glanville, Brian: *Champions of Europe, The History, Romance and Intrigue of the European Cup*. Guinness (1981)

Goldblatt, David: *The Game of Our Lives*. Penguin (2015)

Hawkey, Ian: *Di Stéfano*. Ebury (2016)

Hesse, Uli: *Bayern: Creating a Global Super Club*. Yellow Jersey (2016)

James, Brian: *Journey to Wembley: From Tividale to Wembley*. Marshall Cavendish (1977)

Kuper, Simon: *Football Against the Enemy*. Orion (1994)

Lawton, James: *Forever Boys: The Days of Citizens and Heroes*. Bloomsbury (2015)

McPherson, Archie: *Jock Stein, the Definitive Biography*. Racing Post Books (2014)

Miles, Mike: *Over Land and Sea: A History of West Ham in Europe* Pitch Publishing (2024)

Sewell, Albert: *The Chelsea Football Book Number 2*. Stanley Paul (1971)

Walvin, James: *The People's Game*. Allen Lane (1975)

Wilson, Jonathan: *Two Brothers: The Life and Times of Bobby and Jackie Charlton*. Little Brown (2022)

Publications

Goal

Kicker

Marca

World Soccer